The author is both a U.S. and Israeli citizen. The retail price of the book is $25.00, and it was published in March 1983.

DIALOGUE WITH DEVIANCE

DIALOGUE
WITH
DEVIANCE

The Hasidic Ethic and
the Theory of Social Contraction

MORDECHAI ROTENBERG

A Publication of the
INSTITUTE FOR THE STUDY OF HUMAN ISSUES
Philadelphia

Manufactured in the United States of America

1 2 3 4 5 86 85 84 83 82

Library of Congress Cataloging in Publication Data

Rotenberg, Mordechai.
    Dialogue with deviance.

    Bibliography: p.
    Includes index.
    1. Hasidism. 2. Individualism. 3. Ethics, Jewish.
4. Sociology, Jewish. I. Title. II. Title: Social
contraction.
BM198.R64   306'.6   81-13309
ISBN 0-89727-031-2   AACR2

For information, write:

Director of Publications
ISHI
3401 Science Center
Philadelphia, Pennsylvania 19104
U.S.A.

To my wife, Naomi,
who taught me to enjoy our marriage contract
through the alter-centered art of mutual contraction

Contents

Epilogue: The Philosophical Perspective

Acknowledgments

My attempt to "social-scientize" Judeo-Hasidic ethics has forced me to draw on so many disciplines in which I am not formally versed that in the course of peddling my propositions and shopping for others' comments, I have learned so much from so many scholars in the fields of history, philosophy, and religion, as well as from colleagues and students in the social sciences, that it would be impossible to list all those who have helped either directly or indirectly.

Both here and in several places in the text and notes, however, I shall try to acknowledge my indebtedness in full not only because "a person who learns from his fellow man . . . even one letter, must treat him with honor" (Fathers 6:3), but also because I would like to claim certain rights as well as accept concomitant duties in regard to the present work.

While I take full responsibility for the theoretical propositions developed in this book, my expression of gratitude to experts in various disciplines is intended not as a cover for my errors but as an acknowledgment of the help, advice, information, criticisms, and general encouragement given to me during various phases of the study.

The wise criticism and advice of Shmuel N. Eisenstadt, Robert K. Merton, and the late Talcott Parsons have helped me to crystallize the social-scientific structure of the book. Gershom Scholem, Zvi Werblowsky, David Flusser, Yossi Dan, and Rivka Schatz-Uffenheimer have helped guide and guard my interpretations of complex literature in the field of the history of religion and Jewish mysticism.

I have learned much from Marvin Wolfgang, Ivar Berg, Edward Sagarin, Moshe Chazani, Israel Nachshon, Yona Rosenfeld, and Stanley Cohen about various aspects concerning the sociopsychological implications inherent in the notions of individualism and social control.

I am grateful to Calvin Goldsheider, Harvey Goldberg, Don Handele-man, Brenda Danet, Eric Cohen, Shalva Weil, Dave Macarov, and Monica Shapira for their continuous moral support and for helpful comments offered in regard to various arguments developed in this study.

To Moshe Idel, Gedalya Nigal, Yoav Elstein, Yitzchak Englard, Yaacov Golomb, and Yehudit and Yaacov Shlanger go special thanks for freely providing bibliographical guidance in philosophical and Hasidic-cabalistic literature.

I owe a special debt to Richard Cloward and Josh Halberstam for the invaluable support and encouragement generously given to me in many ways. I also wish to thank Dan Ben-Amos and the wonderful people at the Institute for the Study of Human Issues (ISHI) for the "humane," untiring, "Ishi" ("personal" in Hebrew) care with which they treated and published this manuscript. Last, but not least, I am grateful to the people of the Paul Baerwald School of Social Work for not losing patience with my impatient "shnorering" for various types of *odds* and *ends* assistance given to me as a response to my "endless" requests during the "oddest" times.

Mordechai Rotenberg

Introduction

The interest of contemporary social scientists in studying the possible impact of ethical systems and social or religious ideologies on socio-behavioral patterns reaches far beyond Max Weber's now classic influential model thesis about the relationship between the Protestant ethic and the emerging spirit of capitalism in the modern world. The current interest—for example, in various mystical "philosophies"—expressed by perplexed youth and by sincere social scientists alike seems to stem from the fact that these ideologies deal with various ways of attaining actualizing-salvation goals designed to give meaning to one's life and to mitigate the fears, frustrations, and sufferings that modern life entails while at the same time providing key concepts for understanding human motivation and processes of social change ranging from therapeutic systems to social revolutions. It is surprising, however, that while preoccupation with studying the social implications of Christian and Eastern ethics appears quite superfluous—although the salvation ethics of both are, for example, by and large similarly ego-centered—analysis of possible socio-behavioral patterns emanating from specific Jewish ethics are largely nonexistent, even though Jewish salvation ethics are unique in many ways, especially in that they are essentially other-centered. To be sure, there have been sociological studies of contemporary Jewish communities, but no social-scientific paradigms have been constructed or deduced from specific Jewish ethical systems. This reality may be attributed in part to the tendency of Western students of ethics to enfold Christian and Jewish ethics in the single opaque and engulfing term "Judeo-Christian ethic," or "tradition," referring generally to a nonverified and unspecified tradition of humanism and brotherly love (see Frankena 1963).

Arthur Cohen (1971: xviii) points out in his polemic book *The Myth of the Judeo-Christian Tradition* that "it was only in the late nineteenth century in Germany that the Judeo-Christian tradition, as such, was first defined . . . by German Protestant scholarship to account for the findings developed by the higher criticism of the Old Testament and . . . the negative significance of the expression became primary. The emphasis fell not to the communality of the word 'tradition' but . . . to indicate a dimension, albeit a pivotal dimension, of the explicit Christian experience. It was rather more a coming to terms on the part of . . . the Jewish factor in Christian civilization . . . for the Jewish . . . was all but obliterated, being retained, rather like a prehensile tail in the larger, more sophisticated, economy of Christian truth." It follows that if Christianity does indeed regard itself as the successor or younger brother of Judaism, then, stripped of rhetoric and polemics, it should still be of utmost interest for the social scientist to verify whether the term "Judeo-Christian ethics" today represents a common set of ethics or a historical tribute to that which was once Jewish but is now Christian.

Concomitant with Gershom Scholem's (1972) distinction between Christian "restorative messianism," according to which the future only recreates a past that has already existed, and Jewish "utopian messianism," in which the future entails the past plus a better condition which has never existed before, Cohen (1971: xii) argues that "where Jews and Christians . . . divide irreparably . . . is that for Jews the Messiah is to come and for Christians he has already come." "Where Christianity affirms the completion of history . . . Judaism insists upon the open, unqualified and unredeemed character of history" (p. 158). As it is reasonable to assume that distinct Jewish ethics as such might have at least selectively affected various social patterns, especially in the West, the differential socio-behavioral implications emanating from an open versus a closed conception of a future-oriented history should by no means be of minor significance. Today it is probably generally accepted that hedonistic "here and now" existential behavior is grounded in a nihilistic conception of the world and the future as nothingness and meaningless; conversely, if the feeling of fear and insecurity is related to the "not here and not now" future, which "hangs, like a sword of Damocles, over all that exists," as Zvi Werblowsky (1964: 95) phrased it, then the ontological meaning of future-oriented hope and faith must indeed be understood in specific socio-behavioral terms.

In my book *Damnation and Deviance*, I show how the pessimistic Calvinist perspective on life affected Western social theories and conventional past-oriented psychodynamic "retrospective therapies" in contrast to the optimistic Hasidic "prospective therapy" oriented toward man's future. In the present book, the social-contraction theory will be introduced by drawing on the Hasidic-cabalistic ethic. Thus man's concrete ability to affect his actualizing future and his interpersonal relations is explained as patterned according to the Hasidic-cabalistic doctrine, which posits that by contracting himself to evacuate space for the human world, God in fact bestowed upon man the responsibility and power to determine his own future and to affect God's disposition by his "corrective" behavior.

Thus in contrast to a deterministic-dualistic and Oedipal system of unilateral change which posits an interaction model in which the father/God (i.e., the adult) does not change, in the monistic model of mutual contraction, interaction is bilateral, because man can influence heaven and son may change father. Here, paradoxically, by emulating the Divine, one's personal and social development depends not on an ego-centered *construction* of the self, but on one's inter- and intrapersonal self-*contraction* and opening up to let the natural and social world infiltrate and imbue one's being.

The resulting paradigm of man predicated on the Hasidic ethic thus differs radically and in so many ways from other systems of ethics, notably the Protestant, so that what follows suggests, for example, that while current American popular "I or thou" movements for assertiveness training are patterned according to a noncontracting Prussian-Oedipal male figure, the Hasidic father male image provides a deassertive egalitarian "I *and* thou" model for interpersonal relations somewhat akin to the Japanese deassertive interaction style.

The present social-contraction theory educed from Hasidic ethics essentially comprises a study of a religious ideology and its theoretical implications for the social sciences which in a way follows the Weberian kind of work done by Robert N. Bellah in his *Togugava Religion* (1970b), the study of the values of preindustrial Japan (although he was more interested in the political-economic implications, while I am more concerned with interpersonal egalitarian and therapeutic relationships). I say that my study follows Bellah because for his sociological analysis he systematically used original quotations from texts representing an earlier value system in the way I find it necessary to present the derivation of social contraction. This is to say that although I know few social theories that are not anchored in specific theosophical doctrines, I always wonder why the religious roots in which social thinking is usually grounded are so obliterated that it takes a later generation of researchers to uncover the theological biases and sources of such theories.

As the present study constitutes a natural outgrowth of my previous work on the impact of the static and pessimistic Protestant conception of man on Western social sciences, I have chosen to look into the Hasidic culture as a case study to elucidate social contraction because I found it most interesting and challenging in its social (alter-centered) orientation and in its extremely optimistic approach to deviance, human change, and reciprocity.

The great attention given in this study to the problem of deviance draws on the assumption that the effectiveness of a personality or social system can be best assessed by concentrating on the nature and scope of production and reduction of deviance. It should be stressed, however, that Hasidic ideology is by no means intended to represent Jewish ethics at large, even though the general cabalistic mystical philosophy in which Hasidic norms and ethics are embedded had a much wider imprint on Jewish thinking (dating back to the thirteenth century) and even on Christian theosophy (see Benz 1958) than strictly on the Beshtian eighteenth-century Hasidic movement per se; I would hence dare to suggest that the general functional monistic conception of good (conformity) and evil (deviance) which underlies the social-contraction theory and strives to challenge conventional dualistic structural-functional sociology can be said to concur with Jewish monistic thinking in its broader sense, although one must obviously remember that this very Jewish pluralistic and contractional social structure which allowed the incorporation of the eighteenth-century "deviant" Hasidic movement into its mainstream makes it in fact, impossible to speak about a singular crystallized Jewish ethic.

Moreover, although the Hasidic movement has been in existence for almost three hundred years, it is unfortunate that other than a very few studies of contemporary communities almost no reliable sociological studies describing life-styles in Hasidic communities through its three centuries of growth are available. It should therefore be stressed at the outset that in presenting a social-scientific interpretation of the Judeo-Hasidic ethics, this book attempts merely to construct a social theory as derivable mainly from the writings of the movement's founding fathers, the Baal Shem Tov (Besht) and his two major disciples and interpreters, Yaacov Yosef of Polony and the Maggid (preacher) of Mezeritch. Establishing the extent to which this paradigm reflects past or contemporary Hasidic life-styles would indeed require a social-scientific effort of an entirely different nature. I have limited the analysis to the writings of the movement's three founding fathers, not only because many Hasidic schools of thought have emerged in the interim (e.g., the famous "Chabad" movement), but also because the Besht's basic philosophy, as formulated in the Maggid's psychological "self-contraction" doctrine and Yaacov Yosef's sociological "organic-interdependence" theory, seems to comprise a systematic, integral sociopsychological paradigm which generally guides all branches of the movement to this very day.

Although I lamented the lack of socio-behavioral studies of Hasidic communities, I should point out that in the Hasidic culture, socialization and inculcation of its doctrine are accomplished somewhat as in Zen Buddhism, by reciting and transmitting from generation to generation the legends, parables, and biblical commentaries advanced by the Besht[1] and by the movement's subsequent leaders (the *rebbes* or the *zaddikim*). It should hence be plausible that a social-scientific interpretation of the ideology of a movement that has been in existence now for nearly three hundred years should logically carry not only the value of "another" textological analysis but also be instrumental in contributing to the understanding of the relationship between social ethics and *concrete* behavior that can be empirically tested.

The study of religious myths, ethics, or value systems and their possible impact on social and behavioral patterns may be limited to a paradigm designed to identify *existing* patterns (what "is"), and it may be extended to outline *potential* impacts (what "ought") on behavior. The first type is usually the business of the *sociologist*, the second may be said to characterize intellectual efforts of clinically oriented *psychologists*, or social philosophers who are in constant search for new therapeutic-actualizing paradigms that may help modern man to cope with the increasing stresses that overwhelm him in complex Western society. This book undertakes both tasks: by analyzing the sociopsychological implications of the Hasidic ethic, it strives on the one hand to eschew romanticization of the Hasidic culture and present a social-scientific paradigm that should be instrumental in studying socio-behavioral patterns that may be found to exist in many cultures. On the other hand, it suggests that, as with some Eastern salvation philosophies, some therapeutic-actualizing implications derivable for the Hasidic ethic may be potentially useful to various searching individuals or groups. It is thus the guiding premise of this book that cultural-religious myths not only reflect behavior patterns but also to a large extent shape their divergent expressions. Nonetheless, the difference between the impact of Hasidic ethics on "true believers" living in a genuine Hasidic religious milieu and the interpretation of such norms into modern secular actualization terms must be kept in mind.

By undertaking the broader task of examining the psychological and sociological implications of Hasidic ethics within one pretentiously incorporating concept, "social contraction," the book might suffer from overextension and hence fall short in details. However, I feel that a book must constitute an architectural composition, and only after a long struggle with the comprehensive structure of social contraction did the basic three interconnected levels of social contraction coalesce in my mind. As a result, I felt obliged to present social contraction on a sociological, sociopsychological, and psychological level as one unit, even at the cost of possibly faltering on details. This is also why I was reluctant to publish parts of the book as separate articles. Thus, what I have arrived at is the initial formulation of a theory that I hope will be expanded upon and perhaps revised after being subject to empirical and clinical testing. I did not include in the present volume (as I did in *Damnation and Deviance*) empirical studies that demonstrate how some of my propositions can be tested, not only because some of these are not yet available and because it smoothes the flow of reading, but also because after some preliminary selective experimentation, I firmly believe that from an ethical viewpoint a theoretician should not be the only or principal investigator in studies designed to test his own theories and that it is preferable to have others take the lead in such research efforts.

The emphasis on the paradigmatic nature of this book shows that this study is not intended to compete with the many excellent historical and textological studies of Hasidic literature. Indeed, the wealth of scientific studies of Hasidic texts (available mostly in Hebrew) were of enormous help to me. I should point out, however, that in order to extract and construct my own social-scientific interpretation of Hasidic texts, I relied strictly on primary sources, which I translated to the best of my ability, and used English translations of texts only to the degree that they appeared accurate and superior to what I could produce.

My writing style may at times sin with polemic overtones. As a social scientist who is expected to write analytically, so that objective facts will speak louder than subjective assumptions, I expect to be criticized on that score. I felt, however, that one ought to be consistent with the language in which ethics and ideologies are usually written, and the presumption that a social scientist can hide his biased values or even preaching tendencies is today a verified myth. It is rather, as Robert Bellah says in his introduction to *Beyond Belief* (1970a: xi), that "the work of every man, even a nuclear physicist, is rooted in his personal myth, in the unique and partly unconscious meaning his work had for him." Because we are all raised within particular cultural systems that leave their imprint on us whether we admit it or not, this dictum seems to be especially true when we come to analyze religious ideologies or social ethics. I would therefore like to share with the reader the personal background and experiences out of which this book arises.

I am a descendant of one of the leading Hasidic dynasties, which was transplanted from Poland to Jerusalem after fleeing the Holocaust during World War II. Although my family was semimodernized, mainly in that we were exposed to secular education in addition to Talmudic studies, some of my brothers and nephews still wear the Hasidic costumes of that sect and participate regularly in the Hasidic group gatherings and rituals, as did my late father, Rabbi David Rotenberg. Thus, although I was always a marginal Hasid (not wearing earlocks and costumes), as a child I nonetheless absorbed the Hasidic philosophy, customs, ecstatic group rituals, and general optimistic-fraternal *Weltanschauung* that surrounded me and permeated my whole being at home and in the Hasidic synagogue to which my father took me.

It is hard to convey in words the engulfing or almost entrancing power that Hasidic singing, dancing, and other group rituals can have on a young person like myself, who while rejecting Hasidic man-worshipping and mass ecstasy was enchanted by it in spite of himself, who struggled to keep his marginal position "on the fence" but whom others considered as one who "ought" to be an insider because of his "dynastic" family origin. Because of that ambivalent feeling, and because I felt too emotionally involved, I refused the offer of an anthropology professor at New York University to study my Hasidic community when I first came to study in United States in 1960. It required twenty years of conventional work in the field of criminology and experimental social psychology, and of attempting not so conventionally to struggle with the possible pessimistic impact of the Protestant ethic on Western social sciences, before I was able to generate sufficient courage to present an alternative social-scientific paradigm predicated on Hasidic ethics, which, as I stressed time and again, is by no means exclusively Jewish, but which nonetheless differs radically from both Christian and Eastern (notably Buddhist) socio-behavioral patterns in its alter-centered optimistic social-contractional orientation. I stress "optimistic orientation" because, in the course of my work on the present book, I was constantly haunted by the feeling that a noncynical presentation of an optimistic-joyful ideology of life will inevitably result in a romanticized interpretation of the material, while a cynical version will violate the three-hundred-year-old Hasidic construction of social reality. And after all, social realities are constructed by people, as Thomas (1928: 572) posited: "If men define situations as real, they are real in their consequences."

Thus, in contrast to Bellah (who, as I mentioned, struggled similarly with the problematic impact of personal experience on the analysis of ideology), whose Protestant background led him to feel that his existential writing was characterized by what he termed a "pessimistic optimism" (1970a xvi), I gather that my attempt to "objectify" an optimistic theory of life can at best be described as an "optimistic pessimism." (The "optimistic" referring to the belief in the positive effect that the very analysis of a distinct Jewish ethics may eventually have on social thinking, and the "pessimism" referring to my skepticism about the extent to which Hasidic norms are today identifiable in Jewish everyday life.) In other words, it seemed impossible for me to preserve the aura of an optimistic theory by using a nonoptimistic language to present it.

In my effort to formulate an alter-centered theory of social or reciprocal individualism, I consider myself a follower of Buber's anti-individualistic and anticollectivistic "I and thou" dialogue philosophy, according to which the "I" remains "I" and the "thou" remains "thou," instead of being swallowed into a new dialectic "I or thou" synthesis. (See my *Damnation and Deviance* [1978] and Bergman 1974a.) Being, however, a moral philosopher rather than a social scientist, Buber's social "preaching" entailed the general aura of, or at most the seeds of, social contraction but not its theoretical socio-behavioral components.

Having covered the "why" and the "what" of this book, it is time for a brief overview of the "how," how I am trying to conceptualize social contraction. The theory of social contraction is introduced on three levels, which comprise the three major parts of the book: the sociological level, the social-psychological level, and the psychological level. The major accompanying subconcepts to be used for expounding social contraction on all three levels are "matter" and "spirit." In Part I, the sociological-structural concept of mono versus multiple ideal-labeling is introduced. This concept refers to a social system in which diverse material and spiritual actualization patterns are structurally introduced as equal social ideals, so that the asymmetric exchange between them minimizes the expected ratio of deviance and prevents a hierarchical guilt-debt social patronage stratification. The case of the biblical tribal brothers Zebulun (the sea merchant, or in its neo-Hasidic formulation "the material man") and Issachar (the Talmudic scholar, or in its neo-Hasidic formulation "the spiritual man") is used to explain how sociological mutual contraction (the multiple ideal-labeling system) produces a functional asymmetric or indirect but egalitarian exchange. In such a social system, Zebulun supports Issachar, but Issachar does not become a guilty deviant-debtor (by owing Zebulun an equivalent return or by being deprived of the ability to repay), because his mode of actualization through spiritual studies or ecstatic prayers cannot be measured by Zebulun's yardstick but nonetheless benefits Zebulun indirectly.

In order to explain how alter-centrism, with its multiple ideal-labeling salvation system (Zebulun, Issachar, and others), is structurally functional in reducing the expected ratio of deviance and social gaps, the emergence of the Hasidic movement in eighteenth-century Eastern Europe is then analyzed. By examining the sociohistorical case of Hasidism, it is shown how the dominant positive ideal label of the eighteenth century—that is, "Talmudic scholar" type and its corollary negative ideal label (in the Weberian sense of ideal types) *am haaretz* (ignoramus)—created a sociological situation that caused the unlearned Jewish masses tremendous suffering, because they were labeled negatively and had no opportunity to change their fate. The analysis then shows that Hasidism succeeded, after a long struggle in relabeling the derogatory role *am haaretz* by placing the new positive ideal label *hasid* (which required adhesion to the divine but not to scholarship) on the same level as the Issacharian Talmudic scholar and the Zebulunian merchant. Moreover, this relabeling-transformation process is explained as springing directly from the monistic conception of man, in which lower deviant states (here, the unlearned masses) can and must be functionally reabsorbed into the mainstream by being transformed into new, positive elements.

The new differential conception of *multiple* versus the *mono* ideal salvation-labeling structure is then used to explain how the scarcity of positive ideal labels in relation to negative ideal labels might be crucial in determining the prevalence of deviance in any cultural milieu. Hence, if only one positive ideal label is available for socialization (e.g., to be "rich" or to be a "scholar"), then social processes hindering the fulfillment of this mono ideal label will increase the number of people cast into deviant roles in that society. The eighteenth-century Hasidic movement therefore appears to be a most instructive case in the sociological history of revolutionary movements.

On the social-psychological level (Part II) the concepts of interpersonal deassertiveness via material ("inconspicuous consumption") and spiritual (verbal modesty) contraction is introduced. Here basic tenets of classic interaction and socialization theories will be compared to the interpersonal contraction perspective, and it will be argued that while conventional theories are unilateral in that they make no assumptions about whether the ego may influence the alter (the model or father with whom the child or interacting partner is to identify), the contraction theory assumes a bilateral process of "mutual emulation," whereby father and son—or copier-role-taker and significant model—affect each other. Thus the Hasidic deassertive "contracting father" differs from the Western deterministic type of the Prussian-Oedipal father who, by definition, cannot change after childhood, and thereby places the burden of change upon the weaker "child"-interacting partner, who must annihilate his weak self to become the same castrating, assertive Prussian father. It is hence suggested that since the "father-son" relationship is used in most cultures as a basic paradigm for socialization and interaction, the unique bilateral contracting model might have far-reaching implications.

Following the bilateral-interacting model emanating from the contracting-father image, it is then argued that in contrast to the Western emphasis on "*self-asserting* behavior," connoting an "I *or* thou" interpersonal attitude in which the other may well be designified, an "I *and* thou" interpersonal orientation of shrinking oneself (but not resigning oneself) in order "to make room for the other" can be identified not only in the Hasidic culture but also in communication styles found in Japan and in the secular-social orientations developed in the kibbutz system. Practically, then, this orientation attempts to demonstrate that the principle of *I through thou* behavior, in terms of self-shrinkage in order to accept the "other," differs markedly from the recent popular American training in assertive behavior. By analyzing illustrative cases from the assertiveness-training literature, we can see how, in a Western nation like the United States, the weaker interacting partner (e.g., a minority group member, a wife or husband) is trained to become the same "Prussian king" as his strong partner, instead of training the overassertive partner to deassert himself in relation to the weaker deassertive or underassertive other.

Subsequent chapters in Part II will explore the problem of the alter-centered person's actualiztion through the other without imposing on him or invading his privacy by differentiating between the Hasidic community of *inclusion* and the Western therapeutic model of *intrusion* and its institution-alization process for *exclusion*. It is shown that Western democratic indi-vidualism and its consequent referent of "forced freedom and independence" actually legitimizes *social indifference* because it is believed that people have not only an equal right but also an equal ability and obligation to be independent and to make free choices. Thus people who have suffered all along from impaired "democratic independence" are either neglected in the overdemocratic open society or exiled to the antidemocratic, dependency-fostering total institution. According to the organic interdependency conception of the Hasidic *inclusion* community, the process of communal contraction to make room for others and the notion of mutual responsibility force neither complete freedom and independence on people nor alter-centered actualization on others. The modeling role of the Hasidic *zaddik* is used to explain organic interdependence between the spiritual and material people in the inclusion community.

In Part III, on the psychological level, the functional approach to deviance and deviants is developed by introducing the "ascent through descent" model. It is argued that while deviance may be conceived of as temporary functional waves of "ascent via descent" accompanying the process of modernization and social change (following Émile Durkheim's functional sociology), this functional perspective has never been applied to psychiatric psychopathology per se. Moreover, sociologists such as Kai Erikson and Lewis Coser have interpreted Durkheim's conception of deviance as being functional for the society of "insiders"—because "deviance" sharpens the boundaries between the "insiders" and the "outsiders"—but not as being functional for the deviant person himself.

Thus Western psychiatry, which has taught that *depression* rather than mania is the predominant state in life, has not helped rational Western man to overcome his neurotic fears of the mysterious unknown and uncertainties that exist beyond his realistic, rational "Protestant" world. However, the Hasidic mystical approach of "ascent via descent" taught the desperate Jew of the eighteenth century to perceive mania (ascent) as a predominant, functional state that may be preceded by temporary, functional stages of depression (descent). Accordingly, and similar to Eastern actualizing therapies, man is taught to immunize himself against the fears of the "psychotic" nonrational transcendental world by taking small, functional doses of "psychotic" detachment from reality through ecstatic exercises. In contrast to the Western, nonfunctional, periodic "overdose," escapes from the "rational achieving society," controlled "irrational," mystical, immunization practices may hence become functional "rational" practices that help everyone overcome inescapable uncertainties and fears of the irrational unknown.

Finally, the conception of the "paradox" which summarizes and epitomizes the monistic social contraction theory is introduced. The social conceptualization of the paradox strives to show how such seemingly opposite and polar elements or positions as intuition and rationalism, individualism and collectivism, mania and depression, deviance and conformity, or thesis and antithesis may be functionally related and coexist through mutual contraction. Thus, according to Rabbi Nachman of Bratzlav's Hasidic notion of the "question" and paradox (see Weiss 1974), it is not synthesis which predominates life, it is the in-between state of the creative questioning hypothesis, standing between thesis and antithesis (or rather synthesis), which constitutes life. This Bratzlavian or Buberian I *and* thou conception of the paradox is then contrasted with the "I *or* thou" or either/or Marxist conflict and struggle-oriented dialectic synthesis (in which one class or position must be eliminated) and the existential either/ or sociology of the absurd according to which *either* suicide, destruction, and death *or* a hedonistic-egoistic conception of life, must predominate. Accordingly, even if this book opens up more questions than it answers, it might nonetheless mark the difference between the *baal teshuva*, which is the Hebrew expression for the repenter but which means literally a person who has found the answer, and the *baal kushya* (a man with questions), for whom life constitutes constant hypothetical questioning.

NOTE

1. It is important to stress here, as I did elsewhere (Rotenberg 1978), that whether all or only part of the Besht's literature is truly the Besht's own sayings or part of the literature was forged and related by his students in his name (see Scholem 1976) is irrelevant from our point of view, since this literature has nonetheless been used for socialization among the Hasidim for at least the past two hundred years.

(I)

The Sociological Perspective

Alexis de Tocqueville (1830):

Once individualism has shaped its virtues . . . the individual could no longer feel committed to the chain of all the members of the community. Democracy breaks that chain.

Yaacov Yosef of Polony (1702–1782):

They are each in need of the other as a man and his wife, each one being only half a person. . . . So the scholars and zaddikim should not say that they do not need the common people . . . so, the people should not say that they do not need the scholars. . . . If both form and matter, individuality and collectivity unite, they become one complete person.

(1)

Salvation, Monism, and Social Contraction

As a prospective contribution to the sociology and psychology of religion, this book presents a monistic social-scientific theory that demonstrates how an alter-centered paradigm, as derived from the Hasidic-cabalistic ethic, affects the phenomena of deviance, social change, personal growth, and patterns of social interaction which differ from conventional ego-centered socio-behavioral models anchored in a dualistic theosophy. Thus, the social implications of two essentially theological concepts must first be discussed: (1) the soteriological concept of salvation and its impact on actualizing-motivational patterns, and (2) the concept of contraction as a specific theodicy with its unique effect on the human world.

Salvation and Social Behavior Systems

The extent to which religious ethics or needs shape patterns of cultural behavior and social processes has always generated fascinating and energetic theoretical discussions—by those attempting to document such influences, as well as those endeavoring to deny such effects. In that case, it should be clear from the outset that the present study in the sociology and psychology of religion, which attempts to trace specific behavioral and social patterns to the Judeo-Hasidic salvation paradigm, is hopelessly biased in its guiding premise that specific cultural modes of behavior and social change are primarily grounded in and motivated by underlying religious orientations.

It is a matter of common observation that *rational*, conforming behavior and personal or social change, paradoxical as it may seem, are largely motivated by the inherent *irrational* discrepancies, uncertainties, and unexpected ills that life throws one's way. It is inconceivable, for example, that people would engage in tedious physical exercise if they could be certain of the state of physical fitness and health they would enjoy in the future regardless of how much they exercised. Similarly, wealthy people would seldom worry about the meaning of their existence if their lives were solely conditioned by material or behavioral here-and-now reinforcements, as learning psychologists implicitly suggest.

Likewise, it would seem impossible to explain the unceasing search for mystical, "meaningful" experiences and the willingness of "rational" Western well-to-do people to obey blindly charismatic "false messiahs" to a dangerous or even homicidal (e.g., Manson's cult) or suicidal (e.g., Jones' cult) degree without recognizing the tremendous motivating power inherent in man's need for salvation.

In his introduction to Max Weber's essay on the institutionalization of charismatic symbols, Eisenstadt (1968: xxvi) stressed that "the search for meaning, consistency and order is not always something extraordinary, something which exists only in extreme disruptive situations or among pathological personalities, but also in all stable situations." Accordingly, Eisenstadt (1968) contends that while charismatic symbols tend to be especially articulated during periods of crisis and transition, studies show not only how religious-charismatic qualities permeate routine types of common social activities but also how they are the main carriers and vehicles of social creativity and social change that constantly shape and remold major political and economic institutions of various societies.

Indeed, the Weberian school of sociology (e.g., Weber 1967; Bellah 1970b; Eisenstadt 1977) has shown that man's "universal need for salvation" from the uncertainties, fears, and ills of life may lead either to revolutionary social change and economic modernization in terms of "inner-worldly" ascetic activism, or to world-rejecting behavior resulting in a relatively slow social development or even economic and social stagnation. The psychological literature is similarly permeated with existential and therapeutic perspectives (e.g., Rogers 1965; Frankl 1965) that attempt to explain and teach how one can endow one's life with meaning in order to find unity and peace with oneself, one's fellow man, or the cosmos. Seeman (1959), for example, designates meaninglessness as one of the major referents of alienation. Salvation in this sense would signify dealienating behavior. Thus the study of personal and social behavior motivation is essentially intertwined with the study of salvation patterns. Leading social scientists such as Max Weber and Carl Jung have overtly predicated their theories about man and society on the assumption that motivation is explainable primarily on the basis of specific cultural-religious modes of salvation. Similarly, Shills, for example, maintained that each society is governed by the realm of its values and beliefs which he termed the "central zone," and hence "in this sense, every society has an 'official religion,' even when that society or its exponents . . . conceive of it . . . as a secular, pluralistic, and tolerant society" (cited by Eisenstadt 1968: xxx). It follows that whether we admit or deny the impact of religion on secularized behavior, most of our institutionalized normative behavior and organizational structures are shaped by charismatic religious components. Other behavioral scientists have, however, largely ignored the impact of "religious orientations" on behavior, although the language they use to define such "secular" terms as self-actualization, self-liberation, or psychotherapy are closely akin to definitions of salvation and redemption.

I have used the terms "redemption" and "salvation" with no differentiation. Weber (1967: 148) noted, "It is difficult to completely separate conceptions of salvations from such promises of redemption from oppression and suffering." While it seems that redemption connotes the passive aspect of freedom *from* (e.g., from oppression or suffering), and salvation seems to denote the active aspect of freedom *to* (i.e., to feel secure or to actualize oneself), in the literature these terms are used interchangeably. They seem also to be used as synonymous terms for therapy, liberation, enlightenment, self-realization, and so on.

Scholem, the well-known expert on Jewish mysticism, has suggested that the quest for redemption always refers to one's "wish . . . to be liberated from an existence that by its very nature seems to be connected with suffering, with passion and fear, with ignorance and limitation" (1970: 9). In a comparative study entitled *Liberation, Salvation, Self-Actualization* (1973: 28), Klostermaier claimed that "we can consider all philosophies, religions and also sciences as a way to freedom—not excluding the modern ideologies which claim to 'liberate' mankind, be it from Monarchs, from the Bourgeoisie, from Capitalism, from the establishment in any form . . . [and hence] the core of the salvation myths is the description of the drama of freedom."

The term "salvation" is apparently used to refer to a wide spectrum of behaviors and social processes. Indeed, Tucker (1967: 24), in referring to the most famous movement for secular self-actualization, maintains that "deeply embedded in Marxism is a theme that corresponds to the master-theme of salvation of the soul." Accordingly, man's self-realization means a change from a condition of "enslavement" and self-alienation in the capitalist state to a new condition of "freedom" and liberation of man's creative powers in the egalitarian communist state. Similarly, in discussing Freud's psychoanalytic system, which is probably the most influential secular psychotherapeutic method, Rieff (1961: 361) contends that it "is only one of the most successful and certainly the most subtle, of contemporary ideologies of self-salvation."

As we shall see, various religions have institutionalized infinite modes and roads to salvation, ranging from this-world-oriented, rational-active modes, to other-world-oriented, irrational and inactive methods, or from personal, inner procedures, to collective, externalizing processes. The required signs of grace or redemption may likewise range from inner feelings of assurance-health, inner peace, or meaningfulness, to external signs of intellectual achievement, material success, or political liberation.

To be sure, not all rational religions have produced salvation ethics, and not all religions of salvation have produced ethical systems. Confucianism, for example, produced a rational religious ethical system, but no prescription for salvation. On the other hand, Buddhism is a religion of salvation, but it has no god and it entails no rational system of ethics. Thus it is of little consequence whether our analysis remains within the realm of religious or secular behavior. What seems significant, however, is that we recognize and identify the tremendous impact religious salvation doctrines had on a wide spectrum of behavior—be it suffering, fear, wickedness, sinning, failure, or the like. The unique salvation pattern prescribed by specific religions may thus explain a variety of both secular and religious behavioral systems that emerged in a particular culture.

Most psychological and sociological theories of secular salvation behavior have concentrated mainly on Eastern-Buddhist and Western-Christian ethics, while the behavioral and social implications traceable, for example, to Jewish ethics have largely been minimized. Classic writers such as Weber, whose interest focused mainly on economic behavior, and Jung, who was primarily interested in therapeutic perspectives, admitted that while the road to salvation prescribed by the Western-Christian culture differed markedly from that prescribed in the Eastern-Buddhist culture, the focus on reaching salvation did not differ. Weber (1967: 171) concluded that the Christian pattern requires inner-world action and the Eastern pattern requires other-world inaction, and Jung (see Campbell 1977: 492) determined that therapy in the extroverted West depends exclusively on external redemption, while therapy in the East is an active, introverted, self-liberating process. But both admit that "salvation" in the East or in the West is, by and large, a *self-indulging* ego-centric matter.

It is therefore of interest to explore the psychological and sociological implications emanating from a theosophy with an "alter-centric," or other-centric, salvation system. The specific behavioral system that I have in mind is rooted in what I shall term here the Judeo-Hasidic ethical heritage. The term "Judeo-Hasidic ethics" is used to stress that while Hasidic ethics do not represent Jewish ethics at large, Jewish ethics (which are, as such, essentially embedded in a monistic conception or man) are diametrically opposed to the nebulous yet popular notion of the Judeo-Christian ethic, since Christianity is basically dualistic in its social orientation. Thus, according to Judeo-Hasidic monistic ethics, unlike dualistic systems, salvation is accomplished through the "other," that is, through one's unconditional reciprocity with lower, deviant human elements found either within oneself or outside oneself. Although more will be said about the social implications emanating from a monistic conception of man, I shall say here that by monistic, reciprocal salvation I mean very roughly that in contrast to a dualistic dichotomy between good and evil people (e.g., a Calvinist dichotomy) or good and evil elements within people, a monistic conception of man assumes that evil or deviance is not only an integral part of but possibly even a necessary phase toward salvation, conformity, or goodness. Thus, a monistic conception of man as found in Judeo-Hasidic ethics encourages an optimistic outlook on human motivation and possible corrective behavioral changes.

Accordingly, alter-centered salvation would hypothetically be accomplished via a nonutilitarian or unconditional reciprocal relationship on the *inter*personal level, between people using different actualization systems, or on the *intra*personal level between various weaker and stronger human elements. This means that alter-centered relationships should encompass and explain sociological or social-psychological interaction processes as well as psychological intrapsychic processes. Our concern will be essentially with the diverse behavioral patterns, such as interpersonal exchange and personal-social change processes ranging from communal-welfare organizations and messianic-socialistic trends to therapeutic perspectives, that may be traceable to the functional alter-centric salvation system in Judeo-Hasidic ethics. By functional alter-centric salvation I mean mainly the functional harmony that would presumably pervade a social system in which the needs of group survival correspond to personal salvation patterns, in contrast to systems in which these needs conflict. Thus, alter-centered salvation is essentially featured by *distraction* from self but not *destruction* of self or rather by *contraction* of self rather than *construction* of self.

This brings us to an introductory discussion of "social contraction" as a major point of departure or as a "unique breakthrough" in the history of mankind, in Eisenstadt's words (1977), which attributes cultural diversity in behavior motivation to the source of the universal need for salvation, namely, to the various theodicies explaining not only the roots of good and evil, but also man's ability and motivation to choose between them.

Monistic Theodicy and Social Contraction

Having taken a generally Weberian approach, I have suggested so far that the universal need for salvation from the suffering and uncertainties that life in our imperfect world entails may explain differential motivational patterns, such as ego-centered and alter-centered actualization systems and other cultural variations in behavior patterns. The relationship between suffering and life's predicaments in terms of the *existence* of evil and motivation in terms of the free will and ability to *commit* or *omit* evil obviously cannot be divorced from the age-old problems with which the theodicy deals. Thus salvation from evil in terms of the scope of motivation and will would probably be close to nil according to a theodicy that attributes every ill to the unlimited power of the devil. Hence, speculation about cultural diversity in deviation and salvation patterns has from ancient times to the modern era been intertwined with the specific doctrines and expositions people used to reconcile God's immanent idealism with the world's evils and its faltering realism. As may be well known, explanations about the apparent impossibility that God as the ultimate infinity, perfection, and goodness will himself create or entail finity, imperfection, and evil, were divided between the Gnostic-dualists and the Neoplatonist-monists. Thus, Gnostic dualism, which did not accept the notion that the good God would create evil, believed (as did the ancient Persian Zoroastrians) in the doctrine of two separate kingdoms: that of evil and that of divine goodness. Hence in the cosmogenic process, as well as in man's life, the power of darkness or evil was explained accordingly as constituting a separate, independent entity that clashes with the power of light and goodness. The monistic Neoplatonists, who insisted on God's immanence and unity, accepted the inherent conflict between good and evil, between the spiritual world of purity and the material world of profanity. But concomitant with their monistic conception of God, they reconciled the existence of evil, not as a new creation or a separate entity but as the absence of light and goodness. Accordingly, there is no contradiction or schism in God's harmonic idealism, but evil may emerge where God's light is dimmed or absent.

While the Neoplatonist theodicy explains evil as a passive phenomenon (i.e., as a lack of goodness), a major "active" monistic theodicy explaining the possibility of human free will and earthly evil, which will be used here as the basis for our social paradigm, is the cabalistic notion of divine *contraction*. Accordingly, it is not God's passive "absence" which facilitates evil, but God's active purposeful self-contraction to evacuate space for the human world. It is God's volitionary dimming of his own brightness which made the creation of the world and its apparent evils possible. Thus, according to the Jewish mystical cabalistic doctrine of *tsimtsum* (contraction), God's self-shrinkage, condensation, or withdrawal into himself to evacuate primordial space for the human world is a dynamic ebb-and-flow process of regression and egression, of *tsimtsum* and *hitpashtut* (embracing or expansion), of dimming his own light but staying in the background to bestow light whenever necessary. Contraction is hence not a one-time act of total withdrawal but a continuous, dynamic process of the dimming or covering of[1] (see Ergas 1926) the brightness of the divine light, which is not "absent" but which leaves its "impression" (*reshimu*) where it shined so that it will not blind or burn the human world it created, but will be there, as the sixteenth-century Jewish cabalist Y. Luria (see Vital 1980:

Vol. 1, p. 25) stated, "according to the measure needed to give them [the worlds] light or life." This process involves, then, as Scholem states (1941: 261–63), a double-strain of "light which streams back into God and that which flows out from Him. . . . Just as the human organism exists through the double process of inhaling and exhaling and the one cannot be conceived without the other, so also the whole creation constitutes a gigantic process of divine inhalation and exhalation." Here the first step of creation begins not by emanation but by the commonly conceived act of God's (the *En-Sof*, or Infinite Being) self-contraction. Consequently this dynamic ebb-and-flow process, which as in most ethical systems serves as a model (*imitatio Dei*) that man is urged to emulate, constitutes the essence of the dynamic monistic[2] theory of evil and deviance as it assumes paradoxically that evil exists not as an inevitable absence of goodness or "godness" (because the idea of a godless vacuum is heretic)[3] but, as the founder of Hasidism, the Baal Shem Tov ("Master of the Good Name," shortened to "Besht"), will subsequently phrase it in the eighteenth century (see Besht 1975a: 8), as the "throne of goodness." Thus "evil" is nothing but "an instrument for the good goals of the good God," as Tishby (1975: 12) indicated. The cabalistic doctrine of contraction hence entails the seeds of the philosophy of the paradox (about which more will be said later), because it conceives the coexistence of polar positions or elements as functional and necessary components of creation and progress. Accordingly, the process of contraction made it possible for the element of divine sternness (*midat hadin*) to emerge in the world as Y. Luria is cited (see Tishby 1975: 24) as saying, "in the power of sternness that was exposed there with the contraction." But at the same time unity and harmony are possible only through the coexistence of contrasts and the interaction between this element of sternness (harshness) and the element of divine compassion (*midat harachamim*), because the world can exist only through the continuous dynamic interaction between matter and spirit, between good and evil, between the I and the thou.

The monistic yet paradoxical basis for an "I and thou" alter-centered salvation through mutual contraction and expansion can now be better understood in the words of Buber (1960: 104):

> How could the divine infinite (*en-sof*) become a contracted God which roams the worlds to carry out his creation through acts of contraction? . . . Why did the infinite divine, as an absolute personality, vis-à-vis stands nothing, become a personality which stands vis-à-vis a receiver? . . . because of the desire to find a receiver,[4] so that the divine will be able to bestow His light upon it.

To be sure, Jewish theosophers were not the only ones to use the notion of contraction as a monistic principle explaining how salvation and motivation can be understood only in terms of man's free will to choose between good and evil. The fifteenth-century German philosopher Nicolaus Cusanus (see Bergman 1974b) explained, for example, the possibility of the world as a contracted, concretized maximum that is fashioned according to and created by God, who is the abstract, absolute maximum.[5] While God unites within himself all contrasts, the world's monism is only a relative con-tracted approximation of the divine unity which strives to emulate God, but in which the elements are in reality only identical by and with themselves. The sum of all numbers, contends Cusanus, constitutes a unity like Plato's "idea," but each number fulfills a distinct function which cannot be inter-changed with any other. Thus, contraction (*contractio*), which features only the human world, is a realization but also a limitation of reality.

Similar to Cusanus, and influenced by him, was the notion of contrac-tion used both by the sixteenth-century Italian philosopher Giordano Bruno and by the seventeenth-century German philosopher Gottfried Wilhelm von Leibnitz (see Bergman 1974b). For both of these philosophers, the monads (substances) of the infinite aggregate were conceived as contracted godly elements. Thus contraction preserved the idea of monism because it explains the possibility of what Leibnitz called the "pre-established har-mony" (between the monads) in the world.

While Cusanus, Bruno, and Leibnitz reconciled monism by explaining the world in general contractional terms, it was Friedrich von Schelling (1775–1854) who, influenced by Jakob Böhme, used contraction in a language akin to cabalistic terminology to explain how salvation in terms of human motivation or free will to commit or "omit" evil may be reconciled with a monistic philosophy.[6] In his later (1809) philosophical exposition *Of Human Freedom*, Schelling (1936) writes that monism may be possible not as a Spinosian pantheistic determinism but as an organic whole in which the organs have their relative freedom to choose between good and evil while together they constitute an organic unity. Thus God created both light and darkness, both love and hatred, and both good and evil, and thus God comprises within himself both the ideal and the real. Accordingly, fire and poison are not inherently bad but only *dangerous*. When fire, like poison, is used in small, controlled quantities, it may heal or give light or warmth, but when it gets out of control it becomes dangerous and devastat-ing. It is therefore the disconnection between opposites, the separation between the ideal and the real (which somewhat reminds us of the cabalis-tic notion of *perud*), which explains how the contracted dark elements (which, as we shall see later, do not resemble the cabalistic use of contrac-tion) may grow to become dangerously autonomous evil entities through the process of motivation and free will or free choice.[7]

To understand how the principle of divine contraction fashions human behavior, it must be pointed out here that Schelling's monistic contraction theodicy explaining how the ideal (good) principle can lose its dominant position in the world and give free reign to the contracting dark side of the real (evil) has recently been used by several philosophers (e.g., Bergman 1977 and Marx 1980) to expound how such universal wickedness as a Holocaust is possible. Thus Marx (pp. 11, 12) wrote, for example, that "on the basis of his conceptual determination of the 'Real,' Schelling was able to show that the human being bears necessarily within itself a great and essential danger. . . . Because the contrasting force of the Real is at work in him, and because he alone has freedom of choice, there is in the human being ever the danger of the lordship of evil." Because Hasidic-cabalism developed a motivating-salvation philosophy that appears, in its optimistic free-will perspective (based on the Beshtian notion that "evil is in the throne of goodness"), to be diametrically opposed to Schelling's pessimistic monism (see Tilliette 1970),[8] although both are seemingly grounded in the contraction principle, we should thus now turn to introduce contraction in terms of the concept of will and *correction*.

Monistic Contraction and Correction (Tikkun)

It is of central significance to our social-contraction theory to stress that the Christian use of contraction, whether borrowed from the Jewish cabala or not, refers essentially to the contraction of the earthly-human world or to the dark-real elements within God, in Schelling's terms, while in the Jewish cabalistic sense, contraction refers to God's light and to his volitionary positive self-contraction (see Funkenstein 1974) to evacuate space for the human world by dimming his brightness or his eternal light so the world may exist. Thus, according to cabalism, especially later cabalism, divine contraction is explained as a functional cathartic cosmic process known as the shattering, ("breaking of the vessels") which refers to a kind of divine breaking for the sake of differentiation and correction, as Y. Luria stated (see Vital 1882, *Shaar* A.A. 1): "and here this contraction . . . is called breaking for the sake of correction." This functional cathartic "breaking of the vessels" (*shevirat hakelim*), which followed the process of contraction and which has many explanations in the literature of mysticism, presumably caused a diffusion or shattering explosion of the divine light, and the sparks of that light flew either back into its divine source or downward into the abyss and depths of the earth. In this way, it is said, the good elements (i.e., the divine sparks) came to be mixed with the so-called vicious elements (i.e., the shells [*kelipot*]) (see Scholem 1941). So man's salvation (*tikkun*) requires a constant effort to restore the divine order by raising or uplifting to its divine source the holy sparks that are scattered in the world. According to the major cabalistic document, the *Zohar* (which originated according to the religious tradition during the pre-Talmudic era and according to the scientists during the late thirteenth century), man's corrective actions in this world actually lend strength to divine activities: "In the earthly activity the upward activity is awoken, if a man performs properly down [on earth] so strength is awoken properly upwards" (cited in Tishby 1971: vol. 2, p. 434). Moreover, according to Hasidism, which brought heaven down to earth by reinterpreting Lurian cabalism in an optimistic-operational salvation language accessible to the masses, there is now actually no evil in the world. What appears to be evil is only disguised by "shells." Hence in every earthly matter (*gashmiyut*) such as eating, rejoicing, copulating, and even sinning, there are holy sparks that may or must be redeemed by peeling off the "evil" shells, so to speak, and raising them back to their divine source, and "correcting" part of the primordial breaking. Salvation means now that man must learn to see the good element inherent in every possible event and experience. Moreover, salvation in terms of motivation means not only that man has the free will to choose between commission and omission of the evils of this world but also that he has the obligation and power to "correct" heaven which through the divine process of self-contraction lends itself to be influenced by man's spark-lifting endeavors inherent in the concept of *tikkun* (correction).

It is this dynamic conception of the self-contracting God, which can nowhere be found in Christian or other theodicies, that may also construe the difference between pessimistic and optimistic monism as well as the difference between a deterministic and unilateral versus a dynamic bilateral interaction theory. Thus, if Leibnitz's monism refers to predetermined or "preestablished harmony," if Cusanus' monism conceives of the world (not God) as a contracted maximum, and if Schelling's contraction refers only to the dark-real side within the divine, then the God image that follows from this conception and that man is urged to emulate represents a static Prussian-Oedipal father image (about which more will be said later) which may not be influenced by man, and change and interaction refer unilaterally only to the weaker interacting partner—the son.

Indeed, Rudolf Otto (1976) indicates that according to both Meister Eckhart's Western monism and to Sankara's Eastern mysticism, salvation is a matter of static being which is opposed to all dynamic alterations, changes, and becoming. Similarly, Flusser (1964) suggests that, while already according to Flavius in ancient Stoic monism even man's free will and moral choices are predetermined, according to the Jewish Pharisees man's moral performances may have decisive consequences concerning the occurrences of events. Thus, according to the Greco-Christian static theology the son strives to become the God/father through ascetic withdrawal from others (e.g., saints emulating Jesus), while in the Hasidic-cabalistic theodicy the dynamic God/father contracts himself to become a son who may be influenced by human beings. Moreover, this bilateral dynamic and future-oriented process of interaction between man and God follows from the Jewish concept of trust (*bittahon*) and covenant, which made man a partner to God's creation, as Werblowsky (1964) indicated. Thus the notion of covenant in terms of the relative stability of the social order may be understood in contractional terms as God's willingness to bind himself to his creation so that man can be a complementary partner to God's creation and thus have an impact on the cosmos through God's creative actions, which may now have fairly predictable results in agriculture, science, and society. The half-circled arched rainbow after the flood thus symbolizes not only the reliable future-oriented promise of vitalizing rain versus devastating flood, but also the mutuality of the contracted God, who provides one-half of the circle (i.e., cosmic regularity) symbolized in the rainbow, and allows man to complete the other half through his productive creative efforts on earth. The notion of covenant in terms of contraction and expansion is then further symbolized on an extended human level in God's command to Abraham (see Gen. 17:10) to circumcise himself and his offspring (the literal meaning of the Hebrew *Brit* is circumcision or convenant), that is, to contract his male organ,[9] the symbol of fertility and manhood, and thereupon God promises Abraham expansion: "And Abraham shall become a great and mighty nation" (Gen. 18:18). This bilateral interaction process between heaven and earth, father or mother and son, which involves a continuous contractive and expansive ebb-and-flow, give-and-take dynamic interrelationship is nowhere described more vividly than in Luria's own cabalistic "spark-lifting" terms of mutual contractive and expansive attraction process between heaven (light and rain) and earth (seeds and plants) (see Tishby 1975: 125):

> And the matter of rain which comes down from above causes to draw out the plants . . . as supreme light descends from the holiness above and then the holy sparks which are in the abyss of the shells rise towards the descending light and they cleave and ascend . . . since these sparks are from the holy and they are imprisoned in iron chains in the depth of the shell, and they desire passionately to ascend to their source and they cannot until they will be assisted by the heavens and then they rise with great passion two drops against one drop.

The picturesque image of the earthly plants yearning to be raised by the bilateral efforts of the earthly plants and the heavenly lights, that is, by the process of mutual expansion, is applied by Luria elsewhere (see Vital 1890: Vol. 1, p. 149) to explain how the educational relationship between the mother and son should be fashioned through the "I and thou" alter-centered descending contraction: "Mother must step down from her rung to contract her richness . . . when the sinning of the lower are magnified and they have no strength to receive upper influence, then the supreme mother must lessen her light so that we may be able to receive it." Contraction refers hence to a mutual alter-centered dynamic process in which one side expands and ascends while the other side contracts or descends, so that the weaker interaction partner may have space to grow by affecting or influencing the stronger side, which contracted for that purpose. Here it might be of interest to call the American reader's attention to the fact that the Hebrew term *chutzpa*, which dates back to the Talmudic era and has been popularized in a derogatory sense in the American vocabulary, is rooted precisely in these contractional terms, according to which God as a dynamic "personality" allows man to influence him. In the Talmud (first to sixth centuries), for example, it is stated already that *"chutzpa* even toward heaven is effective [useful and legitimate]" (see Talmud, *Sanhedrin* 105a). Thus from Abraham's daring (*chutzpa*) toward heaven in his famous attempt to bargain with God about the conditions under which God would or would not destroy Sodom (Gen. 18), to Reb Levi Yitzhak of Berdichev's famous arguments with God, *chutzpa* becomes a symbol for man's capacity to affect God and change his decrees and consequently man's future by his actions and justified "complaints" toward God.

Summing up the theosophical sources, the Neoplatonistic definition of evil (and man's motivation or will to choose evil) as absence of goodness, and the cabalistic contractional definition of the world's evil as a volitionary ebb-and-flow process (according to which ostensible evil is "the throne for goodness") it would appear that the difference between these two interpretations is that Neoplatonistic monism is *static*, because contraction refers unilaterally only to the world and divine darkness, and hence earthly evil may grow to become an independent power, while cabalistic monism is dynamic,[10] since contraction refers bilaterally to God's own light and hence "evil" is correctable and transformable.

Adhering to a Kantian, or rather Platonic, belief, which presumes that our introjected preexisting "ideas" may affect the real world through our outward projection, I have indulged in a somewhat lengthy discourse to document the theosophical sources of contraction in order to establish that contraction was not merely an esoteric Hasidic notion.[11] As the contraction theodicy is intended here to relate how the cosmic notion of contraction may explain behavioral patterns of man who is urged to emulate the divine, contraction as *imitatio Dei* may in fact be understood in the anthropological sense of myths or symbols (see Turner 1972).

If we are now to step down from the theosophical to the operational social level, the term "contract" would refer both to the process of shrinkage and condensation and to the process of drawing together. By considering these definitions in combination, contraction would mean then that by the act of condensation the said entity does not lose from its strength but only reduces its visible size or volume. The drawing together implies, however, that by this process of condensation the other part or party is drawn to the contracted part to take his place in the evacuated space, and hence the strength of the resultant contract between the parts or parties will be stronger than the powers each partner possesses separately.

This proposition differs not only from the East-West mystic definition of God as a "one without division or parts" (see Otto 1976), but also from Lewin's (1964) classic statement that "the whole is more than (or different from) the sum of its parts" (p. 146). The present assumption states that the sum of contracted parts is more (stronger) than the sum of raw or uncultivated parts, that is, that "there is nothing more complete than a broken heart," as the Hasidic saying goes. A careful examination of Thomas Hobbes' (1969) "social contract" philosophy will illuminate the above.

NOTES

1. The insistence on interpreting contraction and expansion in terms of God's light being at times hidden or covered was pronounced by many Jewish thinkers. Thus even a non-Hasidic rabbi such as Chaim of Volozin (1871: 31a) states that the "interpretation of contraction is not . . . disappearance . . . to create a vacuum [but] covering and hiding."

2. While Scholem (1941), and especially Tishby (1975), suggested that the cabalistic (mainly Lurianic) notion of evil entailed some Gnostic-dualistic motives (in spite of its essential Jewish monistic and Neoplatonistic *Weltanschauung*), the extreme monistic overtone in Hasidism is unquestionable. It should also be pointed out here that, while according to the Lurianic cabala it is possible to understand the first act of divine contraction as a negative process, according to Cordovero's cabala the same primordial divine contraction process is construed in essentially positive terms as emanation (see Ben Shlomo 1965).

3. It is remarkable that in English the expression "I am free" carries precisely the Neoplatonist passive meaning of neutral absence, referring mainly to time and not to one's existential state of being. Thus "I am free" means "I have uncommitted free time." By contrast, in the Hebrew everyday language, to describe someone as being "free" (*chofshy*) is really to call him "secular." This concurs with the notion that uncommitted or free-floating empty space and time are heretic, as "there is no space without Him" (*Leit atar panuy miney*) (Maggid 1927: 58).

4. The human-social parallel of this contractional give-and-take principle might be found in the popular Talmudic saying "More than the calf wants to suckle, the cow wants to nurse" (*Talmud, Pesachim* 112.a).

5. I am grateful to Yitzchak England for drawing my attention to the Christian treatment of contraction.

6. Although there is apparently sufficient evidence demonstrating a cabalistic influence on some of Schelling's ideas (see Schulze 1957), as well as Jewish influence on Cusanus' thinking (see Guttmann 1899), and although the notion of contraction (*tsimtsum*) was already known in the third century (see Scholem 1941) and used by the Jewish Nahmanides in the thirteenth century (see Scholem 1977:

105), the question of the origin of the term is not so relevant from the present perspective as the difference between its Jewish and Christian interpretation.

7. One should differentiate between these two terms which are often used synonymously. The act of choosing connotes a cognitive rational process presumably controllable by man. The state of willing denotes essentially an emotional desire.

8. Idel (1980) has recently demonstrated how the Jewish philosopher Franz Rosenzweig refuted Schelling's negative theory of the "somber basis" of the divine, which explains contraction in terms of the dark-real side within God.

9. Indeed, the Maggid (1927: 63), the disciple of the Besht, founder of the eighteenth-century Hasidic movement, refers to the circumcision as a symbolic act of personal contraction.

10. Hence, the proposed dynamic contraction theodicy, anchored in an egalitarian social orientation, should be differentiated from the active "secular" theodicy which emerged during the early Enlightenment. While the latter utilitarian "secular" theodicy was indeed intended as a pragmatic "program for analyzing and remedying the evils that befall man in society," as Ernest Becker (1968: 31) maintained, its egotistic orientation probably caused more social evils than it prevented, since the achievement of "maximum individuality within maximum community. . . . was an unattainable paradox" (ibid.: 141).

11. Ross (1980) has demonstrated recently how the cabalic notion of contraction was not only accepted among wide circles of Jewish non-Hasidic groups as an ontological theodicy but interpreted (although not exactly in Hasidic terms) into "concrete behavioral norms" even by so-called Lithuanian *yeshivot* (rabbinical colleges), which in earlier times comprised the major opposition to the Hasidic way of life.

(2)

The Social Contract
and Social Contraction

The Guilt-Debt Contract

In explaining how men should give up their sovereign power to the government out of self-interest and self-defense against mutual and external annihilation, Thomas Hobbes states:

> The only way to erect such a common power, as may be able to defend them from invasion of foreigners, and the injuries of one another . . . is to confer all their power and strength upon one man, or upon one assembly of men, that may reduce all their wills, by plurality of voices, into one will. . . . This is more than consent or concord; it is a real unity of them all . . . made by convenant of every man with every man in such a manner, as if every man should say to every man, I authorize and give up right of governing myself, to this man or this assembly of men, on this condition, that thou give up thy right to him. . . . For by this authority given to him by every particular man . . . he hath the use of so much power and strength . . . that by terror thereof, he is enabled to perform the will of them all. (1969: 176, 177)

Hobbes' formulation suggests that the "common power," the "real unity," that gives the government or a governor the power "to defend them all" is *stronger* than the power each individual member of society may possess. Paradoxically, it is produced by each one "giving up" his right through the contracting and reduction process in the strength of separate individuals. Hence, a social contract achieved through a society's mutual *contraction* reduces the possibility of individuals' *counteraction*.

Hobbes' social contract theory was apparently used as a convenient bedrock doctrine for the rational-egoistic *Weltanschauung* that the Protestant theosophy promulgated in Europe during the seventeenth through the nineteenth centuries, and consequently it was interpreted in utilitarian ego-centric *Zeitgeist* terms. In the resultant picture of Hobbes' man, people saw his "lonely wolf" rather than his collective "Leviathan." The latter was seen to be motivated solely by a material "guilt-debt," an "I or thou" conception of society, and not by an "I and thou" approach to interpersonal relationships.

By the "guilt-debt" conception, I am referring to Friedrich Wilhelm Nietzsche's (1969) use of contractual-guilt. The ethical term "guilt" (which in German is *Schuld*) took its origin from the material concept of "debts" (*Schulden*), and thus interpersonal guilt, according to Nietzsche and Martin Heidegger, is based on the contractual notion that someone "owes" something to another (*ist schuldig*). For Nietzsche and Heidegger, as for most other "man-centered" philosophers associated with the Protestant school of German idealism, interpersonal guilt is hence featured by mere material contractual universalistic and instrumental relationships between people. Accordingly, salvation from "guilt" is not an interpersonal matter, but a personal, ego-centered process associated with intrapsychic sin, to be reached when concerned only for oneself. Thus, if salvation is sought through ego-centric achievements, interpersonal relationships can be conceived only in material contractual terms. In such relationships, the weak, deviant "debtor" will always remain beholden to the strong creditor, since it is not in the latter's interest to reduce his strength or to contract himself in order to create a contract of selves. As a result, the gap of natural inequality inevitably widens.

Thus, in guilt-debt relationships, if the other does not repay something equivalent to what he owes me, all the rules of indebtedness apply to him. I can then degrade him, oppress him, increase his guilt feelings, and even enslave him (see Mauss 1954) and thus also inevitably increase his resentment of me, since "each to his own" salvation predominates. This seems to be how the Protestant individualistic doctrine of salvation has made its second coming under the disguised secularized garment of philosophical anthropology. Immanuel Kant interpreted the Protestant individualist inner court of conscience into an individualistic salvation doctrine of moral cognition: Nietzsche preached salvation (from the need for salvation) through one's egoistic will to power; Heidegger spoke of a solitary man who can communicate only with himself; and Sören Kierkegaard's "Single One" stands alone before God. Thus, in sailing under the flag of a new humanistic "self-salvation army," which in "rejecting the idea of salvation . . . replaced it by a kind of self-affirmation" (see Tillich 1965: 19), man finds himself in desperate loneliness. And hence, argues Buber (1967), with this increasing solitary image of man "each solitude is colder and stricter than the preceding, and salvation from it more difficult" (p. 167).

This "I *or* thou" approach to salvation, in which the strong creditor does not contract his strength to meet the other, has also—as I have pointed out elsewhere (Rotenberg 1978)—laid the groundwork for a long tradition of self-indulging salvation-psychotherapy.

The alternative, the alter-centered theory of "reciprocal-contraction," requires that a differentiation be made between its two major components: (1) the structural nonutilitarian *contractual* nature of alter-centered salvation; and (2) the functional *contractional* nature of alter-centered salvation. Since utilitarianism has been traditionally used to refer to ego-centered motivation and functionalism to group conditions, I am referring by a nonutilitarian contractual relationship to social contracts between people that require each partner to give something or to do something for his salvation that is not directly utilitarian for himself. Consequently, in the functional contractional relationships, which are a result of the nonutilitarian contract, theoretically no side in the contract can become a strong creditor or a weak debtor, for each partner must contract himself in relation to the other in order to make the salvation-contract possible. The resultant contractional relationship becomes utilitarian for each side, because it is functional for mutual survival and for the maintenance of the social system since there is no widening gap to disrupt these relationships.

The Issachar and Zebulun Contract

The ancient sociological exchange system of the nonutilitarian alter-centric salvation pattern, which emanated from the biblical-tribal "Issachar and Zebulun" model (referring especially to its neo-Hasidic "matter and form" formulation), will be used here as a paradigmatic case to explicate and elucidate sociological (alter-centered) contraction. The most successful succinct description of the Issachar and Zebulun contract emanating from mutual contraction is to be found in a short story by the Nobel Prize winning author, Shumel Yosef Agnon:

> When Issachar came to take up his place in paradise . . . they said to him: Issachar, in the world from which you came, from whence was your livelihood? Did he say to them: I had a brother and Zebulun was his name, and he made a partnership with me. He sits on the seashore and sails with merchandise and earns and gives into my mouth and I sit and study the Torah. Did they say to him: if so your Torah was Zebulun's because if Zebulun would not have engaged in trading you would not study the Torah, and you consumed your paradise during your lifetime. . . . Said Zebulun: all the goodness which I received came to me only due to Issachar my brother who studied the Torah, it follows that it was not me who supported Issachar but Issachar supported me, and now I shall take his place in paradise? . . . Zebulun did not return to his place in paradise due to Issachar's sorrow and Issachar did not enter instead because of his love for Zebulun. Said the Almighty: Issachar and Zebulun you contracted yourself each for the other. . . . I shall expand your place.

At this hour Zebulun's lot in paradise expanded and space was found also for Issachar. And to this day Issachar and Zebulun sit in paradise and study the Torah alike, and enjoy the divine light, and the Almighty bestows his honor upon them. Since Zebulun supported Issachar and Issachar supported Zebulun's destiny, the Almighty bestowed his honor upon both. (Agnon 1959: 35, 36)

Agnon captured the two essential components of contractual alter-centered salvation. Not only is one's salvation realized through doing for or sharing with the other, but salvation through the other is reciprocally uneven and materially nonutilitarian. The recipient or debtor does not have to return to the creditor whatever he received, but he must accomplish something else, which indirectly and independent from this uneven reciprocity benefits the creditor. Hence there is neither equality nor inequality, because the salvation-actualization efforts of the two partners are not comparable; consequently, there is also no guilt-debt relationship. Issachar's actualization depends on his studying the Torah for himself and for Zebulun, independent of the latter's support or gratitude; Zebulun's salvation depends on his supporting Issachar, although the latter has no material debts in relation to the former.

In his analysis of gift-exchange systems in various primitive tribes, Malinowski (1961) describes a somewhat similar commercial exchange system termed *kula*, according to which arm shells and necklaces are passed around in a sort of circular movement from west to east and from east to west respectively, and consequently the receivers do not have to return something equivalent to the givers. In the *kula* trade system this circular exchange movement is, however, but one aspect of exchange, based on the principle of obligatory equivalent returns between creditors and debtors.

Nonetheless, an asymmetric exchange system most closely akin to the Issachar and Zebulun contract can be found among the Brahmins (see Mauss 1954), who solicit and receive gifts but make their return wholly by religious services. Here the exchange is so structured that in order not to lose his superiority and to prevent the danger of dependent guilt-debt relationships, this caste pretends to refuse gifts and "then compromises and accepts only those which are given spontaneously [because] the bond that the gift creates between the donor and the recipient is too strong for them" (see Mauss 1954: 58).

While a proper discussion doing justice to the elaborated theories coming out of the sociological exchange school is beyond the scope of the present narrow contraction perspective, I should nonetheless mention that while giving and receiving in social systems of kinship[1] or friendship is instrumental and direct, it is nonetheless essentially unconditional and, consequently, at times unilateral. Unilateral reciprocity in such cases might still eschew socially dysfunctional guilt-debt relationships, although it is unequivocal in that it does not require or facilitate equivalent repayment, at least in the case of offspring, in relation to their parents (see Eisenstadt 1971). It should be stressed further that, while typical patron-client relationship exchange is usually structurally unequal or unconditional, exchange in such systems is nonetheless anchored in hierarchical class stratification and power differentiation (see Eisenstadt and Roniger 1980),[2] which is markedly unlike the Issachar and Zebulun equal status exchange model.

Most interesting here is also the case of Japan, where interpersonal dependent relationships based on the notion of *amae* (see Doi 1973) are fostered as regulative mechanisms of social control and where, accordingly, return of a debt means cutting off relationships, while the nonreturn of a debt connotes friendship, trust, and eternal gratitude.

In discussing what can be termed the "structural-functional" mechanisms of interpersonal dependence in Japan, Doi (1973: 88) quotes an episode from a story by Natsume Soseki:

> I once borrowed three yen from Kiyo. Five years have gone by but I still haven't returned it. Not that I can't, I just don't! . . . and I've no intention of feeling an obligation to return it immediately, as though she was a stranger. It would be as though I didn't take her kindness at its face value—like finding fault with the goodness of her heart . . . to accept a favor from one who's not one of your own people and to do nothing about returning it is doing him a favor, because it means you're treating him like somebody who matters to you. If you pay your own share, the matter ends there . . . To have a feeling of gratitude inside for a favor done you— that's the kind of repayment no money can repay.

Although one might wonder whether the feeling of gratitude might not be as enslaving as the Western guilt-debt relationship, especially when borrowing is unilateral, this case is cross-culturally illuminative.

For the sake of analytical consistency, a conceptual differentiation between sociological and psychological contraction must be made here. Sociological alter-centric contraction means that the cultural system offers several ideal labels or types for salvation (e.g., Issachar, Zebulun, and/or others) which because of their equal status as idealized goals for salvation and their alter-centric prescriptive salvation norms, have to be contracted to facilitate the coexistence of multiple salvation-actualization systems. Psychological contraction refers to interactive behavioral norms prescribing how people should contract their selves in relation to other people or in relation to various mental states within themselves. Sociological alter-centered contraction can be understood by studying structural relationships between various salvation systems, such as those disseminated by the Issachar and

Zebulun contract. Psychological alter-centeric contraction can be understood by examining the dynamics of intrapersonal and interpersonal behavior norms prescribed by Hasidic ethics.

As I shall demonstrate, however, the Hasidic behavioral ethics did not
develop in a vacuum, but seem to have drawn heavily on the Issachar and
Zebulun alter-centered contraction perspective.

The Ideological-Historical Roots of the Issachar and Zebulun Model

To understand how the Hasidic neo-Issachar and Zebulun model emerged,
we must at this point examine briefly the socio-historic origins of the
Issachar and Zebulun alter-centered contract. The earliest sources concerning the Issachar and Zebulun contract are the legends and commentary that
evolved around the biblical descriptions of these two tribal brothers. The
first elements of the legend were based on Jacob's blessings to his sons in
Genesis and on Moses' blessings of the tribes in Deuteronomy: "Zebulun
shall dwell at the haven of the sea; and he shall be an haven of ships . . .
Issachar is a strong ass crouching down between two burdens" (Gen. 49:13–
14); and "of Zebulun he said, 'Rejoice, Zebulun, in thy going out; and
Issachar, in thy tents' " (Deut. 33:18).

In the Talmudic period (specifically from the second to fifth centuries
A.D.) Zebulun was described as a merchant, and Issachar's burden and tents
were described as the burden and tents of Torah. Moreover, the fact that
Zebulun was mentioned first in both blessings, although he was younger
than Issachar, gave birth to the famous interpretation used also by Agnon
that Zebulun and Issachar made a partnership. Zebulun dwells at the haven
of the sea and goes out sailing with his merchandise and earns and gives
into the mouth of Issachar, who sits and studies the Torah.[3] And therefore
Zebulun came before Issachar since Issachar's Torah was due to Zebulun
(Rashi, Deut. 33:18). From a historical point of view it is of interest to
stress that in spite of some evidence indicating that Zebulun was indeed a
sea merchant and Issachar a Talmudist and a judge, it was in fact a legend,
gradually transformed into an ideology, which was also eventually translated
into a contractual and contractional tradition instructing the rich (not
necessarily Zebulunian sea merchants) to purchase their salvation by supporting poor Talmudic scholars (see Beer 1968).

We should differentiate between the two important exchange systems
that followed from this tradition. The predominant pattern was the
straightforward tradition of alter-centered salvation in which Zebulun the
merchant supports Issachar the scholar. Although here the ideal model for
self-actualization was studying the Torah, Zebulun's alter-centered salvation
seems to have reached a higher level than Issachar's because he was mentioned first in the biblical blessings. The second pattern seems to have insti-

tutionalized an exchange system of trading and arbitration. According to this tradition, Issachar divided his time between cultivating his land and studying Torah, while Zebulun only exported Issachar's products and imported the goods Issachar needed from abroad. While the alter-centered salvation motif is preserved in both systems, the first case contains a negative-parasitic element, which I shall address later, and the second system bears the seeds of the unique interpersonal and economic exchange that subsequently developed.

Indeed, for a time there seems to have been a certain struggle between these two alter-centered salvation systems, which was reflected in the ideologies expressed by early (second to third century) and later (third to fifth century) Talmudic scholars. The historian Beer (1968) describes a case of a Talmudic law that was cited in the name of a person named Azarya only because he was a merchant who supported his brother Rabbi Shimon (see Rashi, Talmud, *Zevachim* 2:1). On the other hand, it is said that the famous Talmudist Hillel refused to be supported by his brother Shevna, a rich merchant. This implies that Hillel favored the second system and hence advocated that scholars should both work and study (see Talmud, *Sota* 21:1). In general, maintains Beer (1968), although there is some available evidence from Talmudic preachings that members of the Issachar tribe either rented out their fields in order to free themselves for study or divided their time between study and self-supporting labor (and hence only used Zebulun's marketing services), in fact the rabbis gradually began to demand in their public preachings that the Talmudists (i.e., the Issachars) should devote their entire time to studies and that the merchants (i.e., the Zebuluns) should support them completely. Thus the Talmudists who lived from the second to the fifth centuries institutionalized the Issachar and Zebulun contract through the tradition of public appeals and the formation of welfare organizations in order to support poor scholars. What appears most significant, according to Beer, is that leading solicitors such as "Rabbi Hiyya Bar Abba made Zebulun the supporter of Issachar the scholar. The Israeli and Babylonian Amoraim [Talmudists from the third to fifth centuries] learned from him, and so did the preachers and biblical commentators throughout the ages" (1968: 180).

To lead the reader directly to our major paradigmatic case study, it would be useful to skip now from the Talmudic period to the eighteenth-century Hasidic culture, in order to demonstrate how the Issachar and Zebulun model was revived in Hasidic spiritual-material terms as a neo-Issacharian-Zebulunian alter-centered contraction model.

The People of Form and the People of Matter

The key concepts here are "people of matter" and "people of form." They were introduced by Rabbi Yaacov Yosef of Polony, who was the Besht's contemporary and literary disciple and who laid the groundwork for the Hasidic philosophy by interpreting the Besht's doctrine in biblical commentary and books.

According to the Hasidic monistic conception of man, earthly physical matters (*chomer*) can and must be converted into spiritual forms (*tzura*). The functional relationship between "form" and "matter" assumes that one is impossible without the other, on both the intrapsychic and the interpersonal levels (see Dresner 1960). Thus, in Hasidic literature the terms "form" and "matter" are used to refer to psychological states within people (with which I shall deal separately), to "people of form" (*anshey tzura*), who have presumably reached a high level of spirituality, and to "people of matter" (*anshey chomer*), the ordinary masses who live in the earthly, material world.

According to Rabbi Yaacov Yosef (1963), early Hasidim used the doctrine of "form" and "matter" strictly to reestablish the alter-centered contractional relationship that prevailed between Issachar and Zebulun (see Nigal 1974). Thus, in approaching the rich "people of matter" the early Hasidic leaders emphasized that it is functional for the salvation of the rich to support the "people of form" (referring to the old-style Talmudic scholars), because through their cleavage to the "people of form," so they too will be uplifted and redeemed. Moreover, these early Hasidic leaders stressed that this system of mutual help is functional for the maintenance and survival of the entire community, as the "people of form" have a moral influence on the "people of matter," and the latter reciprocate by bestowing material goodness upon the former (see Nigal 1974: 28).

The structural-functional organic relationship between the "people of form" and the "people of matter" is then extended by Rabbi Yaacov Yosef and other Hasidic leaders to the sphere of adhesion and prayers, which epitomized Hasidic alter-centered salvation. Functional system maintenance on a horizontal level is portrayed in terms of functional organic interdependence between the "people of form" and the "people of matter." The prayers of the "people of form" are spiritual; they constitute the nation's soul and bestow spirituality on the "people of matter." The prayers of the "people of matter" are intended to maintain or supply the material needs for themselves and for the "people of form"; hence, the "people of matter" constitute the nation's body. Thus, a horizontal structure of "organic solidarity" is created, for the soul cannot exist without the body, and the body cannot exist without the soul (see *Toldot*, Rabbi Yaacov Yosef 1963: 269). Elsewhere, Rabbi Yaacov Yosef portrays the "people of matter" as the feet of the congregation and the "people of form" as its eyes. This description gives the organic interdependence of these two "peoples" a most dynamic dimension, for when the feet are low, the head is also inevitably bent (see Nigal 1974: 24).

Thus theoretically Yaacov Yosef's organic solidarity, or rather organic interdependence, model refers not merely to what may be pictured as a vertical Durkheimian or Parsonian universalistic, affectively neutral interdependence but to a horizontal structural status equality that should consequently prevail between Issacharian form and Zebulunian matter on the *inter*personal and the *intra*personal levels. Hence, stresses Rabbi Yaacov Yosef (1963: 243),

> Since similar to the individuality within one person, the soul and form is not to feel superior over the body and say that it is a holy soul, . . . and even more so the body is not to be arrogant over the soul as it holds the soul, . . . as they need each other like a man and a woman, each one being half a body. So it is in the collective, the Talmudic scholars and righteous are not to say that there is no need in the masses, since they support the Torah, . . . and even more so the masses are not to say that there is no need for Talmudic scholars, or to feel arrogant against them since their livelihood is due to them, . . . and so, each one is half and with both together, matter and form whether in the collective or within the individual, it becomes one full person.

Thus, the Issachar and Zebulun monistic alter-centered contraction model was reconstructed in Hasidic matter-and-form terminology.

In summing up the introduction of the sociological "matter and form" paradigm, which for purposes of convenience and historical consistency will hereafter be termed the "Issachar and Zebulun" or material-spiritual contractional model, there emerge two sociological patterns that call for some socio-historical illustrative verification. These patterns, which are today by no means exclusively Jewish, are: (1) The interactive "alter-centered salvation" pattern (i.e., actualizing salvation through the contracted other) and (2) The structural "multiple ideal labels" dimension (facilitating actualization through multiple alternative social ideals).

Although the interpersonal "alter-centered salvation" exchange pattern and the "multiple ideal labels" structural dimension are interrelated (because it is the very contraction of the material ideal label Zebulun in relation to the spiritual ideal label Issachar which creates the organic alter-centered actualization system), I shall deal with these patterns separately after the following general introductory statements.

From a general socio-historical perspective, the Jewish congregational tradition of organizing welfare institutions and forming economic exchange patterns such as banking and trading, as well as the tendency to identify with messianic and utopian-socialistic movements, can be traced to the contractional alter-centered salvation norm.

Although the idea of salvation in Judaism is quite complex, as we shall later see, in relation to the first pattern Scholem (1972: 1) states that while generally "Christianity conceives of redemption as an event . . . which is reflected in the soul, in the private world of each individual, and which effects an inner transformation . . . the Jewish categories of redemption, is a community." Similarly, Buber (1958a) maintains that while preoccupation with one's own salvation is the highest aim in Protestantism, in Judaism one is redeemed only through the other "thous" in the community to whom one is responsible and who are responsible for him. Hence, such Talmudic imperatives as "One who solicits mercy for his fellow while he himself is in need of the same thing will be answered first" (Talmud, *Baba Kama* 92a) or "All Israel are sureties[4] one for another" (Talmud, *Shevuot* 39a) have featured the Jewish communal welfare system for many generations.

In Mahayana Buddhism, where salvation or freedom is attained by obtaining knowledge and enlightenment (*bodhi*), salvation is similarly alter-centered in that the knowledge (*bodhi-sattva*) that one acquires is for all beings and not for oneself (see Ishizu 1970). But in this case there is only one salvation goal, and alter-centrism does not lead to an interactive, this-world activism (see Murti 1970). In general, however, it must already be pointed out here that alter-centered salvation may be, as we shall see later, functional or dysfunctional for the maintenance of the social system.

In alter-centered cultures, with a multiple, contracted ideal-labeling system, people must contract themselves in relation to others, because there is more than one yardstick to measure actualization or salvation. The Besht's (1975b: 17) systematic use of the biblical verse "In all thy ways know Him" (Prov. 3:6) may represent a typical multiple actualization ideal that corresponds behaviorally to the Issachar and Zebulun structural multiple ideal-labeling dimension.[5] In cultures predominated by only one, non-contracted salvation goal, which I term the "mono ideal label" system (e.g., the Protestant "superman" or "supermaterialist"), inequality is inevitably perpetuated. Since by law of nature not all people are equally endowed to be intellectually or materially successful, interaction is regulated by guilt-debt relationships, and this increases the probability of widening social gaps and ratios of deviance, because the less endowed "debtor" will always "owe" something to the stronger creditor. This seemed to have been Blau's (1975) point of departure from Homans' (1961) utilitarian, ego-centric, and consequently guilt-debt oriented exchange theory. While Homans insisted that the course of human action is motivated by people's self-interested maximizations of returns and minimization of losses, Blau admitted that the natural differences in the amount of talent, resources, and power that exchange partners possess create social imbalances that widen the gap between the deprived debtor and his selfish, crediting exchange partner. Our model intends to expose the futility of the *equality* myth by the apparent *utility* of a social structure with multiple ideal labels as it differentiates between multiple *roads* to salvation and multiple *modes* of salvation.

Because the sociological examination of the functionality or dysfunctionality of the alter-centered salvation pattern in terms of its contribution to the maintenance of the general social system is deeply embedded in the problem of altruism (i.e., degree of instrumentality in interpersonal relationships), we may begin our analysis of the first pattern by contrasting alterism with altruism.

NOTES

1. It is of interest that typical Western exchange theorists (see Burns 1977) regard husband-wife exchange as unequal mainly because the wife does not repay in equivalent material productivity matching that of the husband and is for that reason considered to be in a subordinate position.

2. It may be noted in a similar fashion that while Blau's (1964) imbalanced exchange category may at times be functional, as in the case where subordinates receive benefits and protection, inequality and social gaps are still maintained in such relationships because of the imbalanced power, although exploitation and oppression are not immanent. Similarly, the "asymmetrical exchange" among Hindus and other South Asian cultures described by Marriott (1976: 112) is used mostly as a basis for social differentiation and power rankings, whereby "those who give are to be recognized as differing from and standing in rank, power and quality . . . above those who take."

3. In the Testaments of the Twelve Patriarchs (135–104 B.C.) Zebulun is said to have told his sons, "I saw a man in distress through nakedness in wintertime, and had compassion upon him, and stole away a garment secretly from my father's house, and gave it to him" (see Charles 1917: 69). Here Zebulun's alter-centered salvation might be the first description of "Robin-Hoodism."

4. The Maggid of Mezeritz (1927: 63), one of the Besht's two major disciples, has said that the Hebrew word *arevim* (sureties, responsible) should be read *meoravim*, "intermingled."

5. The Talmudic parallel to the multiple-actualization ideal-labeling principle is the notion of "these and those are God's living words" (*Gitin* 6:2), which stands for the principle of legitimizing the diversity of legal opinions.

(3)

Contractional Alterism vs. Contractual Altruism

Researchers have agreed without serious difficulty that psychological altruism refers to "behavior carried out to benefit another with anticipation of rewards from external services" (see Macaulay and Berkovitz 1970: 3). There is less agreement, however, as to whether altruistic behavior patterns can be induced without external social pressures or concrete reinforcement systems. Freedman (1970) has demonstrated, for example, that people who were manipulated under experimental conditions to feel guilty in relation to others showed an increased tendency to expiate their guilt in many instrumental ways, among them by expressing a willingness to help others. Thus, as "instrumental altruism" is a contradiction in terms (see Kaufmann 1970), embedded either in contractual guilt-debt relationships or in an ego-centric reward-and punishment system, many psychologists question the usefulness of altruism as a psychological research construct in the first place.

The obsolescence of studying psychological altruism seems to follow directly from its very Protestant definition; it can be best understood by considering the meaning of sociological or collectivistic altruism. The sharp dichotomy between an egoistic, individualistic life-style in which the "I" exists only for himself, and the altruistic, collectivistic life in which the individual lives only for others (see Gordon 1951)—and in which he is entirely discounted and immersed by a collectivist or totalitarian society (see Buber, 1967 and Tucker 1967)—has long been a feature of Western interpersonal behavior. Westerners have grown accustomed to the social pendulum that swings them back and forth from extreme individualism to extreme collectivism. Hence, if altruism is studied not in terms of self-contraction to help the other but in terms of a contractual relationship between noncontracted creditors and discounted debtors, then research obviously leads to a dead end, because the gap between the mono-ideal creditor (i.e., the Nietzschean "superman" or "supermaterialist") and the weak debtor can never be minimized. Consequently, "altruistic," guilt-provoking, and non-

(28)

returnable help extended in an ego-centered salvation culture by egoistic creditors is doomed to be rejected.

Alterism, on the other hand, refers to functional interpersonal behaviors prevailing among multiple unequal creditors who "benefit others" via contraction, but not destruction, of their self or the alter's self. Zebulun owes something (support) to Issachar, and Issachar owes something *else* (studying) to Zebulun, but neither of them is an altruistic, guilt/hate-provoking creditor, because it is the mutual contraction of their crediting positions that keeps their contract going.

The philosophical difference between functional *alteristic* relationships and guilt-loaded *altruistic* relationships can be considered also from a social-philosophical perspective. In their attempt to refute the claims of egoists who insist that "in doing altruistic things for others . . . we are seeking our own good" (see Frankena 1963: 20), believers in the existence of altruistic impulses used either J. Butler's line of argument "that we sometimes want to do something for others and that we are so constituted as to get satisfaction out of doing so" or David Hume's thinking that "there is some benevolence, however small . . . kneaded into our frame along with the elements of the wolf and the serpent" (ibid.). While Hume admits that we wolfmen have some *kindness* in us, and Butler concedes that we are so *constituted* to get satisfaction out of doing things we *want* to do for others, both see altruistic impulses as *innate* traits unrelated to ego-centered guilt-debt relationships governing everyday interaction. Alterism assumes, however, that the meaning of "altruism" in terms of the motivation to "do things for others" must be examined from a social structural-functional point of view and not from an innate, deterministic, and individualistic viewpoint.

Thus, the ambition to propose alterism as a term preferable to altruism requires a more extensive examination of the age-long controversial question concerning the possibility of altruism from a social-structural point of departure.

In their struggle to study the existence of altruism, classic philosophers were divided between the internalists and the externalists. The internalists, who were influenced primarily by Kant, believe that moral behavior might be autonomic and hence motivated by the truth inherent in ethical propositions that are independent of external psychological interests. Externalists, following J. S. Mill, G. E. Moore, and mainly Thomas Hobbes, hold that behavior is motivated by psychological utilitarian sanctions that are external to pure ethical principles. Hobbes, for example, maintained that motivational energies are derived solely from a universal desire for self-preservation and that hence man must at times help the other with whom he has signed a social contract, so that the other needy, deprived person will not annihilate him. The help extended to him, is, however, purely egoistic. Genuine altruism is thus nowhere operative, because a person can feel only his own toothache, as Wittgenstein (1965) has shown and as the solipsists declared (see Nagel 1975), and therefore people cannot be interested in the welfare of others more than in their own welfare. Consequently, altruism is essentially an enlarged form of egoism, although it requires a calculated consideration of others' needs.

This philosophical dispute between the internalists and the externalists would have remained futile from the present social perspective if both sides had not admitted that altruism, whether egoistic or not, requires a recognition of the reality of others of which I am part, as Nagel pointed out. Accordingly, if "altruism"—whatever the definition—refers to the interchange between individuals and others, it can be assessed only in structural-functional terms concerning one's ability to recognize the reality of others and in terms of the impact one's behavior has on specific others whom he is to help and on society at large.

We can now examine Hobbesian self-preserving egoistic altruism by confronting the solipsist assertion that man cannot feel the other's pain. We begin with three questions:

1. If man can feel only his own toothache, how can he defend himself by helping the other without being able to know what's good or painful for him?

2. Can behavior be defined as altruistic even if the receiver does not enjoy it or even suffers from this help (i.e., is the definition of altruism dependent on the effect it has on the receiver)?

3. Can altruistic help be effective and structurally functional if it is unilateral (i.e., when the receiver is deprived or exempt from the opportunity to return an equivalent repayment)?

Considering the first question, the solipsist Hobbesian assertion that a person can feel only his own pain or pleasure should be refuted first on the grounds that if this would indeed be true then egoistic-altruism (helping others for self-defense) would be impossible, because if I don't know what's bad or good for the other then I don't know how and when to help him, and consequently the other would annihilate me. We can thus assume that since people usually do not annihilate one another, man must possess some empathic ability to feel, or cognitively recognize (see Rotenberg 1974), the pain or pleasure of others. But the assertion that man *must* be empathic for self-preservation is not proof that he can indeed identify the other's pain or pleasure. The present alteristic perspective would suggest, however not only that is he able to recognize others' pain or pleasure but also that man's full cognitive emotional recognition of his *own* pain and pleasure is learned only through the comparative process of experiencing with others or through others what he later identifies as his own pain or pleasure.

We know, for example, that even seemingly "primary" appetites for food, fame, sex, and so on, are not always similarly satisfying. The same physical or social act of eating or lovemaking may be at one time very enjoyable and at other times less enjoyable. We may say to ourselves, "I should have done it differently," "I should have begun my speech to the audience with a different phrase or tone," "I should have cooked the meal differently." But then again, we ask ourselves, "Why? This is precisely the way I did it last time, and then I enjoyed it!" The answer seems to lie in that our self-actualizing salvation can be attained only by comparing and sharing our experiences with others. One cannot really enjoy smoking pot without learning to feel how others in a group react to marihuana (Becker 1963). A mother's vicarious satisfaction from feeding her child flows directly from her own comparative eating experience. We may learn to appreciate modern art or music through others' influence, to the absurd point that we may conceive of yesterday's ugliness as today's new beauty. A rich man receives his real reassuring pleasure from the accoutrements of wealth only after he observes how his guests enjoy them. Likewise, our feelings after a novice-eccentric experience can be enhanced or ascertained much better after we test how others felt during the same or a similar experience. We "enjoy" or "suffer from delusions" to the extent that others in our social group describe such experiences as enjoyable or as disturbing. While in ancient times "holy" people enjoyed "visions," today "sick" people suffer from (the same) delusions or "hallucinations." Hence, an experience receives its complete cognitive and emotional actualizing meaning only through social comparison, that is, only after we do for others what we believe is good for ourselves, or we enable them to experience what we want to experience and sense their feelings in relation to the particular experience.

Thus, the meaning of my own pain or pleasure is acquired through my empathic ability to recognize its comparative impact on many others. We may thus deal now with our second question. Once this ability to recognize the other's pleasure or pain has been established, is the definition of my "altruistic" act of giving dependent or independent from its effect on the receiver? On first consideration, why shouldn't my blood donation be considered altruistic, even if the receiver died in spite of my contribution? That is, why shouldn't we accept Titmuss' (1970) definition that it is this very impersonal, anonymous situation which eliminates the need to express gratitude, which makes blood donations altruistic? If, however, we take this argument to its very bitter end and examine it from a broad structural-functional angle, our confidence in the truism of this definition of altruism would be somewhat shattered. Let us assume that one donates a roast of beef to a vegetarian, or that the rich creditor gives the poor debtor things that are not most urgent on the latter's preference list. It seems obvious that, from a social structural Hobbesian point of view, if many creditors would "help" many debtors without considering what is good or bad for them, society would disintegrate, because the "wolves" would destroy one another, and hence giving cannot be impersonal but must be directly assessed according to its impact on the other and on the society at large. Accordingly, only giving a roast of beef to a meat lover would be functional because it fits the receiver's needs.

But here we come to our third question: if altruistic giving must be personal (matched to the other's need) can it be functional if it is unilateral? That is, is it structurally functional if debtors will be deprived, exempt, or unable to return an equivalent gift or repayment? Will it perpetuate the widening guilt-debt social gaps between debtors and creditors? Later I shall describe in more detail the dangerous social consequences discussed by Mauss (1954) that emanate from the inability to return equivalent gifts in societies that are regulated by symmetric exchange systems. Here it will be sufficient to conclude that, from a social structural point of view, altruism is impossible as an indirect impersonal act because the possible harmful effect resulting from no assessment of its specific impact on others would cause mutual annihilation, and it is likewise impossible as a direct, personal, *unilateral* act, because inability to return equivalent gifts widens the guilt-debt social gap between the deviant, underprivileged debtors and the gifted, strong creditors.

Alterism is, however, structurally functional because it assesses giving according to its impact on others and society at large and because it does not require equivalent return, yet it does not deprive the debtor of his need to repay. Zebulun supports Issachar directly by assessing empathically his needs, but Issachar is neither oppressed by the demand for an equivalent return nor deprived of his need and privilege to repay something else which facilitates actualization and which minimizes social gaps because it is not measurable by Zebulun's yardstick.

It follows, then, that Zebulun supports Issachar not because of his innate *surplus* kindness or his fear of mutual annihilation, and not because he gets an egoistic satisfying kick out of it, and not because he expects the other to return the debt. Rather, self-realizing salvation derived from Issachar's studying or teaching or from Zebulun's support is functionally dependent on others enjoying a similar redeeming feeling from the one doing for or giving something to another. According to egoistic-altruism, individuals are self-sufficient creatures capable of reaching full actualizing salvation experiences all by themselves; hence, giving or doing for others is a "free addition" to interpersonal relations. Thus, the "surplus" conception of giving constitutes the Western unilateral welfare model of egoistic-altruism. On the other hand, alterism assumes that real satisfaction and salvation are attainable only through others; hence, doing for others is neither altruistic nor egoistic, but the very essence of bilateral experiential actualizing salvation.

Altruistic relationships must therefore by definition come to a dead end—not only because eventually debtors will run out of credit, but mainly because if interpersonal altruism involves guilt-debt relationships, it becomes self-contradictory and inevitably self-dissolving. Alteristic relationships, however, encourage continuous unequal reciprocity. In this sense the difference between alterism and altruism is that in the former motivating salvation norms and social relations function in harmony, while in the latter they are contradictory.

This seems to be the underlying assumption advanced by Durkheim's "Jewish functional perspective," which rejected Weber's (1968) Protestant functionalism, positing that Hobbesian-utilitarian mutual self-interests regulate a social exchange system as market behavior. Durkheim's contention that an egoistic salvation system comprised of self-interests would lead to social disorder and breakdown (see Pope et al. 1975)—and that hence shared moral norms and not individual motivation undergird the existence of the social order and behavior motivation—presupposes, however, a somewhat naive deterministic view of society. It assumes that moral obligations stem from the sacred element inherent in society's power without explaining the relationship between norms and behavior motivation. The perspective suggested by the Issachar and Zebulun paradigm assumes that an alteristic salvation system explains the functional survival of a social system as well as the forces motivating behavior. It is thus not charity or philanthropic behavior per se that differentiates between altruistic contractual behavior and alteristic contractional relationships. While altruistic charity or philanthropic behavior characterizes many Western and non-Western social systems, various unique positive and negative alteristic sociological styles can be identified in several Jewish traditions.

As the Hasidic culture that emerged in eighteenth-century Eastern Europe will be used as a major case study to explain the theory of alter-centered contraction, at this point the possibility of balanced (symbiotic) and imbalanced (parasitic) alter-centered contraction may be illuminated by a brief description of sociological patterns of communal welfare systems and messianic universalistic trends that are traceable to the ancient Zebulun and Issachar tradition. I shall use the terms "balanced" (symbiotic-positive) and "imbalanced" (parasitic-negative) "alter-centered contraction," and not the traditional sociological terms "functional" or "dysfunctional" relations, because parasitic interaction may be functional for the survival of the social system at large. The terms "symbiotic" and "parasitic" come to feature a constellation of relationships in which the give-and-take of parties, while being structurally indirect (asymmetric), are balanced or imbalanced respectively in terms of their contribution to the social climate or moral atmosphere of a given social system.

Balanced (Symbiotic) Alter-Centered
Contraction and the Mutual-Aid Tradition

In their classic anthropological study of the Jewish small town (*shtetl*) in Eastern Europe, Zborowski and Herzog observed that the pattern of giving and receiving "provides the central mechanism by which the community functions. The interweaving of individual benefaction with collective community service, of the voluntary with the compulsory, of religious injunction with civic obligation is essential to the organization and behavior of the shtetl." (1952: 194) A famous anthropologist is said to have stated that the Jewish *shtetl* was the bedrock of the Jewish "*statel*" (i.e., Israel). Since the organizational pattern of the poor Jewish *shtetl* in Eastern Europe is a good prototype for the famous Jewish mutual-aid systems and welfare organizations that evolved in the modern world, it would seem sufficient to illuminate the alter-centric nature inherent in this welfare tradition.

While the English words "charity" or "philanthropy" imply an altruistic act of giving unilaterally to the needy, the Hebrew word for charity, *tzedaka*, is derived from the word "justice" in the social sense. The notion of *tzedaka* is accordingly interconnected with a whole set of man-to-man (*bein adam lechavero*: interpersonal) commandments ranging from extending good wishes, advice, food, and clothing to loans and charity. The alter-centric orientation stipulates, however, not only that "giving" is functional for others, but also that it constitutes one of the major self-actualizing modes of salvation in the sense of the "one who solicits mercy for his fellow . . . is answered first." Hence, report Zborowski and Herzog, giving "is not an act of simple altruism, for the donor profits far more than the receiver." The story about the beggar who threatened to leave his congregation and thus prevent the fulfillment of their alter-centered need to give is a good illustration. The ideal salvation label *baal tzedaka* (master of charity) is "one of the most honored titles a man can win" (ibid., p. 195); in addition, the Bible states that *tzedaka* will save from death" (Prov. 10:2 and Talmud, *Baba Batra* 10a), which implies that not giving to the needy may ultimately bring death on the total community.[1]

Similarly Poll (1969) observed that in a contemporary Hasidic community, soliciting letters sent by an anonymous contributory society emphasized heavily the alter-centered goal of giving by indicating that it actually is beneficial for the health and prosperity of the donor. The epitome of this multi alter-centered salvation pattern is accordingly reflected in its "unequal reciprocal" nature. Thus, Zborowski and Herzog observed, "the giving pattern is always complementary rather than symmetrical. The deed itself will not be returned . . . . This is a positive goal . . . to put what you have at the service of others, be it wealth, learning or energy" (pp. 198, 199). To prevent or minimize the possibility of guilt-debt social gaps, which might evolve from unilateral altruistic receiving, the Talmud states that "the one who loans money is greater than the one who gives *tzedaka*" (Talmud, *Shabbat* 63:1), and Maimonides (*Matnot Aniyim* 10:7) stated that the highest degree of *tzedaka* refers to one who loans to the poor, "makes him a partner or offers him work to strengthen his hand until he will not depend on people." Here loans should be understood in terms of the famous Jewish interest-free loan societies known as the *gemachim*,[2] in which theoretically there is no creditor who might oppress the debtor—somewhat similar to Merton and Gieryn's (1978) case of "institutionalized altruism." According to Jewish tradition, these societies operate on the basis of the egalitarian principle that all possessions—land, slaves, money, and so on—belong to God, who divides them equally among people, and hence they must eventually be returned to the original owner (for that reason the Hebrew conception of slave carries with it a temporary status) or be redivided not later than the specified year of the Jubilee; therefore there is in principle no crediting oppressor. Nevertheless, it must be stressed that whether Zebulun indeed contracts himself in relation to Issachar, or turns him into a guilty debtor, remains an empirical question that differs with time and social contexts. But from a theoretical point of view, the Zebulun and Issachar welfare system represents an ideal type (case) of sociological alter-centered contraction in which the *unequal reciprocity* provided by multiple ideal salvation labels (instead of a single, e.g., "supermaterialist," ideal), presumably facilitates the minimization of social gaps and deviance as well as the maintenance of society due to the "indirect" symbiotic salvation system. Moreover, it seems reasonable to speculate that the well-entrenched tradition of establishing functional and well-organized alter-centered welfare institutions, which can be identified in most Jewish communities since early times (see Bergman 1940), is associated with the "social contractional" model presented above. From this perspective, the difference between Western altruistic charity and Jewish alteristic welfare is in the differential salvation needs that motivate them. Altruistic charity is ego-centric and inevitably falls within the guilt-debt category, while alter-centered welfare is by definition other-directed and hence can be functional for both the individual and the collective.

Imbalanced (Parasitic) Alter-centered Contraction and the "Shnor" Tradition

Weber (1967: 249) was certainly correct in his observation that "one element particularly characteristic of modern capitalism was strikingly—and perhaps completely—missing from the extensive list of Jewish economic activities. This was the organization of industrial production . . . or manufacturing in domestic industry and in the factory system." To explain this reality, one could easily follow the apologetic line of argument and suggest that Jewish disengagement from manufacturing and industrial production was due either to persecutions, which indeed uprooted and/or forbade the Jews to work in the professions, or to their preference to engage in "money-lending,[3] which requires relatively little continuous labor" (Weber 1967: 255) and thus frees their time for studying the Talmud, as Weber believed.

One should realize, however, that although the above arguments seem essentially correct—in spite of the fact that serious "Zebulunism" in terms of complex banking and trading often requires more time investment than industrial activity—and although at times Jews worked very hard in manual labor (see Roth 1940), it was also the poorly applied Jewish work ethos that made Jews disinclined to purchase their salvation through hard work and hence invited exploitative interpretations of alter-centered salvation. That is, the lack of a strong "salvation through individualized hard work" ethos seems to have called for a broad, lax definition of "Issacharianism," which thus disrupted the ideal egalitarian "Issachar and Zebulun" structure and legitimized an exploitative appeal to Zebulun's alter-centered salvation needs. Thus, the institutionalized legitimization of the norm of *shnor* (soliciting money to support the needy), which was heavily based on Zebulun's need to redeem himself by supporting the Issachars—now broadly defined as scholars (preferably Talmudic), do-gooders, farmers (mainly those who rebuild the Holy Land), or simply needy people—created a semi-"guilt-debt" tension between the Zebuluns and the Issachars.

A discussion of the *halukah* will suffice to elucidate how *shnor* behavior (not necessarily the exploitive type) became institutionalized. The *halukah* ("distribution") refers to the organized collection of monies by Jews in the Diaspora for the support of their brethren in the land of Israel. This tradition of supporting Jews, presumably Torah scholars, in Israel was customary already during the Talmudic era (first to sixth century): "During the Middle Ages and especially during the following centuries, this method of support . . . became widespread and encompassed the whole of the Jewish world" (*Encyclopedia Judaica* [1971], vol. 7, p. 1207). The fundamental idea on which the *halukah* (which can be identified in contemporary "appeals" in the Diaspora) is based is the conviction that the land of Israel holds a special position in the religious and national consciousness of Jews. Hence the people living there serve as the representatives of Diaspora Jews, who actually should be living there themselves. As the *halukah* epitomizes the Zebulunian alteristic need for salvation, it may be an obvious source of tension inviting systematic attempts appealing to that need. Friedman (1977: 3) reports, for example, that by the end of the nineteenth century the absolute dependence of what can be termed the too broadly defined "Issachars" in Israel on the "Zebuluns" abroad (mainly in the United States) created an inevitable tension-loaded structure of relationship between the two groups due to the aura of imbalanced give-and-take in which "usually the 'receiver' felt deprived and the 'giver' feels, often, that he has given more than he can afford to." Indeed, it would seem safe to suggest that the soliciting methods that evolved from the *halukah* system served as a kind of prototype for *shnor* behavior on an individual and collective basis. Thus, by appealing to the alter-centered salvation need, messengers and letters were sent out from the land of Israel to "brothers" abroad, emphasizing that the donations to be given were vital to the *salvation* of the *donors*, either because the Jews in Israel pray for them, or because they study for them, or because they redeem them in some other form.

Here are a few passages from *shnor* letters sent from Israel during the nineteenth century. One famous public message simply stated that because of the merit of the Jews in Israel (mainly of those who study Torah), Jews exist in the Diaspora: "Due to the merits of those that sit in the land and keep her [Israel], due to the merit of the Torah which is being studied in Jerusalem, Diaspora Jews can live; without them they don't have a merit because it is there where God ordered his blessings on food and economy" (Rivkind 1888, quoted in Rothschild 1969: 48). Another *shnor* letter emphasized that the Jews in Israel suffer for the sake of their brothers abroad, and that "the land and all its inhabitants are those that suffer the reproach and pains for the rest of our brethren, the sons of Israel who are scattered in the Diaspora; therefore, we all, the entire house of Israel, are obliged in life savings" (Hageez 1836, in Rothschild 1969: 49). While in many letters the poverty and suffering of the Jews in Israel are simply dramatized and played up with a pleading request to send rescue money, the appeal to the alter-centered salvation need is maintained in most. In the following letter two intertwined alteristic elements—praying and redeeming—are stressed: "And this is our way to pray . . . for all those sitting in the Diaspora that He will gather the dispersed from the four corners of the earth to our land and our righteous redeemer will come" (Rothschild 1969: 61). Similarly, "And so right is the commandment of strengthening those sitting in the holy land, which outweighs all commandments, and Israel cannot be redeemed but via the charity done with God and his holy land" (Rothschild 1969: 62).

It is by no means being suggested here that people supported by the *halukah* were all parasites and not Talmudists, or that Jews in Israel did not eventually work hard to rebuild the country. Moreover, it is not being suggested that in other cultures a similar alter-centered salvation *shnor* pattern cannot be identified.[4] The *halukah* is used only to demonstrate how the alter-centered salvation norm of *shnor*, which appealed to the contractional salvation component, that is to the equal status of the receiver and donor, became an institutionalized behavior pattern. Thus, in face of the relatively weak tradition of preaching salvation through industrious hard work[5] (as the Protestant work ethos dictates), contractional alteristic salvation seems often to have catered to parasitic needs on the individual and collective levels and to the consequent development of *shnor* behavior (see Leibowitz 1979).

Alter-centered Salvation and Messianic Universalism

Another pattern of alter-centered salvation seems to carry mixed functional and dysfunctional features, from the social-system survival point of view, because its universalistic orientation is highly utopian, on the one hand, yet extracommunal on the other. The first, more functional components of universalistic salvation, which entails important therapeutic implications (about which more will be said later in Part III) is its future-oriented utopian messianism.

Scholem (1972) distinguishes between two major forms of messianism: the *restorative* form and the *utopian* form. Restorative messianism refers to promises of recreating a past that once existed. Hope is turned *backward* to the reestablishment and the reproduction of an original ideal state. In utopian messianism, forces are also directed at reestablishing an ideal past, but nonetheless hope is directed toward a future that supposedly will be better than anything that has ever existed in the past. While restorative messianism lies at the heart of the Christian chiliastic belief, which posits that salvation has already happened in the past (see Flusser 1970) and that Christ's second-millenarian coming will restore Christ's reign on earth, the essence of Jewish messianism is the utopian future-oriented hope that the Messiah's coming will create a collective universal state of peace and brotherhood that has never existed before.

Thus Isaiah's prophetic vision "It shall come to pass in the last days, that the mountain of the Lord's house shall be established in the top of the mountains, and shall be exalted above the hills; and all nations shall flow unto it" (Isa. 2:2) has been used as a motto for Jewish future-oriented utopian messianism for hundreds of years. Indeed, Scholem (1970) states that Jewish future-oriented utopian messianism[6] stands for

> the reintegration of all beings into a state of peace and harmony. . . .
> This reintegration is much more than restoration . . . it is rather the
> utopian hope that redemption will contain much more than any past. . . .
> This hope for a reformation that is at the same time revolution is at the
> heart of the messianic idea. It is this vision and this hope which are the
> contribution of Judaism to the understanding of redemption. (p. 12)

In a similar vein, in his philosophical discussion about images of the future, Polak (1973: 19) linked Jewish survival to its positive perception of the future: "The endurance of Jewish culture . . . lies in its fervently held image of the future, which has survived diaspora and pogrom alike. The prognosis of the dying Christian culture—if it can be said to be dying—lies in its dying image of the future." Thus, in differentiating eschatological and utopian images of the future, Polak concludes that the contemporary popular existential "here and now" pessimistic hedonism is "the wrong response to the challenge of the future [because] nihilistic images are paralyzing" (p. 21), whereas Jewish survival is no mystery at all, because from the time of the prophets, the Maccabees, and Hasidism it drew its living strength "from this burning expectation for the future" (p. 49).

While Polak's eschatological vision about the West's doomed future seems highly overstated, and while the problem of future time perception involves obviously more complex psychological processes that are beyond the scope of the present study, it nevertheless seems plausible that the positive (utopian) perception of the future was functional in terms of Jewish social-system survival because peoples' belief in the reality of their future may be related to their ultimate ability to construct it. The second, less functional aspect of universalistic salvation refers to the tendency to extend alter-centrism from the inner ethnical-communal social maintenance sphere to the cosmopolitan universalistic "messianic" domain. Thus, the "other" through whom one sought salvation was not always an ethnic "brother."

One must only notice how Isaiah's alter-centered imperative "I will also give thee for the light to the nations, that my salvation may be unto the end of the earth" (Isa. 49:6) inspired nineteenth-century leaders of reform Judaism or twentieth-century Jewish philosophers such as Buber, who defined Jewish *raison d'être* and salvation in strictly "Isaiahan" universal-messianic and alter-centered terms. According to Buber (1963: 187–191), for example, collective salvation is accomplished by assigning Israel to Isaiah's teacher/model task, which should ultimately bring universal peace and unity: "The people of Israel was charged to lead the way . . . the messianic prophecy whose central focal point is the effort of the people of Israel for the redemption of humanity."

Using a similar Isaiahan messianic terminology, such Jewish reform leaders as Samuel Holdheim (see Plaut 1963: 138) stated, "It is the messianic task of Israel to make the pure knowledge of God and the pure law of morality of Judaism the common possession and blessings of all the peoples of the earth." Most interesting here is how the Jewish communist Leon Trotsky (1970: 332) refuted the anti-Trotskyist crusade launched against him by his ex-comrades, the other Russian communist leaders, on the grounds that while "to us internationalism is not an abstract idea . . . to be betrayed on every opportune occasion," "they" led it to "self-contained national development and the old . . . Russian patriotism" (p. 520). The universalistic "alter-centered salvation" language comes through even clearer in Jewish historic interpretations of Russian revolutionism. For ex-

ample, in 1918 the socialistic revolutionary historian Angelo Solomon Rappoport explained Jewish revolutionarism as follows: "From Isaiah down to
Lassalle, the cry for justice and equality has been reiterated by the Jews, but
it has always been *universal* . . . to distribute to every one the greatest
possible sum of well-being . . . such is part of the mission of Israel" (p.
259). Thus, the extraterritorial universalistic form of alter-centered salvation seemed to have been less functional for Jewish survival when it clashed
with other more ego-centric salvation norms in the sense of "don't help
others to save your own skin" (see Levin 1977).

In conclusion, the sociological sources of the alter-centered contraction
theory have been introduced through the use of several illustrative socio-
historical interaction patterns rooted in the Issachar and Zebulun Jewish
ethics. Adequate substantiation of these patterns would require separate
studies, but I believe that the limited purpose introduced here has been
sufficiently developed. Issacharism, Zebulunism, or utopian Isaiahan alter-
centered behavior were used as *ideal* types. As stressed earlier, this is not to
suggest that such sociological patterns feature contemporary Jewish groups,
nor is it to imply that exchange patterns of this sort are not to be found in
other cultures or that Jewish alter-centrism should serve as an *idealized* type.
The major points of the present theory come to demonstrate, however, that
in contrast to ego-centered salvation cultures, in alter-centered societies
salvation, self-actualization, liberation, or therapy can be accomplished not
by *fulfilling* oneself, or rather by *filling* the self, that is, inflating the ego to be
full, but by contracting the self in order not to be too "full" (i.e., ego-in-
flated), so that sufficient "filling" will be left for the other. The sociological
cases presented above come to demonstrate how this "social interfilling"
salvation pattern (facilitated through the availability of multiple, contracted
ideal labels), generates various functional (and sometimes less functional)
interactive exchange patterns. The functional component in alter-centrism
stresses that social contraction connotes not an altruistic or quietistic elimination of the self but only the contraction of self. This facilitates the
funcitonal unequal reciprocity between multiple ideal labels, to be distinguished from the dysfunctional, "egalitarian" reciprocity where everybody is
equally compelled to live up to *one* ideal label. We may now turn to the
second structural sociological pattern emanating from the social-contraction
theory, that of the multiple ideal-labeling conception.

NOTES

1. Since alter-centered giving, as conceptualized here, must be functional for social-
   system survival of the total community, and because its effect must be "seen" and
   not only known, one might question the operational meaning of the Jewish
   imperative norm of *"matan beseter"* (giving anonymously), which would resemble
   Titmuss' blood-donating altruism. The answer to this apparent problem might be

found in the following Hasidic popular story: A very stingy rich man was once reproached by the rabbi of the small Jewish town where he lived for not giving *tzedaka*. To the evasive rich man's answer that he gives *matan beseter* (anonymously), the rabbi is said to have responded, "How could it be that all the sins which you would like to commit anonymously are known to everybody and precisely this humble merit of giving *tzedaka* is completely unknown?" Thus, giving anonymously is normative but its alter-centered effect on the total community must be somehow assessable and known.

2. While the free-loan institution is not exclusively Jewish, and while no attempt is intended here to protect Jewish "financial honesty," the contemporary peculiar survival of the *gemachim* stands to testimony that it is rather the alter-centered salvation dictum of "unto thy brother thou shalt not lend upon usury" and not the double standard of "unto the foreigner thou mayest lend upon usury" (Deut. 23:20) which underlies the Jewish moneylending tradition. That is, if indeed the gradual development of economic relations made it internationally indispensable to legitimize the taking of interest from brothers and others alike, as Nelson (1969) has shown, then the question is not why Jews took interest from others (as Weber [1967] and Sombart [1963] stressed) but why Jews *do not take* interest from brothers although today recipients may not only profit from such a free loan by depositing it in a bank (as often happens) but since a loan returned after a year or so loses in its original value due to the rising inflation, recipients practically earn money even without depositing it for interest. It should be noted further that the biblical word *nochry* (from whom you may make interest) in Hebrew means "foreigner" and not Gentile (i.e., not Jewish).

3. Baron et al. (1976: 10) have shown that already during the Babylonian exile (ca. 600–500 B.C.) Jews "assumed an important role in banking and far-flung commerce." And Sombart (1963) cites several sources showing that Jews preferred to earn their livelihood from moneylending and trading even during times when they were encouraged to work in other professions.

4. Upon a visit to Father Flannigan's Boys Town in Omaha, Nebraska, which is presumably the first and one of the most successful projects constructed from money solicited through letters, I was told that it was in fact a Jewish *shnorer* who conceived and administered the soliciting-letters system for Father Flannigan.

5. Active asceticism, in terms of a strong work ethos, which developed among German Jews under Samson Raphael Hirsch in the nineteenth century, was apparently influenced more by a Weberian-Calvinist *Zeitgeist* than by Judaism per se (see Fishman 1971).

6. To be sure, this presumably utopian, future-oriented tendency is by no means exclusively Jewish. A future-oriented action perspective was eminently pronounced in phenomenological sociology. Schutz (1967) has argued, for example, that in relation to social action "all projecting consists in anticipation of future conduct. . . . I have to visualize the state of affairs to be brought about by my action before I can draft the single steps of such future acting from which this state of affairs will result" (p. 20). Schutz's "future-action perspective "is, however, in no way anchored in a conception of "otherhood," not even in the ego-centric sense of Mead's (1934) future-oriented process of "taking the role of the other," by which others are utilized to construct selves.

(4)

Structural Deviance and the Mono vs. Multiple Ideal-labeling System

I shall begin my comparative analysis of the two ideal-labeling systems by confronting traditional sociological theories, which I argue are grounded in a mono ideal-labeling and ego-centered conception of man, with questions following from the social-contraction perspective, which is embedded, as I contend, in a multiple ideal-labeling alter-centered social conception. More specifically, since I maintain that it is the structural dimension of multiple ideal-labeling that is functional for the minimization of deviance, social gaps, and the maintenance of a social system, because in the multiple ideal-labeling system there is not only one "elitist" actualization ideal but a variety of ideals, then the most useful method for defending such a proposition would be to begin by examining theories that purport to explain social mechanisms which minimize or prevent deviance and social gaps.

Two sociological schools—the structural-functional and the interactionist-labeling schools—have dealt seperately but nevertheless inadequately with the problem of deviance (see Rotenberg 1978). The perspective developed below is an attempt to integrate these two schools into a broader structural-functional system. The functional school in sociology has long assumed that problematic social processes, institutions, or patterns of behavior are to be understood by analyzing the impact of such problem areas and "by establishing their consequences for larger structures in which they are implicated" (Merton 1958: 46–47). Thus, from a functional perspective the study of deviance is important and instructive because it indicates how consensus prevails and how society exists and survives in spite of, or rather due to, conflict and social problems (see Coser 1956; Erikson 1966). Within the general arena of functional "social survival" there remain the questions of which particular cultural systems contribute to the minimization or maximization of the phenomenon of deviance and why deviance is functional for some parts in a social structure, while for the other parts it is dysfunctional.

Labeling theorists have hitherto limited their analysis only to studying the impact of *derogatory* (negative) labeling on the incidence of deviance, which implies that *positive* labeling may not necessarily have a derogatory effect. Attempts to assess the relationships between positive and negative labeling or between societal reactions and the broader question of functional social survival are almost unknown. By considering the impact of labeling on deviance within a broader structural-labeling framework, the following analysis will show how positive labels may affect deviance. But first, the structural-functional perspective of ideal-labeling requires some conceptual elaboration. As pointed out earlier, the term "ideal label," as used here, refers to a positive or derogatory ideal label or type used by societies to socialize, label, and relabel their members *relative* to an ideal label. An ideal label stands for a set of desirable or nondesirable behavioral systems. It differs from the term "role model" in that ideal labels do not refer to concrete people and consequently do not entail the charismatic components implicit in the definition of role models. While social types (Strong 1943) refer to idiosyncratic, transient types emerging in small groups, ideal labels are derivations from the broader cultural normative prescriptions for salvation and socialization, which thus transcend the existence of small groups.

Functional labeling and socialization processes usually operate on a continuum between two polar ideal labels. Thus, if at the negative end we find the ideal labels "lazy bum," "thief," and so on, and at the positive end we find the the labels "gentleman," "industrialist," or "scholar," individuals would be labeled *relative* to these terms. For example, "Joe is quite a thief," "Joe is a hopeless lazy bum"; and vice versa, "Joe is a perfect gentleman," or fairly rich, industrious, or quite a "scholar." Moreover, socialization might proceed by contrasting two polar ideal labels. "Be a Talmudic scholar (*Talmid chacham*), a philanthropist (*baal zedaka*), or a 'do-gooder' (*baal maasim tovim*), but don't be an ignoramus (*am haaretz*)" are typical educational imperatives of traditional Judaism. Thus people might be labeled on a relative basis in relation to several labels: "David is a great *baal zedaka* and quite a *Talmid chacham*," or "*but* quite an *am haaretz*." Although the disqualifying adjective "but" is used in labeling David, he will enjoy a positive status as long as the major qualifying adjective "great" is used in relation to one of the accepted positive ideal labels.

As people are not equally endowed or motivated to pattern their behavior according to various labels, the scarcity and rigidity of positive ideal labels in relation to negative ideal labels might be crucial in determining the ratio of deviance to be expected in different social structures. Hence, if only one positive ideal label is available for socialization, for example, to be "rich" or to be a "scholar," then the probability for the prevalence of deviance will be high.

It is with a structural-functional labeling model in mind that we may examine the impact of positive ideal labels on the phenomenon of deviance and thus consider the alter-centered contraction theory in relation to other sociological theories of social relations. In others words, we will ask not only whether a particular social theory explains how functional survival of a global social system is possible, but also how its ideal-labeling system minimizes or maximizes differential conditions precipitating social gaps, alienation, and deviance within its various segments. Let us begin with Durkheim, one of the fathers of functional sociology, and his classic theory about the division of labor in modern society.

Social Contraction and Organic Solidarity

To explain what links people to society, what creates the collective conscience or social solidarity, Durkheim (1964) posited that in traditional or in what for unknown reasons he called "lower societies" it is social resemblance that attracts people to one another in a mechanical manner. Crime in such a social system is accordingly defined as an act contrary to the strong common conscience. Paradoxically, it may be functional, because it consolidates the functional system of punishment and the moral order of society, which sanctions anything threatening the social likeness. With his devout "functional" faith in the essential goodness of human nature, Durkheim, believed that in the old *Gemeinschaft* type of society,

> not only are all the members of the group individually attracted to one another because they resemble one another, but also because they are joined to what is the condition of existence of this collective type. . . . Not only do citizens love each other and seek each other out in preference to strangers but they love their country. They will . . . hold to it durably and for prosperity, because, without it, a great part of their psychic lives would function poorly." (p. 105)

Durkheim thus assumed that in the small *Gemeinschaft* all people know one another, love one another, and conform to the common moral code because it is functional for their survival. In contemplating what will happen in the "advanced society," with its complex division of labor, Durkheim admitted that as "differences become more numerous, cohesion becomes more unstable . . . and . . . the role of the collective conscience becomes smaller as labor is divided" (p. 364).

Consequently, the question as to whether anomie or cohesion will predominate in modern society becomes a subject that calls for serious concern and consideration. From his speculative-functional armchair, Durkheim, assured us that it is this very specialized division of functions that makes people organically dependent on one another and creates social solidarity. Thus, the more that labor is divided and specialized, the more people are dependent on a moral order to regulate and integrate the functions of individuals. As a result, people become more and more dependent on one another and on the moral-legal order. In the organic solidarity that is a feature of modern advanced society, "the individual becomes cognizant of his dependence upon society; from it come the forces which keep him in check and restrain him. In short, since the division of labor becomes the chief source of social solidarity, it becomes at the same time, the foundation of the moral order." (p. 401)

In other words, according to Durkheim, modern society need not be overly concerned about excessive anomie or alienation to be produced by the division of labor because the *interdependence* emanating from this division of labor will not only "restrain" people, but actually becomes "the chief source of social solidarity and the moral order." Apparently Durkheim did not live long enough to explore the ratio of anomie and deviance produced by modern technological society, for most likely he would have had to reassess or revise his functional-utopian prophesies concerning organic solidarity in advanced societies.

Let us examine the meaning of organic interdependence from the alter-centered contractional perspective. I explained earlier why in the Western ego-centered salvation culture, with its one superman, materialist ideal label, interpersonal relations are inevitably characterized by guilt-debt, *"schuld"* behavior. This means that unless give-and-take, or interdependence, is on an equal basis—that is, unless the thing given is equal in value to the thing taken—there will always be a strong creditor to pressure the debtor, who will feel guilty, weak, oppressed, jealous, deviant, or resentful. Hence deviance will expand as a result of the law of "natural inequality." In an alter-centered salvation culture, however, while Zebulun and Issachar may not be equally endowed their interdependence may be sustained, because what they give to each other is not assessed with the same single-ideal measurement.

Here the case against Durkheim's concept of organic solidarity is that specialized division of labor in modern technological society by definition requires universalistic and affectively neutral interdependence (see Parsons 1964) to assure the delivery of equal, nonaffective bureaucratic services to everybody. Consequently, universalistic interdependence may not, from a logical point of view, prevent alienation, or necessarily create solidarity. Our dependence on a bus driver neither prevents nor enhances our feelings of "solidarity" or "solitarity" (especially in a place such as New York City, where bus drivers do not carry change to prevent adverse interaction). In other words, while Durkheim assumed that organic solidarity will prevail because everybody will partake in the division-of-labor network, he did not explain how in the Western, ego-centered, achievement-oriented and affectively neutral society, the rich and talented will be dependent on the weak deviants in a way that they will experience solidarity with the poor, or vice versa. Therefore, he did not foresee how many of the dependent, alienated debtors would gradually drop out altogether (and often not join it in the first place) from this division-of-labor network and most probably become antagonistic toward it because they resent their role of always "owing something"; because equality demands that everybody live up to one ideal label; because the creditors do not contract their selves to make interdependence equal; because, in short, contractual egalitarian interdependence in terms of feeling mutual solidarity is a myth.

Thus, theoretically, in Durkheim's utopian social system, the proportion of deviance cannot be expected to decrease, because the Western contractual and universalistic definition of organic interdependence will always force deviant debtors out of the division-of-labor network into alienated loneliness, defiant subcultures, or dependency-fostering total institutions. In short, consideration of deviance and social gaps in Durkheim's terms of "the anomic division of labor" considers only the problems of the *"inanomics,"* who partake in the division of labor network, but largely disregards the *"exanomics,"* whose problems are inimical to the mono ideal label labor-oriented society.

Social Contraction and Functional Reciprocity

Let us now consider alter-centered contraction vis-à-vis Alvin Gouldner's conceptualization of reciprocity. Gouldner (1966) begins his analysis with a functional assumption stipulating that, similar to other sociological concepts, social reciprocity must explain how reciprocal relationships contribute to the stability—that is, the survival and the ongoing maintenance—of a social system. Accordingly, empirical analysis must explain how and which specific compensatory mechanisms operate to maintain social stability when functional, balanced reciprocity is disrupted. This might be due to tensions rising from power differences, exploitations, or altruistic or egoistic dispositions of reciprocating partners.

As Gouldner was concerned about Western egoistic-exploitative culture, in which "people are more ready to receive than to give benefits" (p. 141), he criticized Parsons' (1964) concept of complementarity. According to Gouldner, Parsons presumably uses complementarity as a synonymous term for reciprocity, which fails to account for the "implications of differences in the degree of mutuality or in the symmetry of reciprocity" (p. 139). Thus, argues Gouldner, since complementarity means that one's rights are another's obligations, and vice versa, then a "complementary" egoistic social system "of rights and obligations should be exposed to a persistent strain in which each party is somewhat more actively concerned to defend or extend his own rights than those of others" (p. 141).

To reconcile individualistic egoism with social stability, Gouldner insists that "we need to turn to the reciprocities processes because these, unlike pure complementarity, actually mobilize egoistic motivations and channel them into the maintenance of the social system" (p. 141).

One may sympathize with Gouldner's insurmountable endeavor to explain how prevention or minimization of the "persistent strain" producing deviance and instability operates in a society where there are many movements dedicated to individual and "civil rights" but not to "civil obligations," a society in which the stronger and more gifted creditors are by definition required to purchase their salvation through their egoistic achievements. But what logic does Gouldner use to fill the theoretical gap left presumably by Parsons' conception of complementarity, which assumes that a social system is self-perpetuating "once a stable relation of mutual gratification has been established"? (p. 142). What is there in Gouldner's definition that better explains system maintenance in face of egoistic salvation norms? According to Gouldner, the "norm of reciprocity, in its universal form, makes two interrelated, minimal demands: (a) people should help those who have helped them, and (b) people should not injure those who have helped them" (p. 140). A quick glimpse at Gouldner's statement (which forces us once more to deal with the problem of symmetry in social exchange) will reveal that there is no qualitative difference between his definition and the definitions of Talcott Parsons, George Homans, Georg Simmel, and Bronislaw Malinowski, who presumably stipulated that in reciprocal relations the amount to be returned must be roughly equivalent to what was received. That is, Gouldner, like the others, assumes that in an egoistic salvation culture, interpersonal relations are motivated and regulated through contractual, guilt-debt relationships. Allegedly, the only difference between Parsons and Gouldner is that the former believes that social survival results from internalized feelings of mutual indebtedness in terms of *duty*, while the latter explains the internalization of the norm of reciprocity in *utilitarian* terms; that is, stability is maintained because creditors and debtors will not harm each other as long as debts are not repaid. By implication, then, Gouldner's assumption that system stability is maintained and deviance is prevented because we should "expect to find mechanisms which induce people to remain indebted to each other" (p. 143)—that is, because debts are never paid in full—is not substantially different from Durkheim's (1964) functional notion of organic interdependent solidarity. Durkheim similarly assumes that solidarity prevails because people will always be dependent on or in debt to one another.

While I agree that because of the law of "natural inequality" the weak, ungifted, deviant, loser-debtor will never be able to repay his debt to the talented, strong lucky creditor, I think that the dynamics of guilt/hate in the contractual-debt relationship has been overlooked or misunderstood by Gouldner. While Gouldner's formulation takes cognizance of the debt aspect, it ignores the resultant guilt (hate-causing) factor that is predominant in reciprocity in a mono ideal-labeling system. Gouldner's naive conclusion that in reciprocity "the sentiment of gratitude joins forces with the sentiment of rectitude and adds a safety-margin in the motivation to conformity" (pp. 143–144) refers apparently only to the society of "insiders," that is, the society of successful, strong, well-to-do, "elect" creditors who are capable of living up to the one predominant ideal label of "supermaterialist." This formulation, however, also suggests that, in contrast to what Kant (1960: 28) termed the "propensity to hate him to whom one is indebted," once an "outsider" (i.e., a member of the "dependent" poor, failing, or deviant class) has been supported, psychotherapized, or otherwise helped, he will no longer deviate but be "grateful" to his helpful creditors—as long as he does not repay his debts. Yet studies of deviant conduct or criminal subcultures have demonstrated unequivocally that in a contractual guilt-debt social structure, deviant debtors usually want not to *shake* but to *break* the hand that feeds them. Moreover, in examining reciprocity in terms of contractual guilt-debt relationships betwen crediting "insiders" and indebtful "outsiders," the problematic requirement that reciprocity must be based on "roughly equivalent repayment" is magnified. It is this very structured inability to return a "roughly equivalent" payment that characterizes the asymmetric helping relationships in total institutions, in therapy, or in charity and elicits further deviant "reaction formation" (see Cohen 1955) or other hostile responses to helping behavior. Moreover, a structural stipulation that defines reciprocity in terms of "roughly equivalent repayments" implies that if repayment is not equivalent, then the law of *lex talionis* may be set in operation, in which case the creditor will use the retaliating negative norms of reciprocity—an "eye for an eye"[1]—in relation to the debtor's unpaid entity.

Indeed, in his classic study (mentioned earlier) of gift exchange in various societies, Mauss (1954) pointed out already that while symmetrical gift-exchanges or the primitive tradition of *potlatch* destructions (which may be equated in our society to Thorstein Veblen's concept of "conspicuous consumption") regulate the major social and economic mechanisms in most societies, he was highly aware of the dangerous social antagonism and gaps that arise from this symmetric-equivalent reciprocal creditor-debtor relationship. Mauss hence states (1954: 41) that in most societies "the obligation of worthy return" is imperative. "Face is lost forever if it is not made or if equivalent value is not destroyed." In the Kwakiutl, Haida, and Tsimshian, indicates Mauss, "the sanction for the obligation to repay is enslavement for debt. It is an institution comparable in nature and function to the

Roman *nexum.* The person who cannot return a loan or potlatch loses his rank and even his status of a free man."

Moreover, as Mauss points out (1954: 62), the double meaning of the word "gift," referring in the Germanic languages to both a present and a poison, explains the "social gift" danger reflected in the classical theme of the attractive present (e.g., a red apple) turning into poison,[2] which imbues many German folk-stories (notably Grimm brothers stories).

Thus, in Gouldner's ego-centric, contractual reciprocity model, the "persistent strain" between the ego-centered need for achievement-salvation and the other-centered need for social stability and survival seem to minimize social gaps and the prevalence of deviance only insofar as "debtors" are indeed able to repay equivalent returns because they are among those who succeeded in living up to the mono ideal label "materialist."

Moreover, here one should mention that the danger of guilt-debt (with its consequent) hate-producing relationship, which may emanate from the inability to return an equivalent payment inherent in symmetric exchange systems, also poses a question concerning the psychological possibility of justice as formulated by Rawls. Concomitant with other "demythifiers" of the "equal opportunity" social doctrine, Rawls (1971: 101) recognized that this liberal "equal opportunity" principle, which called for the elimination of social differences to ascertain an "equal head start," justified in fact "unequal end results" on the basis of natural endowments and personal talents. Rawls hence proposed "to regard the distribution of natural talents as a common asset and to share in the benefits of this distribution whatever it turns out to be. Those who have been favored by nature, whoever they are, may gain from their good fortune only on terms that improve the situation of those who have lost out." In other words, according to Rawls' theorem of fairness, the talented strong "creditors" must give unilaterally to the ungifted, who should cease to be "debtors" because their unfortunate lack of ability is "beyond their control" and hence they don't have to repay. While Rawls' system of "giving according to ability and receiving according to need" concurs in principle with the Issachar and Zebulun exchange structure, the psychological debt-guilt-hate enslavement problem of those who will receive *only* due to lack of personal ability and talent will probably persist. This would be so because as long as there is essentially only one ideal salvation label and one yardstick (e.g., material) to measure one's contribution, and as long as exchange and social relations are based on the psychological expectation of symmetrical equivalent return, the frustrating guilt/debt social gaps could be expected to continue.

More specifically, according to the present viewpoint, deprivation from the ability to repay or rather to contribute to society which in essence blocks actualization outlets, entails the same patronizing, enslaving dangers discussed by Mauss and consequently also the eventual retaliating and annihilating tendency[3] by those deprived from repaying possibilities (who might not feel as being helped) mentioned by Hobbes, although now deprivation and enslavement is only psychological while sociologically the less advantaged are being compensated by the naturally gifted.

In the alter-centered contractional system, however, this psychological strain is theoretically mitigated due to the structural multiple ideal-labeling actualization dimension and the "unequivalent reciprocity" which may be functional in terms of social survival[4] and minimization of social inequality and deviance, because repayment is neither impossible nor measurable by one yardstick. In other words, the multiple alter-centered labeling system enables also the less talented to find actualization outlets that constitute acceptable social contributions.

One can best assess the functionality (in terms of social-system survival and minimization of social inequality and deviance) of a mono ideal-labeling versus a multiple ideal-labeling salvation system by examining whether and how such systems maintain or regain their functional equilibrium during or after a period of transition and/or *social* crisis. To assess the presumed Western mono ideal-labeling salvation system, I have chosen the surplus free time crisis created by the contemporary automated era. To examine the functionality of a presumably multiple ideal-labeling social system, I chose the social crisis featured by despair and social-economic depression which preceded the emergence of the eighteenth-century Hasidic movement in Eastern Europe.

NOTES

1. Here the popular story about the person who refused to accept his neighbor's invitation to attend the funeral of his third wife, because he never had the opportunity to . . . reciprocate becomes paradoxically meaningful.

2. The negative "eye for an eye" *lex talionis* principle of equivalent return was not preserved only among primitive tribes. Thomas Jefferson, the father of the American democratic Declaration of Independence and of the egalitarian individual rights movements, demanded to include, among other requirements, the following stipulations in his "equalitarian system of justice": "Whosoever on purpose, and of malice forethought, shall maim another, or shall disfigure him, by cutting out or disabling the tongue, slitting or cutting of a nose, lip, or ear, branding, or otherwise, shall be maimed, or disfigured in like sort; or if that cannot be, for want of the same part, then as nearly as may be, in some part of at least equal value and estimation, in the opinion of the jury" (cited by Kaufmann, 1977).

3. A good case in point of how lack of talent may precipitate retaliating annihilation tendencies might be the violent extortion mechanism used by members of organized crime. Essentially the difference between a straight business man and an extorter is that the former uses his talents to speculate and make money in spite of the risk of losing, and the latter usually takes money by force either because of lack of talent or because of his reluctance to use his talent.

4. While Singer's (1981) interesting discussion about the sociobiological origins of the "you scratch my back and I'll scratch yours" principle of reciprocal altruism is generally convincing in suggesting that kin and group survival are genetically determined, I think that he would agree that there are two qualities which would make human survival more dependent on structured norms and ethics. For example, while monkeys do indeed spend long hours grooming each other to remove parasites from places they cannot reach without assistance, one should ask (1) whether they reciprocate like humans, on the basis of "how well, compared to my scratching and grooming, do you scratch and groom me?" and (2) are monkeys, like humans, selective in choosing grooms or other commodities to satisfy their primary and secondary appetites in face of scarcity?

In regard to the first question, unequal ability to scratch and groom may serve as a discriminating and retaliating factor not to be found among monkeys.

In regard to the second problem, human selection tendencies in the face of scarcity may determine the strategy to kill the groomer who might steal a selected groom or bridegroom; while it is questionable whether monkeys, like humans, have secondary appetites for scarcities.

It seems, hence, that it is precisely due to the *human* tendency to select and measure grooming exchange on the basis of equivalence in spite of scarcity, that an asymmetric exchange within a multiple actualization system, in which one's scratching actualization (Zebulunism) cannot be weighed against another's grooming actualization (Issacharism), is structurally more functional in promoting group and kin survival than a discriminatory mono (scarce) actualization system with its symmetric guilt-debt-oriented exchange mechanisms.

(5)

Social Crisis and the Mono vs. Multiple Ideal-labeling System

Supermaterialism, Leisure, and Deviance

It was suggested earlier that the current narrow approach of studying the impact of derogatory labeling on deviance should be expanded by exploring the functional relationship between positive or negative ideal social labels and the prevalence of deviance in the broader framework of a social structure. Thus, how should the relationship between deviance and a social structure with a mono-salvation system be assessed? Let us begin by examining in a historical perspective the "surplus free time" crisis presumably created by Western automated technology.

Plato believed that

> God alone is worthy of supreme seriousness, but man is made God's plaything. . . . Therefore every man and woman should live life accordingly, and play the noblest games. . . . Life must be lived as play, playing certain games, making sacrifices, singing and dancing, and then a man will be able to propriate the gods, and defend himself against his enemies, and win in the contest." (Laws 7.796, quoted in Huizinga 1949: 1, 19)

In his classic study of the play element in culture, Huizinga (1949) indicates that while nowadays school refers to systematic, time-restricting work, the word "school" (as many rebelling young students might be interested to know) originally meant "leisure." Consequently, in ancient Greece school was not "an educational system designed to train the citizen for useful and profitable occupations. For the Greek the treasures of the mind were the fruit of his leisure" (p. 147). Thus, according to Plato self-actualization or salvation in life must be reached through playing noble games. Similarly, according to Aristotle, Huizinga points out, "nature requires us not only to be able to work well, but also to idle well. This idleness or leisure is the principle of the universe for Aristotle. It is preferable to work;

(52)

indeed it is the aim of all work" (p. 161). While for the free man in ancient Greece the labels "player" or "leisure man" symbolized salvation, liberation, self-actualization, and attainment of the highest ideals of the Greek culture, after the industrial revolution, Huizinga laments, "work and production became the ideal, and then the idol, of the age" (p. 192). Moreover, states Berger (1963: 25) in ancient Greece,

> work as instrumental or productive activity was regarded below the dignity of a free man, fit only for slaves and women. . . . When Calvinism sanctified work and industrialism ennobled it, what followed was the separation of work and leisure . . . and the relegation of leisure to the status of spare time—time especially vulnerable to the ministrations of the Devil.

What we have, then, in both these cultures—ancient Greece and contemporary Western civilization—is essentially only *one* predominant ideal label for salvation or self-actualization. Thus, if the "productive worker" in ancient Greece was looked upon as a lower-class slave, and the poor or "lazy bum" in Western society is degraded as a deviant outcast, one may predict the ratio of deviance in the respective societies according to the number of people who may have access, ability, or motivation to live up to the one, single ideal label.

Upon the first instinctive lift of eyebrows, one may wonder whether in Western society the "lazy leisure man" is indeed not an "idle ideal man" but, as I claim, a degraded man. A more systematic examination of the meaning of leisure in our society will reveal, however, that it is only the member of the "leisure class" who can prove that somehow he is active or industrious in a Calvinist sense and who hence can constantly provide signs of material success (see Rotenberg 1978), usually in the "conspicuous consumption" manner described by Veblen (1934). The state of grace of a rich but idle hobo or hippie is confirmed only after he displays extravagant, consuming ability; for the real poor, although the road to salvation through leisure is with good intentions *paved,* it leads him not to be among the *saved.*

The difference between behavior motivated by culturally institutionalized salvation norms and ad hoc behavioral goals designed to "keep the masses busy and off the street" receives full expression when examining the paradoxical connection between automation and leisure in Western technological society. Sociologists and economists interested in social problems arising from the growing automation of Western technology have repeatedly claimed that it is not lack of income maintenance but lack of sufficient employment and the consequent excess in free time which threatens to create new and serious behavioral and social problems. Soule (1955: 60) suggested in the 1950s that "if the gain in real income continues for another eighty years as it has for the last eighty, the average family income [in the United States] at that time will be $37,500." Brightbill (1960: 17) likewise predicted in the early 1960s that "the per capita income in the United States will increase as much as 40% within the next 25 years."

On the other hand, President John F. Kennedy, who considered automation to be the "major domestic challenge of the 1960s," maintained that, in the United States 25,000 new jobs would be needed each *week* to meet the demands of automation and population growth. In a House subcommittee hearing, Kennedy's secretary of labor, Arthur Goldberg, testified that in 1962 alone 1.8 million workers would be affected by automation (see Francois 1967: 77). According to sources cited by Piven and Cloward (1972), "in the years between 1950 and 1965 alone, new machines and new methods increased farm output in the United Stated by 45%—and reduced farm employment by 45%" (p. 201). It seems that it is not the lack of sufficient funds to provide everybody with a minimum income but lack of sufficient employment that creates social problems.[1] Paradoxically, however, most relief and economic security programs are, in most Western countries, linked mainly to work records as a major indicator, if not the sole moral indicator, for income eligibility (see Macarov 1980).

It is not my purpose here to take a stand on the difficult economic and social issue of whether there are insufficient funds in a country like the United States to assure a minimum income for everybody or whether the funds are sufficient but simply not available to the right people. Rather, my goal is to point out that wherever there are sufficient sources of income but not enough working hours, "forced leisure" becomes "false leisure" because of the predominating "salvation through work" ideal.

As I indicated above, increases in income and productivity obviously "forced" workers to redivide their time between labor (for additional income) and leisure. As Faunce (1968) pointed out, "In the nongovernmental sector of our economy, output per man-hour has approximately doubled over the past twenty-five years. The benefits of this increased productivity have been distributed between income and leisure on roughly a 60/40 basis, 60% going into greater income and 40% for more leisure time" (p. 73). Faunce further suggested that although various industries are differentially susceptible to further automation and mechanization, "reductions in hours worked per week have occurred at varying rates in different industries in the past and will undoubtedly continue to do so" (p. 74).

Thus, whether in a leading Western country like the United States increased productivity and automation had destroyed more jobs than it has created, as many labor leaders insisted, or whether the contrary is true, as many business leaders believed (see Francois 1967), the question that concerns us here is whether "forced leisure" or paid unemployment in the United States means freedom *from* involvement in work or freedom *to become* involved in leisure (the former does not necessarily lead to the latter) or whether it leads to self-actualization or to social deterioration, and whether the labels "leisure man" and "labor man" are equally acceptable salvation ideals.

Faunce (1968) reported that already in 1847 opponents of the English Ten Hours Work Bill argued that "decreasing hours of work would lead to the moral degeneration of workers [and that] similar outcries were heard in 1926 when the Ford Motor Company inaugurated the five-day week. At that time a chamber of commerce president in a large American city said that 'mankind does not thrive on holidays—idle hours breed mischief' " (p. 72). And what do workers say about their "work-free" time? Faunce noted that, in 1966, after a cotton mill in Leigh, England, began a shift system involving a three-day week at full pay, a newspaper account of this development contained this testimony of one worker: "It was a marvellous experience to begin with. There was plenty of time for fishing and general relaxation. But now I'm just bored, waiting for my friends to finish work. I've tried gardening, decorating, going to the cinema, but it's becoming a drag" (pp. 72, 73).

Berger (1963) admitted that the concern of the cultural elite over mass leisure reflected their fear of the power of the disengaged poor. Accordingly, leisure for "dependent groups" that is designed to "keep them busy" is subjected to the attacks of liberal and radical intellectuals alike. They "accuse the suppliers of mass culture of catering to the lowest levels of popular taste in order to achieve the highest of net profit" (p. 24) and to serve as a device for distraction and intoxicating escape from the hazards of boredom. Thus, compared to ancient Greece, leisure today is no longer the *privilege* of the few, it is the *problem* of many. It seems that the masses did not learn to purchase their salvation by playing Platonian noble games and that leisure did not become their new existential ideal for self-actualization. The problem seems to be much deeper and embedded in the unsettled, inherent contradiction between what Berger termed the value system and the social system. The Protestant value system, which condemned the "lazy man," is incapable of honoring the "leisure man" produced by the situational requirements of the social system. Indeed, if leisure as paid unemployment "fails to give to men . . . the feeling of personal adequacy . . . that only work provides for most adult male Americans" (as Weiss and Riesman claimed, 1963: 169) and if membership in the new Calvinist leisure class can be bought only through what Veblen termed "conspicuous consumption," then it should not be too surprising that taking another part-time job "of a very different sort" is rationalized by many as being "recreational" (see Weiss and Reisman 1963: 172). After all, the Protestant purpose of leisure is mainly to "recreate," restore, or refresh the organism for its primary purpose, "work" (see Berger 1963: 25). Thus a vicious circle of "democratic unfreedom" (see Marcuse 1964) is created. In the "free" leisure class people are forced to work during their "free time" in order to have, as Herbert Marcuse pointed out, a "free choice between brands and gadgets" to be "freely" and conspicuously consumed (p. 7). Faunce's (1968) plea to postindustrial society is to deemphasize vocational training and teach more leisure skills and in this way break the vicious circle created by Protestant work values.

My aim here is not to represent the naive, anti-industrial revolution that takes modern technological comforts and lifesaving devices for granted (as Ayn Rand [1975] has indicated) but to point out how social inequality, social problems, and social deviance cannot be expected to decrease in a mono-ideal salvation culture. Thus I have shown that the inflexible predominance of one ideal salvation label is incapable of contracting itself in order to allow another ideal label to take its place alongside the old one, even when circumstances (e.g., excessive free time) prescribe such a need for the sake of system stability. From this perspective it is of less importance whether and to what extent post industrial technology and increase in leisure are positively correlated (see Gendron 1977) and more important to determine the extent to which leisure activities are equal in status to labor activities.

In Western society new, existential, self-actualizing roads to salvation through leisure activities seem not to be connected to the deep-rooted ideal label "successful worker." Hence, the new leisure salvation movements— including psychedelic and sex-involvement movements (as one sociologist stated, "Kinsey studying sex is surely studying leisure")—appear to be sufficient in keeping people temporarily busy and off the streets, but otherwise they are considered transient, semideviant, and subordinate to the ideal label "productive supermaterialist."

Yet social problems and deviance may be minimized, and social survival may be maintained in a multiple ideal salvation culture, even in the face of a labeling crisis. The socio-historical background of the emergence of the Jewish ideal label *Hasid* in eighteenth-century Eastern Europe is a prime example of how this may be accomplished.

The Convergence of Zebulun and Issachar
and the Emergence of Hasidism

A popular tale in contemporary orthodox Jewish circles goes as follows. A pale, skinny, stooped, ultraorthodox Jewish father drags his small, pale, skinny, stooped son along one of the narrow alleys of their neighborhood. Toward them walks a handsome, tanned, tall, and muscular man (a typical kibbutz member). The father pulls the boy closer to him, points to the muscular farmer, and says, "You see, my dear little boy, if you will not study the Talmud, that's the way you are going to look." In a few words this tale says much about the goals and modes of socialization in this particular community.

In 1939, Alexander Dushkin, an Israeli professor of education, listed five major Jewish ideal types (labels) which he believed emerged throughout the nation's history. These include the "Talmudic scholar," the *Hasid,* and the "Pioneer" (see Dushkin 1939). Dushkin, who unfortunately did not present a fuller sociocultural analysis of these types, believed that each of them is equally important, and so he insisted that each of these types should serve as an equal ideal model in socialization and education. Accordingly, declared Dushkin, "we should not concentrate on one type even if he is most favorable to us" (p. 89).

By and large, the principle of socialization toward multiple ideal labels was maintained throughout Jewish history.[2] Thus the Issachars, the Talmudic scholars, or the "pioneers" (*halutzim*) were not only equal in status to the Zebuluns who supported them, but the Zebuluns, the rich merchants, actually had to struggle to keep their equal place alongside the Issachars, the poor scholars, and "pioneers." Likewise, the poor, pale, skinny Talmudist did not feel subordinate to the tanned, muscular, "kibbutz" pioneer. This does not mean, however, that such a multiple ideal social structure did not face periodic crises. During these times competition between ideal labels and the predominance of one positive ideal label and the concomitant degradation of the others widened social gaps and increased the probable incidence of deviance and social problems.

During the sixteenth and seventeenth centuries, Jews in Eastern Europe, especially in Poland, lived a prosperous and autonomous life—"a nation within a nation" (as some historians phrased it), with their own courts and synods fully recognized by the Polish government. The elected representatives (the *parnasim*) together with the rabbis comprised the town's council (the *kahal*), which in each congregation controlled the religious, educational, and welfare institutions. The famous Council of Four Lands (Great Poland, Little Poland, Ruthenia, and Volhynia) had the authority to legislate taxes as well as religious and cultural matters. Because education was compulsory and the teacher-rabbis were paid by the council, all young men, including those from poor homes, could study the Talmud equally. Thus, maintain Jewish historians, as Talmudic scholarship had rarely reached greater heights in the history of Israel, Poland became a guiding scholastic center for Jews all over the Diaspora (see Dubnov 1975). In other words, during these centuries the contractional relationship between the Zebuluns and Issachars was a living testimony to the functional-survival basis of the alter-centered salvation system with its multiple ideal-label system.

In 1648 the Greek Catholic peasants of the Ukraine, led by Chmielnicki, rose up in revolt against their tyrannical Roman Catholic lords and in the process slaughtered Poles and Jews alike (see Dresner 1960: 24). These terrible massacres, known as the Chmielnicki pogroms, wiped out much of Ukrainian Jewry and brought terrible suffering and harsh decrees to large sections of East European Jewry. From this time on, the central government of Poland was considerably weakened, and as a result the situation of the Jews declined increasingly.

The external problems that shattered the Polish central government were soon reflected in an internal decay of the Jewish communities in Poland. The autonomous Council of Four Lands was dissolved, and the local councils gradually became the government's perverted and corrupted vehicle for extorting taxes from the masses. The weak Polish government, which ignored the plight of the masses, was concerned only with one thing—how to collect taxes. Thus nothing could be done without bribery, including appointments of council members, communal leaders, and rabbis (see Dubnov 1975). The reins of Jewish leadership thus passed into the hands of a few wealthy rabbis and oligarchs. Joseph Dubno describes the late seventeenth-century scene:

> The leaders live in luxury and splendour and do not fear the burden of taxes and other communal levies. They impose heavy burden upon others and lighten their own burdens. They take the lion's share of all honours and distinctions . . . and the congregation of God, the children of Abraham, Isaac and Jacob, are crushed and humiliated, left naked and barefoot by heavy taxes. (Quoted in Rabinowicz 1970: 27)

Thus the "bought" oligarchy of rich rabbis and leaders created a sociological situation that can be best described as a convergence of Issachar and Zebulun into one ideal label of "rich scholar," for now only the rich could afford to study the Talmud. (This does not mean that all rich people were scholars, but all scholars had to be rich.) Consequently the road to salvation merged into one narrow alley, open only to the few privileged, who by divorcing themselves from the ignorant masses shattered the very basis of functional alter-centrism. Indeed, in the eighteenth century only a minute minority was privileged to attend the *yeshiva* (Talmudic college), and for the masses the Torah became a closed book. Thus, contended the historian Dubnov (1975), "the gap between the Talmudists and the masses was continually widening and whoever belonged to the camp of the scholars would look down on the masses and the masses would concede to their worthlessness vis-à-vis the students" (p. 22).

Striking testimony describing the breakdown of the alter-centered salvation principle is given by the concerned eighteenth-century rabbi Yoseph Hakohen:

There was a rabbi of great learning, a master of "pilpul" [Talmudic dialectics], who used to study the "halacha" [law] and "tosphot" [talmudic commentaries] in a hairsplitting fashion. . . . Now, it once happened that, while he was busy studying . . . a poorly dressed woman from the lowest class came to him and placed before him her troubles concerning her livelihood. The rabbi rebuked her scornfully for having disturbed him, and the woman went away with a heavy heart.

Subsequently, upon discussing this woman's "disturbance," this rabbi said,

Is it not written, the study of Torah takes precedence over all? I was busily engaged in . . . a most intricate and complicated law—with only two days remaining before my discourse must be delivered. At such a time this woman came to me. Is it proper for me to put aside my studying in order to judge between one person and another? (Quoted in Dresner 1960: 30)

The compelling description above is one example of how the gap between the poor unlearned and the few privileged Talmudists widened during this social crisis,[3] which, in my opinion was characterized by the convergence of Issachar and Zebulun into one predominant ideal label. The ignorant, poor masses—who at first accepted their degraded, hopeless status and for whom the road to salvation was now almost hermetically sealed—were, like other oppressed people at the time bewildered by fears of the still-fresh massacres and were easy prey to superstitious beliefs in devils and exorcism and to promises of redemption offered by false messiahs. Influenced to a great extent by their Christian neighbors, the Jewish masses were thus given to medieval mystical fancies, devil-hunting, and exorcism of such evil spirits as *dibbukim* (disembodied spirits of the dead that presumably entered the bodies of the living).

The more important socio-historical question, however, is how, in comparison to other oppressed groups, the social system regained its functional survival balance through a structural breakthrough of a new alter-centered ideal label for salvation.

The Hasidic Relabeling Revolution

The revival of Jewish mystic cabalism, with its impact on the emergence of false messianism and, subsequently, Hasidism is best explained as a sociological struggle to create new antischolastic but religiously acceptable ideal labels for salvation. Indeed, Rabbi Moses Isserles observed in 1711 that "students of Kabbala include simple men who do not know their right hand from their left hand, people who live in darkness and cannot explain the meaning of the weekly portion of the Torah" (Rabinowicz 1970: 29).

The story and history of Hasidism has been written many times, and it is not my purpose to conjure up the romantic atmosphere that imbued the emergence of Hasidism in the eighteenth century. However, from a socio-historic perspective it seems remarkable that although the antecedent social symptoms that preceded the rise of the mystical (cabalistic-) Hasidic movement and its early mystagogues (see Weber 1967) who guided it closely resembled Christian practices, the resultant sociological pattern of cabalistic Hasidism differed radically from that of Christianity. Indeed, the Jewish masses, like Christians of the time, believed in superstitious demonology. Similar to Catholic exorcists, Jewish "masters of names" practiced faith-healing and exorcism of devils and *dibbukim.* And, most important, similar to Protestant revivalists and evangelists, the early Jewish cabalistic preachers *(maggidim)* who wandered from town to town were strictly ascetic. Like the Protestant revivalists, they threatened their listening crowds and promised hell's fire in the world to come for those who do not repent and subdue their evil passions in this world (see Dubnov 1975). And yet the inherent difference between alter-centered and ego-centered salvation doctrines underlies why cabalistic asceticism was not transformed, as was Protestant asceticism, into a this-world-oriented secularized economic activism. Rather, it developed into a this-world-oriented, semihedonistic, ecstatic social movement that legitimized economic activities but did not idealize "supermaterialism" as a single goal for salvation.

I have maintained elsewhere (Rotenberg 1978) that, according to the Protestant dualistic sociology of man, which differentiates between the inherently good-elect and the bad-damned people, ego-centric salvation can be functional only for the society of the "elect insiders." On the other hand, according to a monistic gestaltist sociology of man, in which good and evil are but two interdependent sides of the same entity, salvation must be alter-centered and functional for both the "insiders" and the "outsiders." For the sake of social stability and survival, they periodically must be reabsorbed into the mainstream through a process of transformation and relabeling.[4] This distinction between a dualistic functionalism and a monistic-gestaltist functionalism seems highly important for the study of deviance and social survival, or system maintenance.

According to traditional functionalism (see especially Erikson 1966), deviance is functional as a safety valve for the "insiders" and for the demarcation of the boundaries between the society of "insiders" and the deviant "outsiders." Deviance is not functional, however, for the deviants themselves, unless deviant revolutionary movements take over. They then become the new "elect" by defining yesterday's elect as today's damned. In other words, traditional functionalism does not assume the necessity to expand the Hobbesian social contract in order to periodically redefine "wolfian" outsiders as "sheepy" insiders and thus ascertain survival of the whole system. And yet, this has been the underlying conception of functional theories of social change and modernization processes.

On the face of it Hasidism emerged, as many experts maintain, as a response to the physical and spiritual suffering of the poor, "unredeemable," Jewish ignorants (*amey haaratzot*). I have argued, however, that since the single positive ideal label for early eighteenth-century Polish Jewry was the rational (usually rich) Talmudic scholar, *am haaretz* (ignoramus) was used as the ideal derogatory socialization label.

How then did the social system regain its functional balance? Through a structural breakthrough of a new alter-centered ideal label for salvation. The label *hasid*, which was used since Talmudic times to designate "pietists," was assigned a new meaning by the eighteenth-century Hasidic movement. The term now operationally referred to religious self-actualization through group-oriented, ecstatic, and joyful adhesion to God, especially during prayers. The movement's founder, the Baal Shem Tov ("Master of the Good Name" 1700–1760), who is known by the acronym "Besht," is said to have stated that "divine matters were revealed to him not because he studied many Talmudic Tractates and Responsa, but only due to the prayers, as he was always praying with great intention" (Besht 1975a: 44). This was a revolutionary change in traditional Judaism, for by exalting prayer the Besht challenged the major scholastic socialization ideal of Talmudism. Hasidism thus reversed traditional scholasticism and ascetic cabalism by designating sadness and self-torture as the worst of sins and by sanctifying the emotional, ecstatic, and joyful adhesion to God through the art of praying as a countervailing ideal practice to *rational* Talmudism.

It is here that the sociology of the alter-centered contractional salvation structure through its multiple ideal-labeling system receives its full functional expression in terms of social survival. According to the monistic functional relationship between the weak, deviant social elements and the stronger conforming group members, the labels *am haaretz* and "sinner" were not idealized (as false messianisms dictated), neither did the label *hasid* substitute for the old ideal label "Talmudist." Nonetheless, after a long and bitter struggle (see Wilensky 1970) between Talmudic rationalism and Hasidic emotionalism, the functional transformation of the derogatory label *am haaretz* was made possible through the *contraction* of the ideal label "Talmudic scholar"[5] and the reestablishment of the alter-centered functional relationship between the newly defined Issachars and Zebuluns. Hasidism succeeded in relabeling the derogatory label *am haaretz* by putting the new ideal label *hasid* (which now required adhesion to the divine but not scholarship) on the same level with the old positive ideal labels without degrading or substituting them. This is not to suggest that ignorance or poverty became the new, idealized idols for salvation. Tevyeh, the heroic poor *am haaretz* in Sholem Aleichem's *Fiddler on the Roof,* admits that according to Jewish ethics it is no shame to be poor, but "it's no great honor either!"

Thus, sociologically, the new label *hasid* strengthened the old social contract by forcing contraction on other ideal labels in order to make room for it. The alter-centered contractional basis of the Hasidic salvation ethic might then explain the difference between functional, lasting Hasidism and the dysfunctional, transient, "false messianic" movements (i.e., the Sabbatean movement in the late seventeenth century and especially the Frankist movement in the early eighteenth century). These movements, like Pauline Christianity in the first century A.D., attempted in fact to substitute, rather than complement, the old Jewish ideal labels with a new, *single* ideal label ("Sabbatean," "Frankist," or "Christian").

As a point of comparison, let us look again at contemporary Protestant America, which is swamped with oppressed minority groups struggling through civil rights movements to change the single Wasp "superman" ideal-label. Such leading experts on minorities as Cloward and Piven (1974) have said the following regarding the chances of "black power."

> If there is a lesson in America's pluralistic history, it is that the ability of an outcast minority to advance in the face of majority prejudices partly depends on its ability to develop countervailing power. . . . For stripped of rhetoric, the idea of "black power," merely emphasizes the need to augment Negro influence by developing separatist institutions, ranging from economic enterprise to political organization. (p. 255)

In specifying how blacks can be redeemed by developing the "countervailing power" necessary to put them on an equal level with the white majority, Cloward and Piven emphasize:

> The black poor are very poor indeed, and they confront an economy dominated by large scale corporations. . . . Blacks need the resources controlled by municipal officials—contracts for all manner of projects and services to nurture new enterprises . . . especially black economic enterprise and black labor unions to organize the workers in the resulting jobs. (p. 262)

It is not surprising that in Protestant America, with its single Calvinist, "supermaterialist" ideal-label, Cloward and Piven see the attainment of equal, independent economic status and its consequent political power as one of the major, if not the only,[6] pragmatic means to salvation for an outcast, degraded minority. Indeed, one can judge for oneself how successful were such noneconomically oriented movements that attempted to give blacks a new sense of identity and pride by relabeling "black as beautiful." Considering the sociological history of revolutionary movements, it would seem important, however, to point out here that the new road to salvation set upon by the ignorant Jewish masses in eighteenth-century Eastern Europe was not paved by an economic revolution—even though they were similarly not only very poor, but persecuted and tortured by both the hostile general environment and their own community. This combination left them no hopes for redemption, in this world or in the world to come. Thus the Issachar and Zebulun alter-centric system came full circle under the modified revolutionary flag of Hasidism, which added the star of redemption through prayer but did not extinguish the actualizing "spark" of work and learning. Apollo, the god of reason, and Dionysus, the god of emotion, ruled accordingly side by side—not only as rivals but also as equal ideals. The multiple ideal-labeling system regained its structural-functional equilibrium by absorbing the new Hasidic salvation ethic into a neo-Issachar and Zebulun paradigm.

To sum up, by integrating labeling theory with structural-functional sociology, a new, functional labeling model has been developed. I have suggested that the probable ratio of social gaps and deviance, which is important in explaining social survival, can be predicted from the relative availability of *positive* ideal labels in relation to negative ideal labels in any given social structure. This perspective, which assesses the structural impact of positive labeling on deviance, adds a new dimension to labeling theory that has hitherto limited its analysis only to the relationship between derogatory labeling and deviance. I also contend that social stability can be maintained in a multiple ideal-labeling system, because alter-centered, interpersonal salvation and organic interdependence are possible only through the contraction of several ideal labels. The inner contradiction between social interdependence and the ego-centered salvation norms in a mono ideal-label system must inevitably produce contractual, guilt-debt relationships, and not reciprocity in terms of organic solidarity. I have then suggested that prevention of deviance in both systems can best be assessed during periods of social crisis. The need for increased leisure in the age of automation was thus used to show how a social structure with a single ideal salvation label faces difficulty in reducing its social problems during times of crisis, for in Western technological society, actualization through leisure activities seems inexpedient as a means for salvation unless it assumes the same material success as work does. Finally, the case of the eighteenth-century's ideal label, *"hasid,"* was used to demonstrate how, in spite of social crisis, functional social survival and organic interdependent solidarity is facilitated in a multiple ideal-labeling system. It was thus shown how the Judeo-Hasidic monistic sociology of man facilitates the functional revolutionary relabeling and reabsorption of deviants by allowing a new positive ideal label to take its equal place alongside the established ideal labels, even though the new label stands partially in opposition to the old labels. The

A. The vertical-pyramid mono ideal-labeling system

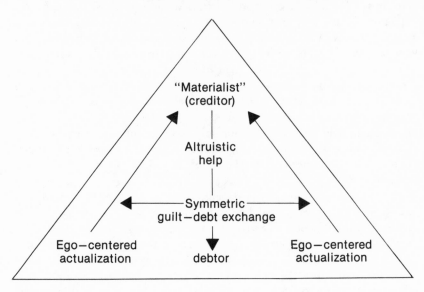

Narrowness at pyramid head, unilateral altruistic giving and disharmony between ego-centered actualization and interpersonal exchange, widens social gaps and expected ratio of deviance.

B. The horizontal-circular multiple ideal-labeling system

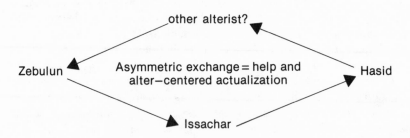

Multiplicity of actualization goals, circular give-and-take, and harmony between interpersonal exchange and alter-centered actualization norms minimize social gaps and expected ratio of deviance.

Figure 1. The mono-multiple ideal-labeling system.

sociology of social contraction further showed that, more than social antecedents, it is the unique (ego-centric versus the alter-centric) salvation norm that better predicts economic versus mystical activism of different societies. In spite of the great poverty that characterized eighteenth-century Eastern European Jewry, Hasidism only legitimized economic activism, but idealized mystical praying.

Three intertwined variables, differentiating between the monistic social contraction model and the dualistic ego-construction social perspective, have been discussed: (1) the dimension of the interactive alter-centered versus ego-centered actualizing salvation, (2) the dynamics of asymmetric versus symmetric exchange patterns, and (3) the structural mono versus multiple ideal-labeling dimension. (See Figure 1.)

The sociological analysis of the alter-centered contraction theory is completed but not yet exhausted. Although Hasidism was presented with a slight "romanticized" overtone, this is only because the Judeo-Hasidic conception of man is indeed optimistic in its monistic approach to human change. It was intended, however, as an ideal rather than an idealized case study, and hence the alter-centered contraction theory should be useful in studying the social and behavioral system of other cultures as well. As Hasidism is anchored in the sociological framework of ancient Jewish alter-centrism discussed above, my next task will be to develop the social-psychological and behavioral theory of alter-centered contraction derivable from Hasidic ethics.

NOTES

1. According to the official figures of the Social Security Administration, actual per capita income continues to grow in America, and hence the rate of poverty will continue to decrease. The dispute between utopians, dystopians, and socialists as to how to calculate the poverty line (see Gendron 1977) is not central to the present perspective.

2. While I think that the recent attempt of Shmueli (1980) to delineate seven major Jewish "cultures" (defined as perceptions of reality and salvation that predominated respectively throughout Jewish history) essentially concurs with the present "multiple ideal labeling" conception, I think that such "Jewish cultures" emphasizing the philosophical, Talmudical, mystical, or enlightened ideals were complementary rather than consecutive. This is not to say that during different periods specific ideals or "cultures" were not more pronouced and accepted than others. Rather, it suggests that due to the pluralistic notion of multiple ideals, one "culture" never eliminated the other entirely but facilitated alternative salvation outlets, that is, either through Hasidic ecstatic prayer, or through Issacharian Talmudism, or through Zebulunian alter-centrism or via any other salvation goal.

3. The philosopher Solomon Maimon (1754–1800) noted in his *Autobiography* (1954) that scholars were careful to wear special clothing which differentiated

them from the Ignorants and that such outward recognizable differences were kept even within one family.

4. A popular story among Jewish social therapists in New York makes a good case for the Jewish, alter-centered, relabeling transformation system. The collective sense of shame and the consequent feelings of congregational responsibility (i.e., the alter-centered need for salvation) concerning increased delinquency among Jewish East European immigrants in New York City during the 1920s and 1930s (see Robinson 1958) were so strong that in order to combat Jewish delinquency Jews founded the Jewish Board of Guardians, relabeled all Jewish delinquents as neurotics, and thus eliminated Jewish delinquency.

5. With the decline of Talmudic studies in the eighteenth and nineteenth centuries, the label *haver* was bestowed on people in Eastern Europe, and especially in Germany, not on the original criterion of Talmudic scholarship, but simply to express respect to good, conforming congregationalists.

6. A good example of how an American alter-centered messianic and antimaterial revolutionist came back full circle to admit that in the United States the only ideal salvation label is money might be Jerry Rubin, the Yippie leader from the 1960s. In an interview for *The New York Times* (July 31, 1980), the former radical defendent in the trial of the Chicago Seven, who became a stockbroker and who in 1967 stormed the New York stock exchange and threw dollar bills from the visitors' gallery, said: "The individual who signs a check has the ultimate power, money is power. . . . Welcome Wall Street, here I come, let's make millions of dollars together . . . let's make capitalism work for everyone."

(II)

The Social-Psychological Perspective

Paul Mussen (1967):

According to classical psychoanalytic theories, the boy begins to fear that his father will castrate him. . . . His consequent fears of punishment . . . constitute the primary forces for the resolution of the Oedipus complex . . . The little boy accepts that he will be vanquished by the father. Identification . . . is as though the boy says, If I am him, he cannot hurt me.

The Maggid of Mezeritz (1710–1773):

The father who sees his son playing with nuts, and then due to his love he plays with him, although for the father this seems a childish act, . . . he contracts his mind and remains in smallness so that the little one will be able to bear him.

(6)

Alter-centered Individualism
and Interpersonal Contraction

Classic lamenters of the plight of Western man, such as Erich Fromm (1960), Rollo May (1950), and others, have consistently shown how the normative interpretation of Protestant individualism has produced a lonely, alienated, and anxious neurotic person who feels an obsessive compulsion to purchase his salvation through individualistic, egoistic achievements.

Consonant with these views, I have argued that alienation is an inevitable by-product not of universal industrialization but of Protestant individualism (Rotenberg 1978). Because of the need to escape from the Western trap of alienating individualism, Western man has been conditioned to oscillate on the "collectivistic-individualistic" pendulum from one extreme to the other. I have thus indicated that, according to Buber (1967), in both conditions people perpetuate their loneliness by running—*from* the lonely crowd or *to* the collectivizing mob. In an attempt to provide the outline of a more promising compromising interpersonal philosophy, I then discussed the Buberian-Hasidic notion of what I termed "reciprocal individualism." This alternative allows people to actualize themselves by maintaining their individualistic *responsibility*, but without necessarily slighting their reciprocal *responsiveness*.

So far our discussion has concentrated on setting the structural-functional, sociohistorical framework for alter-centered contraction. The following chapters will be devoted to the development of the social-psychological components of interpersonal contraction. For this purpose I shall have to develop further the philosophical principles of alter-centered, or reciprocal, individualism, which parallel and underline the alter-centered theory of interpersonal contraction.

The influx of available interaction theories does require compelling arguments to justify a new interpersonal theory predicated on mutual self-contraction rather than on personalized self-construction. Let me stress at the outset, however, that according to classic interpersonal theories, such as Mead's "symbolic interaction" paradigm (1934), the focal concern is not the other, but the *ego-centered* construction of the self through the reflective-manipulative process of taking the role of the other. Hence, interaction in Mead's scheme may stand for a symbolic cognitive process geared to construct, modify, shape, and develop an egoistic self, which must adjust himself to the expectations of significant others only to the extent that they will not hinder his self-indulging development. Accordingly, the "others" are conceived as static or rather passive looking-glasses (Cooley 1902), as inactive objects to be manipulated through impression management for the purpose of eliciting an ever-growing, inflated self-image (Goffman 1959). Such interactions, which are merely "symbolic," may, however, produce and perpetuate narcissistic societies flooded with movements demanding "personal rights," which by definition omit "interpersonal duties." That is, the resultant societies produce cultures in which interpersonal duties are neither fostered nor assessed as central parameters for personality development.

It will be shown that such an egoistic, unilateral, interpersonal concept should hardly be puzzling if one examines it within its Protestant deterministic background. If in the basic father-son, interpersonal paradigm, which is the symbolic universal blueprint of most interpersonal patterns, the God/father is an Oedipal-predestinal one, he obviously cannot change or be affected (as I have indicated earlier) by the son's reactions to him (especially because, in this scheme, personality ceases to change after early childhood). Theoretically, however, according to the bilateral interpersonal theory of mutual contraction, all the son's actions and reactions have an effect on father and heaven (see Besht 1975a: 31).

This conceptualization of interpersonal rights and duties challenges three basic individualistic assumptions that have been inculcated in Western socialization:

1.   It questions the assumption that actualizing salvation requires placing the ego in the center of the world.

2.   It asserts that the individualistic-democratic notions of personal freedom and privacy legitimize social indifference and excommunication.

3.   Consequently, it postulates a bilateral interpersonal concept according to which ego and alter constantly shape each other's behavior.

To construe the functional—though controversial—perspective of a social system in which interpersonal relationships are based on interpersonal contraction and in which interaction inevitably involves what may appear to be interpersonal "intrusion" due to its alter-centered orientation (i.e., theoretically I may sometimes impose on the other through whom I am to actualize myself), let us begin by examining the normative meaning of "contraction" in terms of the cabalistic-Hasidic idea of "active quietism."

Interpersonal Contraction and Active Quietism

To grasp the profound socially functional implications emanating from the interactive theory of contraction, it is useful to differentiate between the social connotation inherent in the concept of contraction and the *a*social, individualistic orientation implicated in classic quietism.

In the history of religions, quietism came to be known as a normative theosophy that prescribes salvation through one's total self-annihilation (*annihilatio*) or self-resignation. The underlying tenet of classic quietism is the pantheistic notion that the fulfillment of God's will on earth can be facilitated only through the absolute elimination of any form of human volition or activism. Molinos, one of the great Christian quietists, accordingly declared, "Activism is the enemy of God's grace" (cited by Schatz-Uffenheimer, 1968: 21). Yet while Christian quietism[1] demanded man's absolute passivity, in contrast to Protestant ascetic activism, both these theologies are essentially individualistic. Salvation is an egoistic matter, accomplished either through lonely activism or through self-withdrawal from the world of others.

Schatz-Uffenheimer (1968), in her eloquent study of the quietistic elements in eighteenth-century Hasidic thought, has already shown that while Hasidism incorporated strong quietistic features, it never required— nor even allowed—complete self-nullification. This possibility was counteracted by the active components that were simultaneously prescribed. According to Schatz-Uffenheimer, however, this paradoxical double strain of Hasidic active-quietism refers mainly to the Hasidic legitimization of self-actualizing salvation by sanctifying such earthly activities as working, and rejoicing, and less to the social sphere of alter-centered salvation.

Nevertheless, it seems impossible to comprehend the profound meaning of Hasidic *active*-quietistic contraction without recognizing its strong social foundations.

The two interrelated cabalistic-Hasidic terms that are of central importance for our discussion of interpersonal contraction are, again, *tsimtsum* (contraction) and *hitpashtut* (expansion). These two major cabalistic terms, which refer to a divine rhythmic process that comes to explain the creation and maintenance of the universe, explain also, as indicated earlier, how through this symbolic process of *tsimtsum,* the deity withdrew, so to speak, into himself in order to *make room* for the material and human world. It is nevertheless important to stress again that this continuous process of divine retreat is not, depicted as a one-time, terminal withdrawal that separates once and for all the sacred from the profane, but is a twofold process of *tsimtsum* and *hitpashtut,* whereby the divine light streams back into the divine realm and flows out to the world. Thus, the act of divine shrinkage and evacuation is paralleled by an act of reaching out and embracing, which according to Scholem (1941) might be equated, as we have said, with an enormous process of divine inhalation and exhalation, much like the human act of breathing.

Now, while the doctrine of *tsimtsum* refers strictly to a divine-cosmic process, human emulations of this divine process can in fact be identified in the applied cabalistic social norms developed in Hasidic ethics. As Schatz-Uffenheimer (1968: 122) points out, "there seems to be no difference between the two, the same as there was no difference between the divine world of talk and the human sphere of talk." Thus, two interactive concepts pertaining to the human social sphere and paralleling the divine processes of contraction and expansion seem important here: (a) *bitul ha'ani* (designification of self) or *anvah* (humbleness); and (b) *achdut* and *hitkalelut* (unification and generalization).

The Hasidic notion of *bitul ha'ani*, or *iyun* (self-designification)— which is derived from interchanging the letters in the word *ani* (I)— became a major imperative in Hasidic personal and, consequently, interpersonal behavior. In the cabalistic-Hasidic mystical tradition, great significance is attributed to the meaning of words that are comprised of the same letters. Thus the Hebrew word *ani* contains the same letters as the Hebrew word *ain* (nothingness). When this play with letters and construction of different words is applied, the quietistic norm of *iyun* (self-designification) is derived. One must strive to designify himself, to approach the level of *ain*, in relation to the divine and consequently also in relation to other people (see Schatz-Uffenheimer 1968). This de-egoistic process of reaching the level of self-insignificance, during which one becomes indifferent to personal needs, paradoxically bestows upon man a new sense of strength. Indeed, in Hasidic literature, the label *ain* often refers to the *zaddik* (the righteous one), who served as a model to be emulated (see Nigal 1974: 40). Accordingly, the Besht (1975b: 19) interpreted the famous saying "If I am not for myself, who is for me?" (Mishna, *Avot*, 1:14) as follows: When I reach the unselfish state of indifference to my psycho-physiological needs, at which I do not feel my own existence and consequently am not concerned about myself, then I shall be so strong that no alien thought or other temptation will be a threat to me. True, in Hasidic literature the notion of *iyun* (self-designification) is usually used to refer to psycho-physiological procedures that help man nullify himself in relation to God. Nonetheless, if one considers such behavioral ethics not as a discrete phenomenon but within its dynamic social context, self-designification (especially in the Maggid's terms [see Schatz-Uffenheimer 1968, 1976]) appears to be interconnected with self-contraction and social humbleness or with social mutual responsibility (if one follows Rabbi Yaacov Yosef's formulations [see Nigal 1962]). That is, if Hasidic active quietism does not allow for total self-annihilation, because it likewise stipulates that not only is it man's active responsibility to redeem the divine sparks through his earthly activities, and assumes that man's earthly activities are capable of influencing heaven (see Besht 1975a: 31), then Hasidic self-designification must be interpreted as self-contraction rather than self-annihilation (as Jacobs [1978] and others erroneously posited[2]).

It is this presumed inherent interdependence between these two active imperatives of self-contracting designification and social unification and the dictum that one should emulate the Divine which differentiates Hasidic active quietism from Christian individualistic and passive quietism.[3] Thus, states the Maggid (1927: 86) the biblical verse "and wisdom will be found from *ain* (nothingness)" (Job 28:12) "means when he [man] considers himself as nothing and makes himself small, God also contracts himself . . . and then he will certainly acquire wisdom." The prescribed advice for acquiring wisdom by emulating God involves not self-annihilation but "making oneself small," that is, contracting oneself and opening up to make space for absorbing the impacts of the surrounding world, which is impossible when one has totally abandoned his self and his active will. This is the source of the unique, paradoxical, yet powerful, social meaning in which the philosophy of alter-centered (reciprocal) individualism and the theory of social contraction find their epitomizing expression. Moreover, the explicit commandment that man should strive to emulate God's traits allows the analogy and application of the Hasidic doctrine of *tsimtsum* to the social human sphere, even though, according to its original cabalistic meaning, it referred only to the divine sphere. Because divine contraction and evacuation *to make room for* the material, weak, human world is, as I have stressed earlier, an act of strength, whereby no power is lost but on the contrary strength is gained through the coil-like process of contraction for the sake of expansion and ascendance, so Hasidic self-contraction differs markedly from the individualistic form of quietistic self-annihilation in its socially functional orientation. Hence, similar to the divine process of *hitpashtut* (expansion)—which parallels or rather complements the process of contracting withdrawal by an ever-new divine reaching out to embrace the world—so the Hasidic human imperative of *iyun* or *bitul atzmi* (self-designification), which is often associated with self-contraction and humbleness, should be examined in conjunction with the social dictum of *hitkalelut* (generalization) and *achdut* (unification). That is, according to the divine pantheistic concept of contraction and expansion, it is in fact impossible for the Almighty to contract himself, for this evacuation would create a vacuum, a godless space, since "there is no space without him" (*leit atar panuy miney*) as the Maggid (1927: 58) asserted. Thus, similar to divine contraction, which therefore must mean only a dimming of the divine light, that is, a hidden presence without the elimination of strength—or, as the Tanya (See Shneurson 1956: 140) put it, "There is no change, God forbid, in the

Divine's intensity"—human contraction also requires that in order to reach the other, one should make his assertive strength less felt, but instead of withdrawing it and deserting the other, leave his strength present in the background, to let the other feel his latent presence in order to give him space to grow and to enable him to enter into a relationship with him.

The dynamic ebb-and-flow process of mutual contraction and expanding embrace, whereby one deasserts his presence but stays in the background to give a hand when needed, is illuminated in the Maggid's interpretation (1927: 59) of the verse "Draw me, we will run after thee" (Song of Solomon 1:4) as follows:

> For example, when a father sees his son playing . . . and the father goes and lets his son see him, and when the son sees him, he leaves his playing in smallness and runs after the father and calls him father! . . . and as the father sees the son running after him, then he goes his way, and then the son calls out more loudly father! father! and runs after him faster. . . . Then he hides his face . . . so that the child will find less interest in activities of smallness (childishness) and he will increase his desire for his father's love. . . . It is thus apparent that the pleasure that the father had subsequently which extended also to the pleasure of the child, could not have been without contraction as the father contracted his love and went away and the son also contracted his playing in smallness.

In other words, the Maggid portrays the interaction-socialization process of contraction and expansion as a game of hide-and-seek, whereby the hiding is not featured as a total withdrawal or desertion of thou but is accompanied by flashes of exposure intended to stimulate and attract the thou into mutually enhancing interaction.

Thus, one may reach the other through self-contraction, by using the mutually attracting or contracting "hide-and-seek" technique and by leaving his strength present in the background. But how is personal growth and actualization affected in both the receiver and giver, that is the role-taker and the significant other, or the copier and the model? Is it a Rogerian (1965) kind of nondirective neutral presence, whereby the contracted nondirective withdrawal and not the expanding-intervening or the embracing is the predominant feature of interaction? Or is it a one-sided kind of copying behavior (see Bandura 1969) or role-taking behavior (see Mead 1934), whereby one person copies the behavior of an assertive model or takes his role, but in which the model or significant other is not presumed to be influenced by this process and hence remains a detached, assertive creditor? To advance an interpersonal theory that not only assigns a dynamic role to the model or significant other, but also assumes that through the mutual paralleling process of contraction and expansion both the model's and the learner's actualizing development are affected, we should begin by explaining how the applied principle of mutual emulation is derived from the cabalistic-Hasidic doctrine of divine contraction.

The Principle of Mutual Emulation
and the Anatomy of "Chutzpa"

The most profound and succinct source concerning the imperative interdependence between divine and socially emulated contraction can be found in the biblical commentary cited in the name of the founder of eighteenth-century Hasidism, the Besht (1975a, 1975b). As stated earlier, the guiding principle of *tikkun* (correction) is that all man's activities are capable of restoring order in heaven by correcting the original divine breaking of vessels; as the Besht stated (1975a: 31), "all his movements, business, and talk leave their impression on Heaven." Hence, according to this paradigmatic relationship between man and God, the son or the pupil may affect and change the father-teacher by his reciprocating behavior. Thus, in regard to the Talmudic stipulation that man should emulate God because "as He [the Almighty] is compassionate so you have to be compassionate" (Talmud, *Shabbat*, 133b), the Besht asks the following rhetorical question (1975a: 39): How can it be that the Almighty, who is pure spiritually, will be compassionate, that is, will contain a material, human entity? The Besht answers, "Only if the Blessed One contracts himself to have [earthly] matter in his thought then He pities us. And whence comes this contraction? It comes when man is compassionate and acts in such a way that the Almighty dresses himself in his [man's] dress and contracts himself, so to speak, and also pities him [man], and this is the meaning of 'as he is compassionate.' "

Although the Hasidic doctrine of contraction formally refers to a cognitive process whereby one should learn to designify himself in relation to the Divine, the Besht's foregoing statements comprise in fact the essential components of a social-contraction theory that pertains to the model's and the learner's actualizing growth. Accordingly, the interpersonal matter of extending compassion to a fellow man, which is the ABC of human interaction, does not proceed from a maximized self that allows the other to copy him, to take his role or identify with him, and who altruistically hands out his "surplus" goods left over from his satiated ego-centered act of salvation. Rather, it proceeds through a contraction process that is gradually forced on the significant model. In contrast to modeling, emulation is not a one-sided process triggered by an assertive static model whose behavior is being copied or manipulated through empathic role-taking tactics, but a mutual, gradually increasing process. Thus man is urged to emulate God in the way he believes or imagines divine behavior to be, and by this he actually "forces" God to conform to his expectations. The principle of mutually emulated contraction assumes that the more one emulates a model's expected (e.g., divine) or real (e.g., compassionate) behavior reached through contraction, the more the significant model is *forced* to increase his own (compassionate) contraction, for "when man is compassionate then he acts so that the Almighty dresses himself in his dress and contracts himself . . . and also pities him." The Besht's disciple phrased it more clearly: "Through your actions and humbleness you should cause the Almighty also to contract himself and reveal himself to you in smallness" (The Maggid 1927: 63).

It is thus the principle of mutual emulation which may contain the operational interpretation of *"chutzpa* behavior." If one dares to challenge the God/father by behaving in a way he believes or imagines justified and appropriate, then *"chutzpa* towards Heaven is useful" (Talmud, *Sanhedrin* 105a), because this behavior is not meant to "kill" or demolish the father, as presumably happens in the Oedipal myth, but only to force mutual contraction, emulation, and space evacuation, so that the weaker interacting partner may grow by daring to challenge and experiment even before he is "grown up." Hence, since mutual space evacuating contraction structurally institutionalizes interpersonal relations, *chutzpa* toward father or toward any other authority or interacting figure need not necessarily lead to the inevitable ambivalent hate toward "father" presumably featuring Oedipal relations as Freud (1938: 308) himself postulated: "The story of King Oedipus . . . explains . . . that we were all destined to direct . . . our first impulses of hatred and violence toward our fathers." Thus *chutzpa* may be defined as behavior imbued with an aura of charm, success, and growth emanating from the daring to challenge superior authority before one is qualified to challenge; to step upward before one knows how to climb, or to be optimistic before one sees the future. My insistence that in the mutual emulation process the contracting partners in the said interaction are forced to *increase* their expected behavior calls for another point of differentiation between traditional modeling and emulation. According to the dictionary, to emulate means to equal or to excel and surpass, while copying refers to imitation or reproduction of something exactly as it existed. Thus, congenial with Scholem's (1972) differentiation between restorative and utopian messianism, the dialectic or rather dialogic process of emulation refers, like in future-oriented prospective-therapy (see Chapter 14), to a utopian reproduction of the model's behavior plus the emulator's own excelled behavior, which surpasses the copied behavior of the model, while copying behavior per se connotes the mere restorative reproduction of a model's performance. In the dialectic-dialogic emulation therapy, the utopian future-oriented ascent of the son may in principle reach a higher level of synthetic, or rather creative hypothetic, behavior which uses the father's modeling as a springboard for personal actualizing growth. But how does the dynamic of *chutzpa* relations (in terms of mutual forcing) elucidate the bilateral mutual-emulation process according to the Beshtian scheme?

In contrast to self-centered interaction theories, the theory of interpersonal contraction assumes that, from a social-functional perspective, effective personal development occurs when ego's emulation of alter's behavior forces alter to conform to and increasingly improve the modeled behavior in accordance with the expectations of ego through an alter-induced process of cognitive dissonance (Festinger 1968). I say alter-induced cognitive dissonance in order to suggest that mutual self-development may sometimes occur even when a person increases his contracted interaction after he realizes that someone (usually a subordinate, follower, or disciple) emulated his inadvertent, unintended behavior, that is, that the other took him seriously. There are times that one patterns his behavior according to the way he "believes" the model intended to act.

Because even in such unintend interactions alter's "investment" creates a cognitive dissonance in the model's mind, which urges him to save face by keeping up his "accidental" modeling behavior, it is logical to assume that in *intended* contractions, such as between father and son, the mutually emulated interaction will enhance the behaviors of both learner and model. Again, because man can influence heaven, the son can affect his father, and the learner can affect his teacher or significant model.

In this context the principle of mutual emulation gives self-designification its social meaning. As the Maggid (1927: 86) has said, "if the *Zaddik* [righteous] clings to the trait of humbleness and is considered *ayin* [as nothing] . . . namely, when he himself is considered as nothing and makes himself very small, it will be seen that the Almighty also contracts his divinity and remains with him." The notion of self-designification is repeatedly mentioned in connection with humbleness and self-contraction (making oneself small). Again, although the main emphasis is on self-designification in relation to the Divine, the social implications given in the examples used by the Maggid lend themselves to clear behavioral norms. Thus, using self-designification in the literal self-contracting terms of making oneself small and humble, the Maggid states that God "is proud of Israel when he [Israel] clings to the trait of humbleness and makes himself small as a small boy and a lad . . . and considers himself to be nothing" (ibid.). Elsewhere the Maggid (p. 63) uses the Hasidic notion of *ain* strictly in the social sense of making oneself small in relation to others, "since a person cannot be bound to his friend but through making himself small seeing himself as *ain* [nothing] against his friend, through this he will bind himself to his friend."

The principle of mutual emulation defined above may now offer a concrete, interactive interpretation to the Beshtian dictum: "If a person had the opportunity to observe a transgression and he should feel [the need] to correct himself . . . then he will bring back the wicked person after he includes him through unification" (Besht 1975a: 21). Upon initial consideration of this imperative, one may wonder why the anormative behavior of the other should be casually related to the same anormative behavior in myself, and, further, how my correction of this particular behavior should simultaneously correct the other's behavior. To understand this process we should distinguish again between the one-directional model of Bandura (1969) or the passive, reflective, looking glass of Mead (1934), and the double-mirror model of the Besht, that is, the dynamic process of mutual emulation. While in the one-way looking-glass model there are no assumptions as to whether and how an A, the role-taker or the copier, affects B, the significant other's or model's behavior during an interactive situation (although it is possible of course, that the role-taker or copier, A, may serve as a B, significant model, during a different interactive situation), the mutual-emulating scheme proposes a situational dynamic, reflective process of double-mirroring, in which both interacting partners are affected simultaneously. The active-dynamic double-mirror concept assumes that if my interacting partner persistently repeats a certain kind of anormative behavior, then my performance in regard to this specific behavior must have been similarly anormative or insufficiently normative and persistent to serve its reflective modeling purpose.[4] Hence my correction of this behavior should reverse the process, for unlike modeling, emulation is a two-dimensional mirroring process. Indeed, Rabbi Yaacov Yosef (1963: 259) interprets the verse "who is a wise man; who learns from everybody" (Mishna *Avot* 4:1) by using the mirror metaphor (about two hundred years before Charles Cooley) as follows: "A wise man is the one who learns from everybody like someone that looks in the mirror; and knows his own faults by seeing the faults of his fellow man." Buber (1978: 241) related:

> Once Rabbi Zusya came to an inn, and on the forehead of the inn-keeper he saw long years of sin. For a while he neither spoke nor moved. But when he was alone in the room which had been assigned to him, the shudder of vicarious experience overcame him in the midst of singing psalms and he cried aloud: "Zusya, Zusya, you wicked man! What have you done! There is no lie that failed to tempt you, and no crime that you have not committed. Zusya, foolish, erring man, what will be the end of this?" Then he enumerated the sins of the inn-keeper, giving the time and place of each, and his own, and sobbed. The inn-keeper had quietly followed this strange man. He stood at the door and heard him. First he was seized with dull dismay, but then penitence and grace were lit within him, and he woke to God.

A more common example of such mutual self-correction might be when a teacher suddenly lowers his voice to bring attention to the fact that both he and his students have been shouting over one another's heads. Likewise, a mother who notices that her child is eating in an unmannerly way while important guests are present attempts to correct her own eating habits in the hope that the child will emulate her behavior, rather than reprimanding him in front of the visitors.[5]

Mutual emulation therefore also entails an operational definition of alter-centered individualism: collective orientation in terms of alter's misconduct is reduced by enhancing ego's individualistic actualizing behavioral responsibilities toward self. According to this "categorical imperative," it is insufficient to act, as Kant declared, so that my action *may* or at most *ought to* become a general moral, natural law. Rather, the ultimate test of my actualizing personal behavior depends on how it *actually* affects my interacting partner or the others in my community. Thus, while Kant's moral autonomy requires, by definition, the absence of any social motiviation to ethical conduct, alterism recognizes that self-actualization is possible only through its tested impact on others.

Nowhere is this individualistic alter-centered orientation expressed better than in Rabbi Yaacov Yosef's organic social theory. Thus, states Rabbi Yaacov Yosef (1963: 335); "when the Hasid witnesses the failure of the generation he should blame himself . . . and when the worldly people witness the failure of the *Zaddick's* action and the generation's Hasidism, they should blame themselves and put their heart to repent so that each will acquit his fellow man . . . and this one [the *Zaddick*] should put his heart to correct himself so that the people of his generation will be corrected and so the people of the generation will put their heart to repent so that the generation's leader will merit." Thus the twofold double-mirroring process of contraction and emulation constitutes the coil-spring concept of "ascent through descent" in its social-psychological sense (about which more will be said later).[6] If I contract myself, that is, descend to make room for the other, his emulation of my real or imagined behavior forces me, through the dynamic double-mirroring process, to ascend (i.e. to improve) my performance. In other words, if one considers the Maggid's psychological self-contraction doctrine and Rabbi Yaacov Yosef's sociological "organic solidarity" theory of mutual responsibility as one integral theory,[7] then the notion of self-contracting *Iyun* in relation to God may be understood in the way it filters down to parallel patterns of interpersonal contracting behavior.

We now should clarify and examine the operational dynamics of specific social-quietistic behaviors involved in interpersonal contraction by contrasting these behaviors with quietistic self-elimination or self-assertive behaviors. I shall begin by considering the element of personal contraction and permeation, in which one dilutes, dims, or contracts his strength yet at the same time retains it in the background so as to let it infiltrate the other.

NOTES

1. According to Meister Eckhart's Christian quietism, God's immanence requires pure nothingness and man's "absolute detachment from everything that is created" (cited in Suzuki 1971: 15).

2. Recent comparisons between Hasidic and Buddhist self-extinction have either claimed that in both processes something is left after ego-destruction (see Heifetz 1978) or that both require total self-extinction (Teshima 1978). According to Suzuki (1971: 30, 41), however, Buddhism is "the doctrine of *anatta* . . . that is, of non-ego" and of "emptiness transcending all forms of mutual relationships," which differs markedly from Hasidic active "spark lifting."

3. This anti-individualistic self-designification is somewhat akin to Castaneda's description (1974: 39) of how Don Juan told him that "as long as you feel that you are the most important thing in the world you cannot really appreciate the world around you." In Don Juan's philosophy, however, as in Zen Buddhism, self-designification is in relation more to the cosmos than to the social world, as in Hasidism.

4. The double-mirroring process, according to which the other's faults reflect my own faults, challenges extreme interpretation of an ego-centered psychology, according to which taking the blame for another person's mistakes might be interpreted as a lack in clearly delineated ego boundaries and as a paranoic-neurotic guilt complex.

5. I think the following example of how the double-mirroring principle of mutual emulation has taught me a lesson in the bosom of my own family might be illuminative. My daughter has recently decided to comply with the norm of not gossiping about people (a part of Jewish ethics and, hence, formally a part of our own ethics). While she has so far not succeeded in depriving us entirely of this vital part of life's enjoyment, her grimaces and other expressions of disapproval (mirroring) during such gossip sessions have forced us to become very aware whenever the urge to gossip comes over us.

6. The major exposition of the "ascent through descent" model, which comprises the psychological part of the contraction theory, will be presented in Part III.

7. The present integrative conceptualization of the Maggidic sociopsychological personal-contraction perspective with Yaacov Yosef's sociological concept of organic unification differs from such psychological formulations of Hasidic ethics as Shoham's (1977). Shoham differentiated between the Besht and the Maggid as representing two major and polar psychological types: the Besht presumably representing the Sisyphean type who aspires unsuccessfully to crystalize (by means of pain and distress) his own separate personality, and the Maggid representing the Tantalusean type, who aspires all his life to return to the pantheistic unity within his mother's womb. While Shoham's existential psychology of the absurd leads to a deterministic interpretation of Hasidic ethics in terms of various dysfunctional life-styles or personalities, the present view considers the Beshtian doctrine as the basic formulation of a psychosocial theory that was elaborated and developed into what lends itself to be conceived as a single integrative, functional social theory by his two major disciples: the Maggid, who reformulated the psychological part, and Yaacov Yosef, who developed the sociological perspective.

(7)

The Prussian-Oedipal Father vs. the Maggid's Contracting Father

There is a story about the congregants of a small Hasidic community who gathered in their local synagogue to pray together on the eve of the Day of Atonement. As they were about to commence their prayers, the rabbi suddenly walked up to the pulpit and publicly declared himself to be a "nothing" and a "nobody." He asked the congregants to forgive him for past boasting and self-indulgences. As the rabbi finished, the president of the congregation walked up to the pulpit, took his place next to the rabbi, and similarly declared himself to be a "nothing" and a "nobody." Following the president, the congregation's richest man (the *gevir*) announced his "nothingness"; then the local judge and other important members of the community all publicly declared themselves to be "nobodies." Finally, the maintenance man (the *shames*) of the synagogue walked up to similarly declare his nothingness, but the congregants all turned to him and protested scornfully, saying, "Look who takes himself to be a 'nobody'!"

Jokes and sarcastic stories always reflect a certain reality. On the one hand, this tale comes to question whether the prescribed norm did not boomerang. On the other hand, while it is imperative to contract and designify oneself in relation to the Divine and in relation to one's fellow men, one has to be "somebody," that is, one must possess strength in order to give up strength. One has to be strong enough to admit weakness through self-contraction in order to make room for others.

The Maggid of Mezseritz (see Schatz-Uffenheimer 1976), who led the Hasidic movement after the Besht's death, is the major exponent of the Hasidic interpersonal contraction doctrine. To construe the social meaning of contraction, I shall thus draw mainly on the Maggid's philosophical formulations. Similar to the Besht, the Maggid expounds the divine process of cognitive contraction in moral-social terms. The Divine's revelation, as it were, in human behavioral terms in turn enables man to emulate God by patterning his behavior in accord with the Almighty's traits. The main exposition of divine contraction, which is found repeatedly in Hasidic writings, stresses that divine contraction was "necessary for the world for without it the world would have been unable to absorb the [divine] light . . . and the world would have been eliminated from existence" (The Maggid 1927: 38).

Thus, to explain why the Divine revealed himself in the Bible in the "contracted language" which is used to describe human behaviors as if the Divine were able to feel pity, anger, regret, and so on, the Maggid says that "the Almighty contracted his brightness, so to speak, in the image of a father who contracts his mind and talks in small [simple] terms for his little son . . . [and] love caused contraction" (1927: 9). As we shall see, the cognitive dimming or contraction of the father's brightness to reach the weaker small son is again not a one-directional process from father to son, that is, an empathetic role-taking process whereby the self-fulfilled and self-developed father "understands" the son by putting himself in the small shoes of his son. It is a process that enables the son to move toward the father who dimmed his "brightness" ("talks in small terms") to make room for the son, for the father likewise actualizes himself as a father-teacher through the educational love that "caused contraction," that is, that can materialize only if the partners contract themselves for each other.

Educational love relationships between God and man, teacher and student, or father and son are used in most theosophical ethical systems as basic patterns for examining socialization and interpersonal relations. The two-directional interpersonal implications of the Hasidic father-son relationship are even more explicit in this passage from the Maggid (p. 63):

> Through your actions and humbleness you should cause the Almighty also to contract himself and reveal himself to you in smallness. As in the case of the father who sees his son playing with nuts, and then due to his love he plays with him, although for the father this seems a childish act of "smallness," nonetheless out of love for his son and so that he should receive pleasure from his son, he contracts his mind and remains in "smallness" so that the little one will be able to bear him, for if he would have been unable to bear his father, then the father would not have derived pleasure from him.

I have quoted the foregoing passage in full because it contains the main cognitive and affective components of alteristic contraction. In order to best understand the difference between altruistic mutual aid or assertive behavior and socially functional alteristic contraction, one should examine the dynamics of educational love relationships. In no interpersonal relations is the meaning of mutual apprehension as important for interactive fulfillment as in love and educational relationships. The egoistic, self-fulfilled, altruistic creditor does not know—and possibly is not interested in knowing—whether he has or has not helped or reached the other with the "surplus" goods that were left over after he actualized himself. Hence, he may feel pride or contempt in relation to the debtor, but he cannot sense his gratitude or reciprocating love. As the Renaissance "psychologist," Juan Luis Vives, stated, "[in the West] passive love, that is, the tendency to be the recipient of love produces gratitude; and gratitude is always mixed with shame . . . which gives one a feeling of being thwarted" (cited in Zilboorg 1941: 193). The loving alteristic person can derive comforting pleasure from his love for the other by contracting his mind and interacting with the loved person on the other's level. If his message is sufficiently contracted to permeate the other, until he feels that the "son can bear it," then the feedback of self-actualizing pleasure flows back to him. From this perspective, the Western derogatory archetype "Jewish mother" is nothing more than an ultimate alter-centered personality whose actualizing needs (through loving or "feeding" others) are rejected by the ego-centered self-insulated "offspring."[1] The two-directional cognitive process of alter-centered contraction is a useful means to explain various interpersonal interaction processes. Two cognitive-contraction phases may be identified. In the first phase, contraction in terms of simple, cognitive concentration explains the emphatic process of contracting one's mind to concentrate on the needs of the person under consideration. Thus, says the Maggid (1927: 88), "If a person must think about something which is vital for him, then this person must contract his thought in great contraction so that he will not think about anything else but what is necessary for him." In the second phase the principle of cognitive contraction explicates how, in interaction between two unequal partners, one can fully convey what he feels or thinks only through narrowing and contracting the matter to be conveyed so that his message may permeate the other, and not by asserting oneself. Thus, asserts the Maggid (1927: 47),

> When the Rabbi wants his student to understand his broad mind, and the student cannot apprehend it then the Rabbi-teacher contracts his mind in talk and letters. For example, when a person wants to pour from one container to another and he is afraid to spill, then he takes an instrument called a funnel, and by this the liquid is contracted . . . and he will not spill. So it is when the Rabbi's mind is contracted in talk and letters which he says to the student, and through this the student can apprehend the teacher's broad mind.

True, a difficult operational question, which immediately presents itself here, is *how* the teacher-rabbi contracts his broad mind in "talk and letters." Within the present theoretical analysis of ethics, it is difficult to provide concrete contraction strategies because they are not easily educible from the literature. One possible interpretation (to which I shall address myself in more detail later) is that if the Besht used simple parables to inculcate his ethical system among the masses—and thereafter they were used as modeling socialization procedures by his disciples—then it seems logical to assume that this use of parables is the cognitive-contraction method for reaching the small son, that is, this is the application of the principle of small talk and letters. What we have then is a doctrine of cognitive-affective contraction with strong interpersonal implications, indicating that one can reach the other, weaker person not through a movement from the assertive altruistic model to the "needy" student or debtor, commonly referred to as "intervention" or, rather, *intrusion* strategies, but through a movement of self-contracting *inclusion* strategies from the needy person to the model. One can make room so as to enable the other to come toward him. As a result, one's being is sufficiently contracted to let the "son" perceive one's "broad mind" by funneling it into the son and by letting the son's reciprocating apprehension and love permeate or infiltrate the educator-father's contracted mind, so that he too will be able to derive his actualizing pleasure. For example, Rabbi Nachum of Tchernobil said that "the Almighty contracts himself and makes himself smaller, so to speak, until he brings himself closer to us into the physical limbs" (see Horodetzky 1951: vol. 2, p. 81).

The ultimate testing-ground for actualizing pleasure through interpersonal interaction thus usually evolves from educational or love relationships, because it is in love or educational relationships that self-fulfillment is meaningless until the interacting partner provides the proper feedback signs that the educational/love message was indeed fully perceived. Hence, alter-centered contraction and not ego-centric, altruistic self-assertion would seem to lead to actualizing salvation in terms of deriving self-fulfilling pleasure. If the father-son relationship can indeed be conceived as a universal paradigm for studying socialization and interaction, then the Maggid's use of the contracting father image should be viewed not as mere rhetoric but as a point of departure for studying education, socialization, and interpersonal relationships. According to most interpretations of the Freudian noncontracting, Austro-Hungarian, Caesarlike—or rather, the Prussian-Oedipal omnipotent father-type—rooted in the stern, uninfluenceable deterministic Calvinist God/father image, the child learns to love his father and to identify with him by transfiguring his envious, competitive fear of the authoritative castrating father into "becoming his father." Indeed, the deterministic Prussian father image with whom we are doomed to identify out of fear and guilt-feeling (due to our wish to kill him) is already immanent in Freud's own writing. Based on the case of a man (whom Freud probably treated) who suffered from obsessive wish impulses to kill first his overstrict "dead" father and through the process of "transference" also strangers outside the family circle, Freud (1938: 307) admittedly constructed the Oedipal conflict paradigm, thus stating that "the Oedipus Rex . . . depends on the conflict between the all-powerful will of the gods and the vain efforts of human beings threatened with disaster, resignation to the divine will, and the perception of one's own impotence." Thus taking a glimpse at how Freud's thinking permeated psychological literature, Paul Mussen (1967: 82), whose textbooks on child development are among the most widely cited authoritative sources on identification and socialization theories, states, for example,

> According to classical psychoanalytic theory, the boy begins to fear that his father will castrate him in retaliation for his aggression and rivalry as well as for his sexual feelings towards his mother. The boy's envy of his father, his hostility toward him, and his consequent fear of punishment and retaliation constitute the primary forces for the resolution of the Oedipus complex and, subsequently, for the boy's identification with the father. . . . That is, frightened by the overwhelming threat of castration, the little boy accepts the fact that he will be vanquished by the father. He realizes that he cannot compete successfully for his mother's love. Identification with the father then develops, replacing the boy's jealous, hostile, and rivalrous feelings toward him. It is as though the boys says, "if I am him, he cannot hurt me."

In other words, the son must annihilate his own little self in order to become the same Prussian, noncontracting, stern father. That is, according to the Western Oedipal model of interaction and socialization, the burden of identification (usually termed defensive) and personal development falls on the shoulders of the poor trembling child—the weaker partner in the interaction—who has to surrender his competitive weapons and work out his ambivalence toward the father in order to be absorbed or dissolved into the strong father-male image. But self-contraction on the part of the father is not a necessary component in the educational process and love relationships. This is of course not to suggest that practically all clinical interpretations dealing with strategies geared to resolve the Oedipal complex rule out self-contraction on the father's part, resulting from interactive experiences.[2] It is only to stress that since by definition psychodynamic theories of socialization do not assume personality changes after childhood, the resulting identificatory father-son interactive paradigm presents a unilateral change process according to which dynamic change possibilities and identificatory efforts are essentially assumed only in regard to the weaker "son" interacting partner.

In a sense, Confucian filial piety requires similar submission and loyalty of the son to his father. In Confucianism, however, the lack of ambivalence that features father-son relationships prevents the son's need for assertive aggression against his father. Moreover, the trinity notion, which is presumed to prevail between man, heaven, and earth, creates a cosmic conceptualization of man according to which *all* people are to dissolve or integrate into the cosmos. Everyone must deassert himself in relation to the world and one another, so it is not one-against-the-other assertion that characterizes the father-son—or any—interaction. Consequently, a son's submission to his father is part of a general deassertion in relation to the cosmos and the world (see Bellah 1970a).

Indeed, one may wonder whether the origins of the stereotypic noncontracting Western male/father chauvinist should not be traced to the very same Oedipal-Prussian father socialization model that is usually used admiringly and unquestionably in the West to raise both contemporary feminists and masculinists alike. Essentially I am suggesting that Freud's fantastic Prussian-Oedipal noncontracting male image is so entrenched in Western culture that such "personal rights" movements as the feminist movement may in fact train women to become the same assertive, noncontracting Oedipal types as the "castrating" males they so abhor, instead of searching for new models that would teach interaction by means of mutual contraction for both partners. One writer for this movement, for example, complains that "by structuring itself according to the male castration complex, civilization sets the conditions under which women are forced to define themselves as castrated" (Strouse 1975: 169). Another writer, who believes that Americans are dominated not by male tyranny but by female tyranny, insists that "what we do try hard to outgrow . . . is our subjugation to female power" and that "the central opportunity for self-deception . . . lies in the shift from dependence on female authority to dependence on male, patriarchical authority" (see Dinnerstein 1977: 188). Condemning *any* form of dependence or self-contraction, the typical response to such agitations can be found in one of the numerous "assertiveness training" books so popular recently in the United States. The authors of such "how to do" books usually advise partners in "marriage contracts" to "always stress the behaviors you want to increase rather than those you want to decrease" (Fensterheim and Baer 1975: 131). Thus, the power struggle between marriage partners results in a dichotomizing division of two authorities in which no one is willing to "decrease" or contract behaviors or desires to make room for the other. Using educational love relationships as a test case for interpersonal relations, Kierkegaard (see Bretall 1946), in his ambivalent rebellion against Protestant Christianity in which he was so hopelessly imprisoned, struggled, as did the Maggid, with the problems of assertion and interaction in regard to love and education by alternately using the images of the God-teacher and the earthly king. Thus, like the Maggid, Kierkegaard realizes that the success of love and educational relations depends on a bilateral process of cognitive and affective union. Accordingly, the unhappiness of a king who loves a humble maiden "does not come from the inability of the lovers to realize their union, but from their inability to understand one another. . . . For love is exultant when it unites equals, but it is triumphant when it makes that which was unequal equal in love" (ibid., pp. 164–165). Pondering over the realization prospects of this love, Kierkegaard then considers the chances for happiness of the king and the maiden:

> Would she be happy in the life at his side? Would she be able to summon confidence enough never to remember what the king wished only to forget, that he was a king and she had been a humble maiden? [And Kierkegaard concludes] For if this memory were to waken in her soul and like a favored lover sometimes steal her thoughts away from the king . . . where would be the glory of their love? (Ibid., p. 166)

Applying this analogy to the educational domain, Kierkegaard then uses God as an alternate image for the king and asserts, "If this equality cannot be established, God's love becomes unhappy and his techings meaningless, since they cannot understand one another" (ibid.).

One by one Kierkegaard rules out several options open to the king: Should the union be brought about by an elevation of the learner? He concludes that deep down the maiden would feel deceived. Should the union be brought about by the king "showing himself in all the pomp of his power? Alas, . . . this might have satisfied the maiden, but it could not satisfy the king, who desired not his own glorification but hers" (ibid., p. 107). Kierkegaard finally concludes that learning and love cannot be realized through what I termed the Oedipal-Prussian internalization of the father's threatening power, or through the Maggid's contracting father-teacher image, but only through God's total self-concealment. He must come to the maiden as an unrecognizable, ungodly *servant*. Kierkegaard insists that this appearance is no mere "contracted" outer garment, "like the filmy summer-cloak of Socrates, which though woven of nothing, yet both conceals and reveals" but "his true form and figure" (ibid., p. 168). Thus, although the ambivalent Christian Kierkegaard comes closest to the Maggid's contracting model of socialization and interaction, in the Christian world, mutual contraction seems to be essentially impossible. One either erases his royal self and becomes a quietistic servant, or one remains an ego-centered, inflated, Oedipal male chauvinist.

We have spelled out the norms of alteristic existence, which means interacting with others through the two interrelated processes of personal contraction and alter-centered expansion and social unification. To grasp the difference between contraction of a father's "small talk" and everyday noncontracting, Oedipal communication, we shall now show how the popular Western socialization system for assertive behavior contrasts with interpersonal contraction.

NOTES

1. On the other hand, it may well be that it is due only to the space-evacuating "contracting Jewish father" that the Jewish mother acquired a domineering image in the male-oriented culture of the West.

2. While Shelleff (1976), in his survey of myths dealing with father-son relationships, has demonstrated, for example, that there is sufficient evidence indicating how and why these presumed hostile murderous feelings may in fact be directed from father to son, and not vice versa, and while the theme of unilateral murder wish and not mutual contraction is evident in these mythologies as well, the overwhelming impact of Freud's parricide conflict model in Western psychologically oriented thinking unfortunately seems still unchallengeable and dominant.

(8)

Assertiveness Training
for "I or Thou" Behavior

I have already made several allusions to the proposition that while contractional deassertive interaction patterned after the Maggidic image of the father playing with his child should theoretically enhance mutual growth and self-fulfillment, the noncontracting training for assertiveness may enhance separateness and alienation—what may be termed an "I or thou" communication style. At first glance this proposition seems paradoxical: how and why should the very essence of communication, that is, enhanced assertiveness and articulative ability, decrease communication instead of improving it?

In support of the above "absurd" proposition, it would seem useful to illustrate, again, with a story. Two Hasidic Jews were traveling together in a train. After a long hour of silence, one of them sighed heavily, from the depth of his soul, you might say. Although the two had never met before, the other immediately responded by saying, "You're telling me?!" This anecdote implies that by using the normative, deassertive, nonverbal language of sighing (which is deassertive in the sense that it is normative to sigh once in a while, as if to say, I ain't so great! It is difficult to be a Jew, to make a living, etc.), the instantaneous understanding that was formed between these two perfect "strangers" was deeper and more meaningful than the understanding that any word language can ever create. Indeed, one may say that in the Hasidic world, the nonverbal, indirect language of sound and gestures is so deeply implanted that it begins with a baby's first cry and ends with an old man's last sigh.

In his Hasidic "I and thou" philosophical formulation, Buber (1967: 3) went even further. He suggested that "for a conversation no sound is necessary, not even a gesture." Chaim Potok (1967) skillfully described how communicative understanding between a Hasidic rabbi and his rebellious "modern" son was reestablished not through each asserting himself and his position but through the father's penetrating, piercing communication of silence to his "deviant," academic, "lost" son.

Studies comparing communicational differences between Japanese and North Americans (see Haring 1956; Nakane 1970; and Johnson and Johnson 1973) have found that a feature of the Japanese interaction style is a calculated amount of vagueness. A conscious use of indirection and circumlocution diminishes assertiveness and fends off possible adverse reactions by frequently resorting to silence and passivity during verbal communication. Moreover, Johnson and Johnson (1973: 457) report, "A child raised in a Japanese family learns that he should not call attention to himself by being loud, conceited or self-centered. Children who take verbal initiative are generally not rewarded." Hence, boasting about one's achievements or those of members of one's family, or being verbal in class, is sanctioned partly out of "a concern for how such immodesty might make the other person feel," that is, that others shouldn't feel "that he is attempting to put them down." Generally among Japanese, ritualized self-deprecation "is less concerned with status considerations than with emotional relationships between peers."

Because both Japanese and Hasidic societies are indeed known to be more collectively solidaric (see Doi 1973; Poll 1969) and more dealienating than the American individualistic culture, it would appear then that training for deassertiveness rather than for assertiveness per se would enhance communication and group cohesiveness, due to its built-in alter-centered concern for others. In other words, the popular trend of treating "communication problems" should paradoxically concentrate on teaching people to talk *less* to one another rather than more. Humorist Tom Lehrer once wisely declared, "If a person cannot communicate, the least he ought to be able to do is to shut up" (cited in Boorstin 1974: 3).

To be sure, the problem is not "to talk or not to talk" or "if I speak, I exist." It seems that it is the sociopolitical value context from which the recent popular assertiveness-training movement sprang that has endowed it with its paradoxical alienating direction. We should keep in mind that the recent fad of assertiveness training is interconnected with the American neo-individualistic trend that constantly fosters new personal and "civil rights" movements. I say "American individualistic" trend because these movements are indeed patterned after the supreme American sacred cow— the archetypical Declaration of Independence movement. And while I have no intention of devaluing the historical significance and contribution of Jefferson's individualistic declaration for humanity and the free world, one ought to remember that movements for independence usually emerge as an outrageous reaction *against* another presumably oppressing group from which the new group strives to be separated. These "personal rights" groups either overlook or ignore Jefferson's own stipulation that "a man has no natural rights in opposition to his social duties" (see Hook 1962: 6). Boorstin (1974: 7) rightly stressed that "the Declaration of Independence was motivated by, among other things, American feelings of anger and outrage against King George III and the members of his government."

Similarly, today, the feminist movement emerged, for example, as a reaction *against* men, from whom the movement seeks independence through assertiveness training. Thus women are trained to be assertive and independent *against* men; men are trained to be assertive and independent *against* women and their universal "Jewish mothers," black "personal rights" movements are trained *against whites,* and whites are trained against "reds"—and the list can be extended endlessly. Consequently, training for individualistic assertiveness *against* seems to boomerang its own communicative goal and to train people for egoism and alienation rather than improved communication.

A few examples, taken randomly from the countless assertiveness-training books appearing daily in the United States will suffice to make our point. As one skims through these books, the first thing that strikes the eye is that the first rule of improving communication, in the sense of "the best way to make a friend is to be one," is nowhere to be found. All books promising happiness begin by listing people's personal rights—not their interpersonal obligations, as if mutual obligations were merely obstacles on the way to happiness.[1] The basic notion of Mead (1934) that self-fulfillment, in terms of self-esteem, is a function of the evaluation of one's behavior by his significant others—in whose eyes one should at least attempt to remain significant—is entirely denied.

In one "against" book entitled *Don't Say Yes When You Want to Say No,* we find the following definition of self-esteem: "The more you stand up for yourself and act in a manner you respect, the higher will be your self-esteem. Hence my basic equation: Assertion = self-esteem." Moreover, continue the authors in their tautological egoistic definition of self, "The assertive training formula maintains that as long as you act assertively, you maintain your self-esteem" (Fensterheim and Baer, 1975: 25, 26). Further, by providing a detailed list of the rights people should insist on in their everyday relations "against" others, another "against" book, entitled *Stand Up, Speak Up, Talk Back,* delineates for us what constitutes and shapes one's self-concept: "A person who has acted nonassertively or aggressively in his relationships for a long period of time usually thinks poorly of himself. His behavior toward others—whether self-denying or abusive—evokes scorn, disdain, avoidance. He observes the response and says to himself, 'See, I knew I was no damn good' " (Alberti and Emmons 1977: 77). Indeed, the utilitarian assumption that selfish maximization of self-pampering and not self-denial and sharing with others produces self-fulfillment appears to be a basic dictum in assertiveness training. Actually, it is training for membership in the cult of egoism. In one book selling happiness through personal freedom from others, the trainee is warned:

> You're in the unselfishness trap . . . if you feel you're *required* to give part of your income to the poor, or if you think that your country, community, or family has first claim on your time, energy or money. . . . They say that the way to be happy is to make others happy. . . . Do you want to make someone happy? Go to it—use your talents and your insight and benevolence to bestow riches of happiness upon the one person you understand well enough to do it efficiently—yourself. I guarantee that you'll get more genuine appreciation from yourself than from anyone else. Give to you. Support your local self!" (Browne 1974: 64).

Let me state loud and clear that it is not the proposition that assertive behavior can sometimes improve interpersonal relations and feelings of personal competency which is questioned here. What I wish to challenge is the basic assumptions that happiness and self-fulfillment are functions of self-pampering and that self-contraction, or nonassertiveness and self-denying in relation to others, hinders self-fulfillment and equals poor self- and social-identity. The narcissistic "self-actualizing" system of "giving and supporting only your local self" must inevitably turn into a self-defeating mechanism that in fact prevents gratification of self needs as Sennett has so eloquently argued. Sennett (1970: 8) explains this absurd reality:

> Narcissism is an obsession with what this person, that event means to me." This question about the personal relevance of other people and outside acts is posed so repetitively that a clear perception of those persons and events in themselves is obscured . . . it makes the person at the moment of attaining an end or connecting with another person feel that "this isn't what I wanted." Narcissism thus has the double quality of being a voracious absorption in self needs and the block to their fulfillment.

In other words, viewed from the present perspective, narcissism means that since giving to another person (be it money, love, affection, or any other form of giving) satisfies the other, then "it isn't really what I want," because I want to give only to myself, although paradoxically I can enjoy often myself only through this or another particular other. Hence, I prefer preventing gratification of my own actualizing pleasure needs as long as I know that I am not in the "selfishness trap" of being brainwashed to acquire happiness by making others happy. Putting the narcissistic "assert yourself—give only to your local self" imperative in role-theoretical terms, the new encounter-exchange style of mutual self-revelation, which should presumably enhance interpersonal relations, would instead lead to separating dead ends. This would be so, because if self-disclosure requires a minimal sense of self-concept, which by definition (see Mead 1934) may develop only through continuous reflective practices of taking the role of others, this reflective process—which inadvertently but inevitably benefits others (who would thus practice their own role-taking skill or at least enjoy the intimate gossip)—will violate the "give only to yourself" dictum and hence create the feeling that since "I can't really feel myself, I can't relate to others and therefore better stop this interaction."

Thus, it is probably true that in the West, where the Hobbesian social contract was so interpreted to teach people what *not* to do with one another rather than what and how to do things together, a person who is self-denying and who does not stand up against others to defend his rights will think poorly of himself and will "evoke scorn, disdain, and avoidance" in others. This is apparently so, because in the West self-actualizing salvation is an egoistic matter patterned after the Prussian-Oedipal male figure who is not expected to contract himself in relation to the other weaker debtor with whom he interacts. Thus, according to this Prussian noncontracting model of interpersonal relations, the burden to resolve the Oedipal conflict in any form of interaction falls on the weak "child." He is compelled to learn how to love through fear and self-assertion, to become the same Prussian male-father, so that all interpersonal relationships result in a division of authority between two noncontracting Prussian "kings." But the price of such narcissistic self-salvation is alienation and not collaboration. Consequently we must ask, Is it really true that a person can be self-fulfillingly happy by giving only to himself? Does the rich man really enjoy himself more when he eats and celebrates all by himself, than when he entertains others, who through their enjoyment of his goodies reinforce the self-fulfilling satisfaction inherent in his possessions? Let us consider how the individualistic movements for assertiveness train the weaker, nonassertive partner to become more egoistic and assertive. Indeed, let the reader judge for himself how in the assertiveness-training literature the stronger, Prussian partner is not told to deassert and contract himself, or to give in order to make room for the other, although admittedly he can enjoy himself more by giving part of his possessions.

Consider how interactive self-contracting put-downs are unequivocally condemned in the following case study taken at random from the assertiveness-training literature:

> Jason has just won first prize in a photography contest. His friend Jerry comes up and says: Hey Jason, I heard you won that contest. That's neat, there must have been a lot of competition. . . .
>   Jason replies: Oh no, there wasn't much to it. I think I was just lucky. I am really an amateur.

While Jason was obviously contracting himself to make room for Jerry, who might have felt that he had no such chances for winning, the authors rule out a priori any positive connotation inherent in deassertive interpersonal contraction:

> Nothing constructive can come out of putting yourself down overtly or covertly. What good does it do? It doesn't make you a better person, does it? Quite contrary: isn't your self-confidence hurt? . . . Practice in not engaging in self-put-down behavior. Try to be nicer to yourself. Like yourself. . . . Be assertive with yourself and think and say self-fulfilling thoughts instead of self-deprecating ones. (Alberti and Emmons 1977: 153–155)

Thus, in contrast to the Japanese or Hasidic deassertive norms (ironically in today's reality probably more Americans behave like Jason as compared, for example, to some typical "Israeli Sabras"), being humble in relation to the other by saying that the contest wasn't that difficult doesn't "make one a better person," but it does hurt one's self-confidence—as if self-confidence were a function not of one's ability to perform but of one's ability to be an imposter-performer. In short, the possibility of contracting oneself to make room for the other just so he will feel more comfortable is utterly and vehemently rejected. Consequently, no mutual contraction is expected in conflicting relationships, and people are *forced* to actualize themselves by asserting and praising themselves all by themselves. In fact, by not deasserting oneself in relation to the other, one is deprived of the double self-fulfilling pleasure of others' praise.

Two cases, again taken at random from the assertiveness-training literature, will suffice to demonstrate how assertive training leads to a divisive contract between two noncontracting Oedipal kings rather than to a binding contract between two contracting partners:

> Seth represented the perfect example of the unassertive man. . . . As an adult, he rarely asked for anything for himself. . . . When he acquired wife number two, she also began to exploit him unmercifully. After working a fifty-hour week at the office, plus overtime at home, Seth vacuumed the floors and did the grocery shopping, even though his wife did not work. She too, walked out, saying, "I've tried to provoke you to get signs of life, but you never get angry and never fight back!" . . . After seeing Seth for individual sessions of Assertiveness Training, I decided upon group therapy with two treatment goals (1) to teach him how to express anger; (2) to train him . . . how to stand up for himself. . . . He carried his new assertive ability over into his life. He stood up to his girl friend, his sisters, his boss. (Fensterheim and Baer, 1975: 28, 29)

> A woman who complained for years of her husband's lack of firmness in dealing with others became upset when he finally sought help, participated in assertiveness training, and began to stand up to *her*. She could

not accept his new behavior and told him she didn't know if she loved him any more. (Alberti and Emmons 1977: 70)

Actually, both husbands should have been potential ideal models for the women's liberation, sharing/collaborating, new-husband types who vacuum the floor, do the shopping, and so on. It would seem that the wife and sisters were the ones who needed deassertive and deexploitative training so they could be content with the male type for which they aspired. In reality, however, the Western woman apparently demands a Prussian, noncontracting type of husband who fits her unchallenged Oedipal socialization background. The result is that instead of training both sides to contract themselves equally toward each other, the rules of assertiveness training determine that only the weaker partner be trained to assert himself *against* the other partner.

True, what is suggested here is that social conflict is functional for group integration. Consonant with Simmel's (1955) theory, I agree that conflict is functional for enhancing group unity, not by subtracting discord from consensus or disharmony from harmony, but by adding these elements to group interaction. However, what Simmel might have disregarded is that, in an ego-centered salvation culture, people are trained to actualize themselves individually and egoistically by asserting themselves against others and hence they avoid or evade the functional ongoing conflict.

The difference between the Western "dividing conflicts" in terms of "I do my thing, you do yours" and the Hasidic "involving conflict" in the sense of organic mutual responsibility and involvement, "when the feet are low the head also bends," is not a minor one. "Involving conflict" follows directly from the Hasidic interpretation of the tradition of "oral Torah" or "oral Law." Accordingly, the "oral Law" (e.g., Talmud, Commentary) should never have been written or printed because it is the basis for a continuous functional debate and free choice that should never cease, as it ties people together (see Schatz-Uffenheimer 1968: 172). Oral debate is the essence of the dialogue and dialectic "contrasting-binding" force among people. If nothing is final (i.e., written) or settled among people, but open to continuous debate, then each interacting member can retain his individuality and responsibility in relation to the matter under dispute, while at the same time also being bound to the other in their continuous concerted search for new tentative solutions. Final, written solutions connote separateness; "involving" conflict implies living relationships (see Rotenberg 1978: 162).

To recapitulate, deassertiveness in the United States—as the prototype for the West—evokes scorn, disdain, and avoidance because it is rooted in the unchallenged Prussian-Oedipal socialization conception. Hence, self-indulging assertiveness *against* others may lead to improved interaction in terms of clear division of authorities, but at the possible price of increased separateness and loneliness. On the other hand, Japanese and Hasidic deassertive contraction *for* the inclusion of others would seem to enhance communication. For the Western Christian man, self-actualizing existence means "to be or not to be! If I assert myself, I exist!" If this Nietzschean superman does not assert himself to rule all by himself for himself, he does not exist. To be B-minus does not exist. Everybody must be A-plus. In this competitive Western individualistic world the rule is "I *or* thou." Either I rule or you rule, but not I rule with thou. One must choose between the Oedipal salvation road, which leads to egoistic activism, or, alternatively, follow the road that leads to passive quietism. In both, this individualistically trained man is lonely. In Kierkegaard's Christian world (see Bretall 1946), the king must come to his beloved humble maiden incognito, as a servant; he must totally erase his royal self, for he is unable to contract himself to make room for the simple maiden he loves or to uplift her to his level, because of the cognitive social gap (either in his or her mind), which cannot be bridged. While Kierkegaard's servant "is no mere outer garment," the Maggidic father contracts his broad mind and plays with his small son, thereby deriving the actualizing pleasure of reaching the son through cognitive affective role-taking (Rotenberg 1974). Hence, in the Hasidic world of Rabbi Yaacov Yosef (1963: 476), who uses a similar parable of a king's search for his son who joined a group of "worthless people," it is sufficient for the king's noble messenger to remove his elegant clothes (i.e., to contract himself), in order to reestablish communication with him and reunite with the lost prince, so that he can be returned to his father.

Having established the self-defeating problems involved in the ego-centered self-assertive type of actualization "against" others, let us now turn to discuss the possibility of alter-centered actualization from the standpoint of one's right to nonintruding privacy.

NOTE

1. A notorious visitor to the United States was once quoted as having said that parallel to the East Coast's Statue of Liberty symbolizing America's insistence on people's individual rights, there should be a Statue of Duty on the West Coast to remind people of their interpersonal duties.

(9)

Alterism, Individual Freedom, and "Exclusion" Systems

To this point, contractional interaction has been discussed from the social-psychological perspective, which relates to the dynamics of alter-centered actualization mainly from the standpoint of the ego. By introducing the principle of self-correction, derivable from the process of mutual emulation, we have shown not only how one contracts himself to make space for the other, but how through actualizing personal development one may affect another's behavior. In doing so, we have presented a radical departure from the unilateral Oedipal father-son paradigm of interpersonal relations, for in the bilateral double-mirroring process of mutual contraction not only does the father/God model affect the son, but the son's alter-centered actualization affects the father/God or the significant model, since each is dependent upon the other.

However, it is one thing to stress that "all Israel are sureties one for another" (*Baba Kama*, Talmud, 1938: 92a) and another to show operationally how one is to actualize himself through the other if, say, the other simply refuses to be helped, changed, or otherwise affected by him, that is, if the other interprets his alter-centered efforts as intrusions upon his right to privacy. Consequently, we cannot deal with alter-centered actualization from alter's standpoint without returning to the age-old controversy over the meaning of personal freedom and the individual's rights to privacy. We shall approach it from a new angle, however, and show how alter-centered actualization is possible without intrusion upon the individual's rights to privacy by postulating the difference between the ego-centered systems for *exclusion* (of intruding deviants) and the alter-centered concept of communities for *inclusion* (by means of interpersonal contraction). But first it is necessary to examine some of the contradictions inherent in the Western individualistic notions of the personal rights of liberty and happiness.

Absurd Freedom and Independence

It is said that the story of man's struggle for freedom and liberty, and his presumed consequent happiness, comprises the history of mankind. Yet the definition of the kind of freedom and liberty that bestows happiness on man has troubled philosophers throughout history. There was a time when the term "free man" was used to describe someone who had legal rights and duties, as opposed to a slave (see Feinberg 1973). In contemporary Western society, freedom is derived mainly from the proclamation in the Declaration of Independence that people are endowed with inherent, inalienable rights to life, liberty, and the pursuit of happiness (or property, in Locke's older sense; see Hook 1962). Earlier I stressed that since the Western notion of freedom and personal rights was molded by the popular and probably somewhat distorted interpretation (see Wills 1979) of the Jeffersonian Declaration of Independence, the many subconcepts associated with peoples' right to freedom and liberty seem to have produced the self-defeating patterns of Western alienating individualism because the struggle to gain independence from others usually leads to extreme expressions of individualism. I have suggested further that in their struggle to free themselves from others the "personal rights" movements tend to overlook how demands for individual rights impinge upon interpersonal duties. This is inherent in the way that the paradoxical Jeffersonian political definition of freedom and the pursuit of happiness has been misinterpreted.

The subconcepts that emanate from Jefferson's popularized concept of freedom are all derived, as Padover (1965), Nisbet (1977), and others have shown, from the democratic Western notion of Protestant individualism and thus include the ideas of equality, independence, freedom of choice, personal rights, and the liberty to do whatever makes one happy as long as it does not infringe on the rights of others. However, an attempt to differentiate between such subconcepts as individual rights, freedom of choice, equality, and independence, on the one hand, and the pursuit of happiness, on the other, will show how these referents of freedom and liberty are at times not only self-contradictory but in fact legitimize social indifference. It is therefore impossible to reconcile them without the proposed alter-centered dimension, which according to Wills (1979) actually featured in the original Hutchesonian definition of freedom adopted by Jefferson.

Let us begin by asking what we mean when we say that people have a *right* to life, liberty, and the pursuit of happiness. It seems obvious that a right is usually a defense against actual or feared abuses or obstacles to the fulfillment of specific needs or desires (see Hook 1962). We would be puzzled if someone would demand a right to do something that most people are normally free to do anyway. Hence, whenever we assert that we have a right, we are actually making a *claim* that others must grant us. If one of three survivors floating on a lifeboat at sea claims his right to breathe fresh air, this demand would be meaningless, because air is not a scarce commodity on the open sea and no one is preventing him from breathing it. But if he claims his right to an equal share of the limited available food, his demand would be valid. A right is therefore "a claim which entails an *obligation* or duty on the part of others in specific times and circumstances" (see ibid., p. 4).

Thus the interconnected concepts of rights and obligations (which were inherent in Jefferson's original "social-moral" definition of rights) are essentially social notions requiring a community, as Hook (ibid.) contended: "Without some common nature or some community of feeling, the sense of obligation could hardly develop; the assertion of rights would have no binding or driving emotional force . . . not even the right of a child to parental care." Thus one may agree with Wills' observation (1979: 213) that "a human right is now most often thought of as a power the individual retains over against the state. But its earlier use was as a power exercised in the name of the state." Hence, a right *against* the state nurtures alienating individualism, which is typical of some contemporary personal rights movements (see Chapter 8), and a right in the *name* of the state would require a community of people.

Having tentatively established that claims of rights require a sense of community and that one person's right involves a claim on another person's duties—or, as Jefferson himself put it, "man has no natural rights in opposition to his social duties" (ibid.)—let us now consider whether the meaning of liberty and the pursuit of happiness is compatible or contrasting, that is, whether it is possible to pursue happiness by insisting on the rights of privacy from, or rather *against*, others. Lincoln is often quoted as having said, "The shepherd drives the wolf from the sheep's throat, for which the sheep thanks the shepherd as *liberator,* while the wolf denounces him for the same act as destroyer of liberty, especially as the sheep was a black one . . . . The sheep and the wolf are not agreed upon the definition of the word liberty" (cited by Hook 1962: 11). It seems the prevailing consensus today is that in order to determine whether the freedom to pursue happiness is virtuous or vicious, one must examine its social effect only to the extent that the right to do whatever one pleases does not injure or offend others. Elsewhere (Rotenberg 1978) I attempted to tackle the difficulty involved in defining the paradoxical meaning of "offending others" by asking, What happens if a "Jewish mother" says to her son: "Do whatever you like, but I will be offended if you don't become a doctor!" Although this situation can easily be laughed off, the paradox of purchasing freedom at the expense of freedom becomes more complicated if we articulate the right-duty conceptualization of pursuing freedom and happiness in terms of offending others not by our actions but by our inaction, that is, by *refraining* from acting with or upon others.

While we would easily agree that a mother cannot exercise her right to freedom by ignoring her child's right to receive her care, we are perplexed as to whether an adult can legitimately assert that he is offended because another adult rejects his need to be dependent on him, to be cared for or be treated by him in one form or another. Here the paradox of freedom becomes entangled with another sacred referent of the Western view of liberty, namely, *forced* independence and freedom of choice and its consequent legitimization of social indifference. Moreover, here paradoxically a member of the "independent classes" may be more dependent on his dependency needs than a member of the "dependent classes" who was never too dependent on such needs.

The Cursed Blessing of Enforced Freedom

Sartre is said to have stated, "Man was *condemned* to be free." In *Nausea* (1959), when asked by the waitress to choose his dessert, Sartre's self-taught man turns white and is unable to comply. Mathieu, Sartre's hero in *The Roads of Freedom* (1951:245), ends his life of hopeless battle against indecisiveness as follows:

> Each of his shots avenged some ancient scruple. One for Lola whom I dared not rob; one for Marcelle whom I ought to have left in the lurch; one for Odette whom I did not want to kiss. This for the books I never dared to write. This for the journeys I never made, this for everybody in general whom I wanted to hate and tried to understand . . . . He fired. He was cleansed. He was all-powerful. He was free.

There is a story about a member of a collective farm who suffered a nervous breakdown while sorting potatoes in the field. When asked what troubled him in his pastoral, peaceful life, he was said to have answered that the task of sorting potatoes required decision after decision—small, medium, or large—which he could not bear any more, so he collapsed. This story and Sartre's irony suggest that the Western interpretation of democratic individualism insists not only that everyone has an equal *right* to independence, in terms of freedom of choice, but also that everyone has an equal *ability* and *obligation* to be an independent choice-maker, even if that infringes on the right to pursue happiness by choosing not to choose or by choosing to be dependent. What's more, the "equal right, ability, and obligation" concept of independence legitimizes social indifference, exclusion, and other forms of ostracization, because it views the other's right to be emotionally dependent as parasitism and intrusion. Thus, liberty and independence in terms of maximal freedom of choice may be one thing, and the equal right to pursue happiness may be another.[1]

The question now is why the necessity to be independent by making maximal free choices is forced upon us in our society. (As Lederman put it [1972: 44], "He who shrinks from taking the risk of a decision is guilty before his conscience.") In other words, if effective free choices and the right to do what one wishes equals happiness, what is the meaning of the statement "I feel free to be your slave"? Would the man who has the ability (and courage?) to choose chains freely be free as long as he is chained, and unfree when he is not as van den Haag (1978: 65) proposed? John Stuart Mill (1910: 157) declared, "The principle of freedom cannot require that anyone should be free not to be free." In an article entitled "On Forcing People to Be Free," Rempel (1976: 24) cites a famous case of a prisoner who, upon release from the penitentiary at Fort Madison, Iowa, petitioned the governor for a special life term in the institution he had come to regard as his home but was *forced* out of prison to be "free." Dwelling on the paradoxical law of freedom that forces the master to give up his bondsman and the bondsman to give up his master, Rempel uses another example of parents who, concerned about the welfare of an *overly dependent* adult off-spring, may expel him from the ancestral nest with the aim of forcing him to be independent and "free."

Although the prisoner and the adult offspring may have made it explicit that their equal right to happiness requires that they remain in a state of relative *dependence*, they were forced to be free, independent, and unhappy.

Viewed from another perspective, Rousseau's "free child," Emile goes so far as to ask his father to free him from his own passions so that he may become his own master in obeying not his senses but his reason (cited by Rempel 1976). Thus, according to Rousseau, Emile perceives that real happiness means independence from sexual passions or dependence on other people in any other form. But since passions and sensuality obviously constitute one of the major means by which people acquire interpersonal happiness, could we really leave out interdependence from the equation that comprises happiness? Wouldn't Rousseau's individualistic definition of freedom lead to an asocial, self-defeating kind of alienating insularity rather than to social happiness?

In essence, freedom in terms of effective independent choice-making and the right to pursue happiness may often represent self-contradictory terms. Here it might be added that while van den Haag's (1978) brilliant distinctions between positive and negative definitions of freedom (which are based on Jeremy Bentham's definition of freedom as "absence of coercion") are indeed very useful and enlightening, even he cannot reconcile happiness and freedom, since admittedly forcing a person to get rid of his toothache might make him happier than not coercing him to visit a dentist. I have already pointed out (Rotenberg 1978) that in a non-Western country such as Japan, not only does the notion of *amae* permit a person to actualize himself through fostering his dependency needs (feeling free to be dependent) but also a person who is unable to *amaeru* (be dependent and pampered) may be considered abnormal and in need of emotional help (see Doi 1973).

What is it then that makes independence such a sacred referent of freedom in the West, even though one's forced independence may at times stand in contradiction to his right to the pursuit of happiness? The fact that Western societies are constructed of natural social systems based on leader-follower interaction patterns stands in contradiction to the notion of forced independence and the consequent legitimization of interpersonal indifference (in the sense of "Get off my back, you're intruding on my right to individual privacy and I have a legitimate right to reject your desire to be dependent on me"). Nonetheless, to accept the natural tendency of people to form leader-follower relationships means to accept people's differential ability and desire to use freedom and independence. We have already quoted Mill's statement (1910: 157) that "the principle of freedom cannot require that anyone should be free not to be free." Yet given a legitimate leader-follower paradigm, where does one draw the line between following and voluntary enslavement?

It seems that the key to this paradox of forced freedom and independence must be sought in the Protestant individualistic definition of self-actualization, which I assert predominates in the West and which postulates egoistic salvation through personal material achievements. As I have indicated earlier, in such an actualizing-salvation structure an attempt to achieve alter-centered *salvation* is considered as *slavation* and hence as a violation of the other's right to privacy (which is a facet of individual freedom) and a violation of one's duty of ego-centered actualizing salvation. This may explain why Bentham's utilitarian definition of maximizing one's happiness, even if it makes others miserable (see Stephen 1950: 311), is more acceptable in the West than one's freedom of choice not to be free, even if it does not really offend others (as Mill implied). In such an ego-centered salvation culture, with its guilt-debt interpersonal-relations system, helping others is a Hobbesian self-preserving act of *intrusion* or intervention extended by the self-fulfilled, egoistic altruist to another, and it either leaves the other in a state of guilt because it deprives him of self-actualization through equivalent return, or it leaves the other in a state of debt, which does not permit him to pursue his happiness through permissive dependency.

Rabbi Yaacov Yosef's egalitarian principle of alter-centered actualization through the interdependence of *unification* is an act of *inclusion*, however, accomplished through ego's self-contraction to make space in his world for the other but not to impose help on him. Organic interdependence is not a collective dependency-fostering concept; it merely defines the independence-dependence continuum in differential terms that allow one to be a dependent receiver in condition X and an independent giver in situation Y.

One can best explain alter-centered *inclusion* by contrasting the Hasidic contraction methods with the *intrusion-exclusion* "helping" method practiced in total institutions for deviants in the West. We shall thus explore the difference between the dualistic systems for exclusion and the monistic inclusion system by demonstrating how people labeled deviant in the West are excluded because they fail to exercise their equal right and obligation to be independent while the monistic inclusion system theoretically minimizes deviance by its built-in mutual-dependence structure and its mechanism for absorbing the weak social elements into its mainstream.

Intrusion and the Total Institution for Exclusion

It can generally be agreed that despite the traditional insistence of psychopathologists that eclectic or specific aetiologies lead to deviance, the primary common denominator of people who actually or potentially populate total institutions can be described as their initial difficulty in exercising their enforced independence and freedom of choice—either because they failed to receive sufficient "personal support" (mental patients) or because they were insufficiently restrained by "social controls" (prisoners). Personal support, as used here, refers generally to permissive dependence, which releases one from making forced choices, and social control refers generally to nurturing-parental fostering of dependence, which helps to restrain one's negative-choice tendencies.

The puzzling thing about this phenomenon is that in a Western society like the United States, where undifferentiated "independence" is among the most cherished of human values and is posited as the sacred-cow criterion of "normalcy" (see Rotenberg 1978), people who suffer from "democratic disabilities"—that is, those who encounter difficulties in being independent in exercising their right and obligation to make free choices in a superdemocratic, open society—are sent to antidemocratic total institutions that foster a parasitic and authoritarian life-style totally incongruent with the free give-and-take exchange system operating in the free community (see Goffman 1956). Studies have shown, for example, that long-term institutional care fosters a desire to remain under care (see Segal and Aviram 1978) and that "traditional approaches, including psychiatric hospitals . . . have resulted in a low level of success as far as restoration to normal functioning in interpersonal relations, adjustment in the community and productivity in work and study are concerned" (see Sinnett and Sachson 1970: vi). Thus it should hardly be surprising that after years of no experience with independent living, in terms of contracts with bureaucratic organizations (e.g., banks, tax, insurance, transportation, and employment agencies or food and

medical-supply services), formerly institutionalized people who were generally excluded from society's division of labor network in the first place or
who "left the conflicting choice-making field" (in Kurt Lewin's [1964]
classic terms) fail to lead an independent, democratic way of life, regardless
of the treatment method applied in the institutions. Nonetheless, social
scientists seem to fluctuate between the two polar dysfunctional positions:
the advocation of "treatment" for deviants within ineffective, dependency-
fostering, antidemocratic total institutions or the recently popular trend of
leaving the deviant in or dumping him back on the superdemocratic, open
community, where he stumbled in the first place and is rejected by the
"community's" hostile reactions and strategies for exclusion (see Segal and
Aviram 1978).[2] It seems that the reason a Western nation such as the
United States is reluctant to structure what can be termed "differentially
democratic" social systems, where dependency is permissibly and differentially fostered in a manner similar to Japanese organizations (see Rohlen
1974) or to the Kibbutz system (see Spiro 1971), and where people with
"democratic disabilities" may voluntarily find some peace of mind and release from the forced independence practiced in the superdemocratic, open
society, can now be better explained. As alluded to earlier, in an ego-
centered salvation system, where individualistic, self-actualizing salvation is
translated into forced freedom of choice, independence, and the right to
privacy, people are punished by exiling exclusion or social indifference if
they fail to maintain happiness independently. Moreover, in such a system
the meaning of therapeutic care is often conceived of by scientists and
laymen alike as averse social control that must be totally rejected. Skinner
(1972: 38) put it this way:

> The literature of freedom has encouraged escape from or attack upon all
> controllers. It has done so by making any indication of control aversive.
> Those who manipulate human behavior are said to be evil men, necessar-
> ily bent on exploitation. Control is clearly the opposite of freedom, and if
> freedom is good, control must be bad. What is overlooked is control
> which does not have aversive consequences, at any time.

Indeed, psychologist Perry London (1969) has portrayed all forms of
psychosocial help, including hypnotism, drugs, and all forms of psychotherapy, as forms of social and behavioral control. Similarly, the recently popular antitherapeutic trend in penology inspired by the report of the Committee for the Study of Incarceration (see Von Hirsch 1976), which advocates
a prisoner's right *not* to be treated, introduced the concept of desertion as a
guiding principle for dealing with criminals. While I agree that neither the
prison system nor traditional "therapeutic" intervention methods of correction have been effective in rehabilitating criminals, the notion of deserting

people who may have been suffering from "forced independence" or desertion all along seems to befit the legitimization of social indifference but not
to help those who may yearn for functionally balanced control-support
systems that legitimize and facilitate some form of increased dependency.

The Committee for the Study of Incarceration (see ibid., p. xxxvi)
declared: "We contend that the ultimate and critical value in a concept like
desert rests in its ability to preserve and promote decent and accepted values
in this society and at the same time to restrain the state from infringing on
individual rights." The question remains, however; Whose individual rights
are we talking about? Those of the deserters, who do not want to be
bothered by the "needy debtors," or the rights of the dependent to be
included rather than deserted and abandoned to the hyperdemocratic streets
of a huge city like New York?[3] If freedom and independence are not op-
tional but emanate directly from the mandatory, ego-centered, equal-right-
and-obligation dictum of salvation, then whoever fails to be independent
can either be helped by a Hobbesian altruist (who through the *intrusion*
process, provides him with surplus goods left over from his own self-fulfilling
actualization) or be punished, through the *exclusion* process, by being ex-
communicated to a total institution (where he is eternally deprived of the
freedom he failed to exercise). Moreover, in the exile of the total institution he becomes an eternal debtor who has no right and no opportunity to
make equivalent repayment to society. Thus the ego-centered salvation
system, which generates either altruistic *intrusion* or antagonistic *exclusion*,
serves, as Erikson (1966) pointed out, to sharpen the boundaries between
the society of insiders and the "asociety" of outsiders.

Exclusion to the dependency-fostering total institution—which can
now be apprehended as an island of exile for "democratic failures"—is
dysfunctional for rehabilitation, correction, or therapy, however, because
once and for all it releases people who have been suffering from "democratic
disabilities" all along from the enforced freedom and independence that
Western society imposed on them. Ironically, however, incarceration may
solve the problems of both the independent creditor and the dependent
debtor by enabling the creditor to maintain his independence from the
debtor's intruding threat of dependency needs or from their Hobbesian
revenging annihilation attempts, and release the debtors from the burden of
forced independence.

In the alter-centered salvation system, where theoretically the principles of horizontal organic interdependence, mutual responsibility, and social
unification prevail, the process of intrusion or exclusion is structurally impossible. As we shall explain in detail later, the alter-centered salvation
system of inclusion postulates the concept of breaking open the vessels to
make room for the world—and the breaking open of the community's
"heart" to make space for others—which follows structurally from the mo-

nistic gestalt salvation imperative that one segment of society, for example, the Issachars ("people of form"), cannot actualize themselves if another social organ, for example, the Zebuluns ("people of matter"), are not functioning properly, because the organic, holistic conception of society assumes that when the "feet are low, the head also bends" (Yaacov Yosef 1963) or when one organ malfunctions the whole body may decay. Thus, in place of a total institution for exclusion, a monistic transformation or reabsorbtion process of inclusion operates to preserve or reestablish the holistic structure of the total community through a mechanism fostering organic interdependence.

We should therefore proceed to examine the meaning of community in relation to the exclusion-inclusion dimension.

Paradoxical Ego-Centric Community Therapy

The key concept explicating the differences between the dichotomizing process of *exclusion* (which proceeds unilaterally, via intrusion, from the altruist to the needy debtor) and the bilateral unifying process of *inclusion* (which proceeds from the needy other to the *alterist*) is the community. While Popper (1950) openly asserted that the individual's actualizing achievements are possible only through his separation from and rejection of all forms of moral or social interdependence, as the Sophists and Socrates believed, Nisbet (1977) and other bemoaners of the "lost community" in Western society seem to be constantly at pains to reconcile the capitalistic, Protestant, ego-centered dogma of actualizing salvation with the concept of community. It seems that Nisbet's (1977: 235) own assertion that "neither personal freedom nor personal achievement can ever be separated from the context of community" is something of a utopian dream in light of deeply entrenched Western beliefs inculcated by such authorities as Jeremy Bentham or George Adams, who proclaimed (in Nisbet's rendition) that "freedom would rise from the individual's release from all the inherited personal interdependence of traditional community" (p. 227).

Considering this antagonistic approach to the Western concept of community, our next question should be: Precisely what is meant by the recent call for leaving, returning, or treating the deviant in the "community"? It is not my intention to reiterate or recapitulate the overcited distinction between Tonnie's medieval family-like *Gemeinschaft* and the contemporary impersonal *Gesellschaft*. Nor is it my purpose to dispute the objective difficulties inherent in recent attempts to reabsorb ex-mental patients (see Segal and Aviram 1978) or ex-prisoners (see Allen 1964) in "community based" programs, because it seems indeed unreasonable to expect that people who originally encountered difficulties in exercising the freedom and independence forced on them by society and were consequently rejected and exiled to dependency-fostering total institutions should be able to function even as "halfway" independent citizens in halfway houses and halfway communities. Instead, I wish to focus on the inherent contradiction between the notion of ego-centered, actualizing salvation and the apparently diametrically opposed concept of community, which requires, by definition, not Warren's (1963) evasive "locality performance" but concrete interdependence and interpersonal commitment (see Rieff 1966). In other words, a community-based therapeutic conception of rehabilitation in Western democracy seems to entail a contradiction in terms, as implied in de Tocqueville's observation in his classic diagnosis of America's individualistic democracy.

In discussing the differences between the old-style community-oriented "commitment therapy" and the modern individualistic type of "analytic therapy," Rieff (1966: 60) relates (albeit in a context that differs from the present perspective) that according to de Tocqueville, in a democracy,

> once individualism has shaped its virtues . . . the individual would no longer feel committed to the chain of all the members of the community. "Democracy" breaks that chain and severs every link of it. The individual . . . has cut off his feelings from communal affections. Individuals learn to feel that "they own nothing to any man, they expect nothing from any man."

Thus Rieff asserts that "an endemic individualism, such as that in the United States, whether doctrinally elaborated or not, may prevent a commitment therapy . . . [which] operated by returning the individual to the cosset of his natal community or by retaining him for membership in a new community" (pp. 62–65). He further contends that in the new individual-oriented democracy, "analytic therapy, which developed precisely in response to the need of the Western individual, . . . creates negative communities . . . which enabled to survive almost automatically by a self-sustaining technology" (p. 63). Rieff thus concludes that "earlier therapists, being sacralists, guarded the cultural superego communicating to the individual the particular signs and symbols in which the superego was embodied . . . . The modern therapeutic idea is to empty those meanings that link the individual to dying worlds" (p. 66).

Hence, if the ideas of commitment and community indeed represent dying worlds in modern Western, individualistic democracies, where individuals learn that they "owe nothing and can expect nothing," we must repeat our question with double force and ask again, What kind of community and what kind of therapy—or rather criterion for normalcy—do those who advocate the return or the retaining of the deviant in the community have in mind? Is it a "halfway" commitment therapy and a "halfway" analytic therapy that prepares people for a halfway life in negative communities whose members owe nothing and can expect nothing from one another? Do these halfway therapies admit the contradiction between an ego-centered self-salvation culture and the idea of interpersonally committed community? Moreover, do the architects of modern democracy, who are reluctant to exercise a more balanced control-and-support system in such huge cities such as New York, ever look in the democratic mirror and ask whether their individualistic principle of universally enforced freedom and independence is indeed equally applicable to all people in terms of their equal ability and desire to be "independent" and their equal right to pursue happiness by being somewhat dependent?

In other words, it seems impossible to reject the idea of pursuing happiness through dependence and advocate the therapeutic merits of returning the deviant to the "community," because such a self-contradictory ego-centered salvation system of "having the cake and eating it too" inevitably produces the dualistic, negative communities of exclusion. However, in "inclusion communities"[4] liberty may be defined in van den Haag's (1978) negative terms of the absence of coercion, not at the expense of happiness but as the freedom to be voluntarily and differentially dependent and happy.

The two intertwined key concepts that explain the functionality of the inclusion community are the alter-centered horizontal interdependence between the "people of matter" and the "people of form" and the concomitant principle of descent for the purpose of uplifting others. Unfortunately, as mentioned earlier, there are almost no sociological studies describing the structure and the interpersonal dynamics of the Hasidic community. It is possible, however, to construe the dynamic relationship between the people of form and the people of matter by analyzing the modeling role of the *zaddik* (who is the prototype person of form) and his relationship with the people of matter in the inclusion community.

NOTES

1. Since the word "happiness" is derived from the word "hap" or "happens," it originally connoted a more fatalistic state in terms of "whatever happens" as compared to its contemporary implicit meaning of ego-centered active pursuing or self-indulgence. It also seemed to concur with Jefferson's original social definition stating that "the surest way to promote his private happiness [is] to do publicly useful actions" (see Wills 1979: 249–252), which suggests a relativistic attitude in the sense that chances for happy happenings are greater for everyone if everyone contributes to the general good.

2. The startling fact is that even such a "liberal" organ as the *Village Voice* (see Witten et al. 1977), which originally carried the call to liberate deviants from the establishment's Bastilian total institutions, found it necessary to denounce the trend of abandoning mental patients to city streets.

3. In his recent study about crime in Switzerland, Clinard (1978) attributes the

impressively low crime rates there to the country's decentralized social structure, which facilitates increased social control and personal support through its close-knit acquaintance system. In discussing the implications that can be drawn from the Swiss case by a country like the United States, Clinard (1978: 155) thus concludes that in both these affluent countries ordinary crime "is far from being produced by economic disadvantages or poverty" and hence to combat crime "large urban concentrations can be controlled by the dispersal of industry and the development of satellite cities which would help to decentralize the size and population densities of the large cities." It would be interesting to see a pilot project on breaking a huge city like New York into semiautonomous satellite boroughs in which a natural leader-follower community may develop in the sense that control and support would not be superimposed but facilitated through permissive dependency and its natural caring and acquaintance system.

4. It should be stated that Yaacov Yosef's holistic organic conception of the inclusion community fostered, at least in its early stages, a policy of segregating communities that resulted in Hasidic separatist communities in relation to the external world.

(10)

Deviance and Interdependence Between Matter and Spirit

To expose the self-defeating and internal contradiction inherent in the Western conceptualization of ego-centered salvation, I have argued not only that independence *ad absurdum* is impossible in terms of the equality of rights and ability but also that the very claim to the right of liberty, privacy, and happiness involves some degree of dependence on a community of others who are obligated to grant these rights (Hook 1962). The negative definition of man's right to liberty and happiness in terms of the absence of coercion (van den Haag 1978) applies not only to the case of not forcing people to be dependent but also to not forcing people to be independent (Rempel 1976). Our next task will be to show how alter-centered actualization is possible without coercion in the inclusion community, which accepts people's differential ability to be independent and does not deny people's natural right of mutual interdependence. In this context, the definition of community would not necessarily be limited to the concept of locality performance (Warren 1963) but would refer to a social-psychological medium that allows people (e.g., people of matter) who have dependency needs in one area (say, irrational cognitive discrepancies) to be dependent on others (e.g., people of form) and the latter ivory-tower "spiritual" people to be dependent on the former in concrete, down-to-earth matters.

Using the case of the *zaddik*, who is a model "person of form" and the center of a community of inclusion, our discussion will now turn to the interdependent relationship between matter and form in such an inclusion community.

Organic Interdependence Between
Material and Spiritual Dispositions

Distinctions between matter and form were made as early as the writing of the ancient Greeks. A simple exemplifying distinction between the two in

Aristotelian philosophy would be the case of a man who makes a marble statue or a bronze sphere, wherein the marble or bronze is matter and the statue's shape or sphericity is the form. Distinctions become more complicated on the human level, but generally speaking the soul was conceived as the form of the body. According to Plato, however, both form and matter existed before the bronze sphere came into being, and all that man does is bring them together. Thus, matter without form is considered only potentiality, and for the ancient Greeks it was "the soul that makes the body one thing, having unity of purpose, and the characteristic that we associate with the word 'organism' (see Russell 1945: 165).

It is important to stress here that precisely this Platonic distinction and relationship between matter and form can be found in cabalistic-Hasidic formulations. The Maggid (1927: 30) states, for example, that "matter is the letters and form the picture of the letters—and the one who understands will understand that both ways are one, but the first is in mere action and the second in generality." Following the cabala, the Maggid uses matter to refer to intuitive potentiality (*Chochma*, which is interpreted as *koachmah*, meaning "some potence" in Hebrew) and uses form to refer to substantiated wisdom (*Bina*, meaning "construction" in Hebrew) which, as Plato suggested, gives unity and purpose to matter.

So far we have discussed Rabbi Yaacov Yosef's sociological theory of organic interdependence between the people of form and the people of matter from a rather simplistic though basic egalitarian and economic perspective, which posits a horizontal mutual dependence between the material Zebuluns and the spiritual Issachars. While body and soul, or matter and form, were conceived by the Greeks (and especially their Christian successors) as essentially separate entities possessing such diametrically opposed characteristics as good and evil (which differs from Yaacov Yosef's monistic conception of matter and form), it is important to heed the psychological implication inherent in the Greek differentiation, for it undoubtedly affected later thinkers—including Yaacov Yosef. Thus Bertrand Russell (1945: 171) indicated that Aristotle's doctrine of matter and form was essentially set forth in the *Nicomachean Ethics*, which postulated, "There is in the soul one element that is rational, and one that is irrational." Accordingly Russell (p. 172) stresses that "Individuality—what distinguishes one man from another—is connected with the body and the irrational soul, while the rational soul or mind is divine and impersonal." The natural division of subsequent philosophies into those concerned with emotions and those inspired by actions, or between the idealists and the realists or the optimists and the pessimists, all seem to have drawn on this classical distinction between matter and form.

One philosophy that seems to be continuous with the dichotomy between matter and form as rational versus irrational entities and also seems pertinent to our effort to differentiate between matter and form in terms of mental-psychological dispositions is Henri Bergson's distinction between matter as intellect and spirit as life and intuition (see Russell 1945). While Bergson (who never denied his mystic orientation and Hasidic origin) saw the whole universe as an arena in which a constant clash between two opposite motions takes place—one of integrating life forces moving upward and the other of a separating force of matter moving downward—he in fact implicitly recognized the complementary functions of the two age-old mental dispositions of the rational intellect and the irrational mystical intuition. Thus, citing Bergson, Bertrand Russell stated:

> The intellect is characterized by a natural inability to understand life; geometry and logic, which are its typical products, are strictly applicable to solid bodies, but elsewhere reasoning must be checked by common sense, which, as Bergson truly says, is a very different thing . . . . The intellect . . . always behaves as if it were fascinated by the contemplation of inert matter. It is life looking outward, putting itself outside itself, adopting the ways of unorganized nature in principle, in order to direct them in fact . . . . Thus logic and mathematics do not represent a positive spiritual effort . . . . Incapacity for mathematics is therefore a sign of grace—fortunately a very common one. (pp. 794–795)

It is not in the salvation of nonmathematical minds that Russell's sarcastic statement that "incapacity for mathematics is . . . a sign of grace" (p. 795) has significance for our social-psychological conceptualization of matter and spirit. Moreover, it is not as if the intuitive-spiritualist does not accept the logic of geometry and the scientific analysis of "solid bodies" (which he very often does not understand), but it is the reality of the unreal, the natural limits of science and rationality and the consequent inability to "put itself outside itself, adopting and directing the ways of unorganized nature" that will preserve the complementary functions of material rationalism and mystical spiritualism for as long as the world exists as it does. This seems to be the difference between paganist idolatry, which worships only the palpable world of solid bodies—such as stone, wood, science, and people—and monotheistic idealism, which accepts science but recognizes its limits and worships the unknown, the supernatural power beyond human reach associated with what Weber (1967) termed the "cognitive discrepancies" resulting from the imperfect world. This complementary relationship between philosophical rationalism and emotional mysticism is also featured in the interdependent complementary relationship between the Jewish philosophical and mystical movements. Accordingly, the mystical approach to Jewish lore, which received its main impetus in the sixteenth century from the Lurianic school of practical cabalism, is not to be understood (as often happens) as opposing the rational-philosophical school in Judaism which faced a serious crisis during the late fifteenth century's "Spanish expulsion." Rather, due to the inherent Jewish multiple-actualization structure, these interpretations and practices are to be seen as complementary or supplementary, practical philosophies. As Scholem (1941: 24) put it, the Jewish mystics could see farther because "they stood on the shoulders of the philosophers."

Drawing heavily on Bergson's (1978) theory of intuition and knowledge, Buber (1974) shows how in interpersonal alter-centered relationships, when the spiritual (intuitive) complements the material (rational) interhuman contact, an "I and thou" unity between two people is created. "Out of the tension between the image of the person and the existing person, a genuine understanding can spring forth; a fruitful meeting between two men issues directly into a break-through from image to being" (p. 83). It is apparent that while for Buber "matter" means the objective rational "it" image we have of a person, and "form" or "spirit" refers to our differential intuitive-subjective experiencing of the real existence or being of the other "thou," the unity between I and thou requires that "out of the tension [a sequential] break-through from image to being" will occur, so that each will relate to the other merely on a spiritual-intuitive level. The present view, however, considers complementarity between materially inclined people and spiritually inclined people not only in terms of the intuitive relationship between two people but also in terms of the complementary relationship these two people may have with their respective external spiritual and material ecologies.

Accordingly, the nature of the I-it (material-rational) or I-thou (intu-itive-spiritual) relationship that people maintain with their spiritual-material ecologies determines their interpersonal relationships as well. It is precisely the spiritual artist's unique interpretation of the uncertainties in life and the world's imperfections (to which both Bergson and Buber have repeatedly referred) and the technological rationalist's ability to organize and system-atize these uncertainties and imperfections that enter into the "I-thou" com-plementary inclusion relationship. Thus the "material-spiritual" (rational-in-tuitive) perspective developed here presents an "I-it-thou" relationship, while Buber's conception appears to advocate only a "spiritual" (intuitive) I-thou interpersonal scheme.

While Bergson's dualistic scheme envisions the psychological-mental disposition of material intellect and spiritual intuition as two *opposing* en-tities—the former power moving, downward and the latter power of life moving upward—Rabbi Yaacov Yosef's organic conception of matter and form may be understood as the interdependent complementary psychologi-cal forces that exist in every person and in every community of people. Although it is not explicitly stated, this organic-monistic conception of matter and form as two halves that need each other on the *intra*personal and *inter*personal levels follows from Yaacov Yosef's conceptualization, for he states:

> Since, similar to the individuality within one person, the soul and form is not to feel superior over the body and say that it is a holy soul . . . and even more so the body is not to be arrogant over the soul as it holds the soul . . . as they need each other like a man and a woman, each one being half a body . . . and with both together matter and form . . . it becomes one full person. (1963: 243)

Therefore it would be misleading to speak of people of matter and people of form as two distinct personality types or two opposing entities, since matter and form prevail simultaneously in every body. However, since in Yaacov Yosef's organic scheme the spirit-soul cannot exist without matter-body, that is, the spiritual soul cannot exist if the material body malfunctions, and vice versa, matter cannot exist if the spirit dysfunctions—we may now examine the interdependence between functional and malfunctional matter and spirit in the social-psychological terms of rational-material predispositions (pertaining to the concrete physical world) and spiritual-intuitive dispositions (pertaining to the mystical-metaphysical world).

The "Matter-Spirit" Conception of Deviance and Conformity

If the tendency or disposition to view the world through rational-analytic spectacles can be conceived of as the result of a mixture of natural inclination and socialization, then we may expect to find that people in whom the material disposition is more developed will have a greater sense of and need for organizational, routinized structures and an enhanced ability to manipulate their physical ecology. As a result, they will most likely have an increased mastery, need, and appreciation of the material-technological world. Moreover, if the tendency or disposition to view the world through intuitive-spiritual spectacles similarly results from a combination of natural propensity and socialization, we might likewise expect to find that people in whom these mystical-spiritual dispositions are relatively more developed will have a greater ability to explain the "unorganized events in nature" or the erratic discrepancies emanating from the imperfect world—such as unexpected death, natural disasters, and depressions, as well as joyful experiences—in mystical-intuitive terms, and as a result they may have a relatively greater need and appreciation for aesthetics, religion, poetry, and mysticism.

As we assume that these dispositions are complementary rather than mutually exclusive, it would in fact be possible to reach higher levels of alter-centered development through mutual interdependence between those in whom either the material or the spiritual dispositions are more manifest, so that each one serves as a modeling guide for others in whom one of these dispositions is latent. Indeed, the Besht (1975a: 57) stated:

> There are two kinds of people: A who behaves according to nature . . . B who behaves metaphysically . . . and when one approaches the other and the above two kinds unite, everything becomes one perspective, as it is known that the one is the throne for the other and when they join . . . everything becomes one.

Moreover, in Yaacov Yosef's (1963: 711) Aristotelian distinction between matter and spirit, both the possible predominance of matter or form in some people and the complementary functional interdependence between them are clearly spelled out:

> There is in the individual person body and soul, and the body is the dress of the soul . . . because there is in man matter and form, and at times form is more predominant than matter, and these are called people of form, and likewise its opposite, are called "matter" and . . . as in the private person, the body and soul cleave together . . . and by the pleasure of the body it causes *the soul* pleasure . . . therefore one has to make the people of matter happy whether in feasting or by singing.

Viewed from another vantage, alter-centered spiritual salvation in the inclusion community may function to maintain the harmony between man and man and between man and his spiritual ecology by attributing meaning to life without relation to the presence or absence of material wealth, while alter-centered material salvation would function to maintain the harmony between man and his material ecology by systematizing and handling problems requiring the routinizing approach that emanates from modern complex technology.

Theoretically, then, the difference between materially and spiritually predisposed people might be not in status or in prestige but rather in mental mechanisms. While the former is mentally conditioned and functionally trained to systematize material ecology, the latter is predisposed to cope with fluctuating moods and circumstances. Various secular and religious gurus, artists, and spiritual therapists seem to represent the "spiritually trained person," while many bureaucratic and science-oriented personalities may represent the "materially inclined person." Moreover, these types often complement each other in families, organizations, and communities in the sense that opposites attract (or sometimes clash) in a natural manner. To be sure, matter and form, in terms of mental mechanisms, are not to be associated with occupations. The spiritual type with his descending prepu-

berty crises and his subsequent orgasmic ascending creativity might therefore be found working as a clerk, though he is more likely an artist. Likewise the material-systematic routinizing type might be an actor or therapist,
though he is more likely to be an administrator.

Matter and spirit may indeed complement each other when, as
sketched above, harmony prevails in such settings as families or close-knit
communities. But it is also possible that disharmony, or rather dissonance,
will prevail between a person and either his spiritual or material ecology. It
is therefore necessary to reformulate the problem of deviance in material-
spiritual terms. In Part III, I shall elaborate on the differences between
these two basic patterns of deviance. To outline the problem briefly, however, what are popularly called mental disorders may actually refer to "spiritual deviance," and what is generally termed delinquency may actually be
associated with "material deviance." Thus deviance may be conceived as a
negative dialectic process composed of three phases.

The first, the *antithetic-question phase*, encompasses the experiencing of
a cognitive dissonance or cognitive strain (see Sarbin 1964) that one may
encounter with regard to either one's material ecology or his spiritual ecology. During this antithetic-questioning phase, which stands for dialectic
dissonance with the normative thesis in one's particular environment, "spiritual deviance" may be characterized by expressions of fear, anxiety, or
uncertainty regarding irrational, mystical-metaphysical elements for which
one cannot find a rational explanation. Here again examples might be
unexplainable death, illness, or feelings of meaninglessness. Likewise, the
"material deviance" typical of this antithetic-questioning phase may be
characterized by vandalistic-violent conduct that represents conflict with
one's material ecology. Here cases of lawsuits and other material losses
resulting from organizational inefficiency might be illustrative of this phase.

During the second, the *hypothetical phase*, both materially and spiritually deviant conduct might be represented by various bizarre and erratic
experiments to solve the dialectic dissonance through semiconforming and
semideviant behavior. Thus periodic violent outbursts alternating with
"preparatory" attempts at stealing (see Matza 1964) may represent the
"material-hypothetical" phase of experiments to resolve the "material dissonance," and one's temporary psychotic detachments or withdrawals from
reality and socially disappointing envirnoments, alternating with neurotic
attempts to hold on to this reality, may represent hypothetical experiments to resolve one's "spiritual dissonance."

The third, the *synthetic phase* of deviance, represents the negative solution (in the absence of better answers) in the anormative dialectic process.
From this dialectic perspective, established patterns of schizophrenic behavior, such as communicating with spirits or enacting the role of the Messiah, may represent the "spiritual deviant" synthetic answer to eschatologi-

cal fears of the metaphysical world in the sense that "if I am the Messiah, no unexpected catastrophe can befall me." Established criminal patterns of instrumental embezzlement, imposture, or theft may represent the "material deviant's" synthetic response to dissonance with his disorganized, unreward-ing material ecology.

Variations according to material and spiritual deviations[1] may obvi-ously be found within mentally disordered or delinquent conduct, and these dimensions should be examined on a continuum rather than viewed as dichotomous. Thus what is commonly termed "psychosis" may be conceived as a spiritual, anormative, dialectic process, and "psychopathy" may be conceived as a material, anormative, dialectic process. The question that presents itself here, however, is whether materially or spiritually inclined people would tend to encounter dissonance according to their inclination. In an answer to this question, I would suggest that dissonance and conse-quent deviant tendencies do not necessarily follow the patterns outlined above, because material and spiritual inclinations are presented here prima-rily as products of socialization, not as personality types. Nonetheless, since socialization goals are presumed to be molded by the fusion of dispositions and socialization trends toward particular ideals for actualizing-salvation, we may indeed assume that to the extent that people with spiritual or material dispositions were socialized to actualize themselves spiritually or materially, their deviating patterns might be largely determined by the degree of frus-tration or anomie they encounter in their perceived ideal salvation area.

In light of the above, Merton's (1958) classic anomie paradigm must be taken as only a partial model, for it explains material modes of deviance and adaptation typical of an ego-centered, dualistic, Protestant world that min-imizes or disregards the differences between material and spiritual devia-tions. According to the "matter-spirit" conceptualization of deviance, one may in fact differentiate between spiritual and material patterns of dialectic anomie (see Figure 2).

While Western material socialization (see Merton 1958) may often train people neurotically to deny or accept spiritual uncertainties—and in this sense the West socializes people to be "functionally neurotic"—Eastern (and Hasidic) emphasis on spiritual salvation trains people to communicate with and master their spiritual ecology through controllable and temporary "functional psychotic" detachments (about which more will be said later in Part III). The dialectic deviant, multiple actualization approach ("in all thy ways know Him") may, however, help to resolve the dialectic dissonance by changing one's actualization ideal from spiritual to material or vice versa. This sometimes happens when a "material" member of a criminal gang breaks his old associations and finds his salvation in a new religious-spiritual value orientation.

Similarly, it may happen when a person who experiences a spiritual

Salvation goal	Thesis: Actualization means	Antithetic deviance	Hypothetical deviance	Synthetic deviance	Deviant label
Spiritual	Neurotic acceptance/ avoidance	Uncertainty, anxieties	Psychotic detachment, neurotic attachment	Messianism, withdrawal	Psychotic, mentally ill
Material	Neurotic achievement efforts	Vandalism, violence	Primary deviance	Embezzling, imposture	Psychopath, delinquent

Figure 2. The Matter–Spirit Anomie Scheme.

crisis (mental disorder) resolves his dissonance by adopting a new material salvation goal, such as working in a routinizing bureaucratic-technological organization that cushions him with a new concrete-material protective sense of being. It should be stressed, however, that such a dialectic solution only shifts the role-dominance focus from spiritual to material or vice versa (whatever caused dissonance), but it does not eliminate one in favor of the new role.

Having generally spelled out the functional and dysfunctional parameters of the complementary matter-and-spirit paradigm of deviance and conformity, we are now in a position to demonstrate how alter-centered actualization may take place in the inclusion community by means of mutual contraction, even when either the material or the spiritual element malfunctions.

NOTE

1. In line with neuropsychological studies indicating that cognitive-thought (i.e., rational) disorders, which are usually associated with left-hemispheric dysfunctions, can be identified among those labeled "schizophrenic" and "psychopath" (see Flor-Henry 1974), while emotional-affective (e.g., irrational) processes were found to be associated with right-hemisphere functioning (see Galin 1974), it is possible that both schizophrenic and criminal behaviors represent "material deviations" and that only manic-depressive disorders (fluctuating emotional-affective moods) represent "spiritual deviations." Indeed, the findings of sociological research indicating that schizophrenia is strongly associated with the Western, rational, stressful, individualistic, and competitive way of life (see Eaton and Weil 1955) may lend further support to the hypothesis that schizophrenic reactions represent "material deviations." On the other hand, clinical studies (e.g., Hommes 1971) showing that depression is related to lesions in the left hemisphere while euphoria (mania) is associated with the right hemisphere might suggest that both pessimistic depressions and schizophrenic isolations (which were labeled in combination schizo-affective reactions; see American Psychiatric Association 1968) are the typical, predominant states of Western, rational, material deviations, while only mystic-manic and ecstatic euphoria are associated with spiritual deviations. I shall address myself to this problem in Part III.

(11)

The Modeling Role of the Zaddik in the Inclusion Community

In discussing his utopian "I-and-thou" community, Buber (1958b: 145) states that "a real community need not consist of people who are perpetually together; but it must consist of people who . . . have mutual access to one another and are ready for one another." Thus more than a "locality performance" (Warren 1963) or an economic organic division-of-labor network (Durkheim 1964), a community—or rather communal feelings—is created through an "I-and-thou" process of socialization for mutual inclusion. However, Buber (1958b:135) also states: "The real essence of community is to be found in the fact—manifest or otherwise—that it has a centre. The real beginning of a community is when its members have a common relation to the centre overriding all other relations."

Elsewhere I have suggested that the communal center, which is the pulsing engine of the community's socializing vehicle, can be understood in terms of the meaning of the traditional Jewish synagogue (Rotenberg 1978). I have thus shown that originally the Hebrew word for synagogue meant literally "a house of gathering" (*beit knesset*), not only for praying but also for meeting members of the community, learning to include others without excluding oneself, and learning the meaning of mutual asymmetric dependence. Indeed, most Hasidic communities are made up not of people who live perpetually together but of people with a common center and leader to which they have a common relation. Therefore, asymmetric interdependence between matter and spirit in terms of mutual inclusion—not superimposed intrusion—may be best learned by examining the modeling role of the *zaddik*, who is the leader and center of the classic inclusion community.

The two interconnected processes that explicate inclusion are (1) material and spiritual alter-centered contraction and (2) interpersonal development through alter-centered deciphering inclusion. It should go without saying that the first prerequisite for manifesting inclusion must be the alter-centered evacuation of space for others by the above-mentioned process of

(120)

self-contracting humility, which draws alter toward ego. Two general principles of contraction that pertain to our matter-and-spirit perspective may be identified in the *zaddik*'s modeling behavior. But first let us consider briefly the Hasidic outlook on the role and personality of the *zaddik*.

The term *zaddik* is derived from the Hebrew word *zeddek*, the literal meaning of which is social justice. Although in earlier Hebrew literature the term *zaddik* is used in a number of different and occasionally contradictory ways, the Hasidic use of the concept usually denoted a "spiritual person" who feels concern for people and leads the community (see Dresner 1960: 276). Indeed, in explaining the double meaning of the verse "The *zaddik* shall flourish like the palm tree; he shall grow like a cedar in Lebanon" (Ps. 92:13), the Besht (1975b: 44), who was apparently aware of these diversified definitions of the term, strived to inculcate and accentuate the *zaddik*'s social role by expressing his unequivocal preference for the first manifestation of the *zaddik*—the date palm who bears fruit, that is, gives and devotes himself to the people—over the lofty, aloof, barren, cedar tree type *zaddik* who keeps his knowledge and wisdom to himself. In a similar vein, Rabbi Yaacov Yosef (Dresner 1960: 106) regards Noah as a symbol of the negative, ego-centered *zaddik*, who may be knowledgeable and righteous but who saved only himself, while Abraham symbolizes the *zaddik* who went out to save others and include them in his community.

In line with this approach to the *zaddik*'s role, the Rabbi of Kotzk (cited by Dresner 1960: 153) once described a noted rabbi to his disciples as a "*zaddik* in a fur coat." In explaining this metaphor, he stressed, "There are two ways to keep warm in a cold room: One can put on a fur coat or one can light a fire. . . . The first man only wants to keep himself warm, the second wants to bring warmth to others as well." The contrast between wrapping oneself in warm clothing and lighting a fire is repeatedly found in Hasidic literature in the context of contraction-expansion (introduced above), whereby no strength is lost through the social contraction that produces the social contract. Hence Rabbi Yaacov Yosef stressed time and again that just as the glowing flame of one candle may kindle many candles while losing nothing of its own brightness, so the *zaddik* must kindle sparks in as many people as possible while keeping his own flame burning bright (cited by Dresner 1960: 215).

The Hasidic *zaddikim*,[1] then, are leaders and model "spiritual people," or "mystagogues" in Weber's (1967) terms, whose function (despite the controversy it generated regarding the creation of a personality cult; see Dubnov 1975) differs markedly from that of the detached, secluded Christian sacred-type saint and hence can be understood only in terms of their prescribed relationship to the members of the inclusion community. The *zaddik*'s role as a leader-model is repeatedly described not as that of an authoritarian leader (although in reality he might turn out to be one) but as a channel (see Yaacov Yosef 1963: 345) or tube whose task is to role-model and mediate between man and the concrete physical or the inscrutable metaphysical world. The *zaddik* is the channel (ibid., p. 345) that draws from above and below or "the vessel which brings water to irrigate the field," as Dresner (1960: 142) put it. Since a channel or tube receives at one end what it dispenses at the other, Rabbi Yaacov Yosef (1963: 242) states, "If he who receives *shefa* (richness) does not hand it over to others, it will be cut off from him. . . . If he wants to receive, he must give to others." Thus, permissive interdependence in terms of giving and receiving does not connote dualistic individualism, whereby a person is cast into the role of a guilty debtor. Neither does it imply collective dependency on a mob or a tyrannical leader. On the contrary, alter-centered interdependence (or alter-centered individualism) means that each partner retains his individuality and responsibility in the communal give-and-receive transaction. Put otherwise, such an alter-centered society may be compared, as did Schopenhauer (see Wells 1971: 273), to hedgehogs clustering for warmth and unhappy when packed too closely or scattered too sparsely. Hence the mediating role of the *zaddik* is to serve as a model—not as a savior—for spiritual and material salvation from inexplicable ills, uncertainties, and the consequent "cognitive discrepancies" that confront us all in our "imperfect world," as Weber put it. Buber (1978: 4), for example, describes the mediating-modeling role of the *zaddik* as showing the way to salvation but not providing it for the individual. In his plastic language:

> How was man, in particular the "simple man" with whom the Hasidic movement is primarily concerned, to arrive at living his life in fervent joy? . . . How retain unity in the midst of peril and pressure, in the midst of thousands of disappointments and delusions? . . . the griefs and despairs of life itself. . . . How shall those loftier concerns be approached? A helper is needed, a helper for both body and soul. . . . This helper is called the zaddik . . . he can teach you to strengthen the soul . . . until you are able to venture on alone. He does not relieve you of doing what you have grown strong enough to do for yourself. . . . The zaddik must make communication with God easier for his hasidim, but he cannot take their place.

Theoretically, then, alterism should foster individualistic mutuality and not collectivizing total dependence. I realize that by highlighting the mediating but nonetheless leading role of the *zaddik* as a model, the organic scheme of an egalitarian, mutually interdependent community might be somewhat distorted. True, the Hasidic community was hierarchical in the sense that it did not eschew or evade the naturally human tendency to form leader-follower social structures. Thus one might mistakenly perceive the hierarchy as a unilateral social structure in which the materially inclined person is dependent on the spiritual leader but the spiritually inclined person is independent. The reader is urged to remember, however, that this hierarchical structure means only that the spiritually disposed people are the equivalent of the eyes or head of the community, while the materially inclined people are its feet, or, in a different metaphor, the "spiritual man" lives on the second story, while the "material person" resides on the ground floor. The organic scheme of interdependence is preserved in both meta-phors, however, in the sense that when the feet are in the pit the head also bends, and it is the feet that must be used for climbing out. Likewise, the spiritually inclined people residing with their heads in the clouds will suffer more if the ground floor, where the materially inclined people reside, col-lapses under them (see Yaacov Yosef 1963: 43).

To return to the *zaddik,* his general modeling task in the inclusion process (which is actually a communal reformulation of the contracting self-designification process of *iyun,* discussed earlier) is self-contracting hu-mility to make room for others. Thus Dresner (1960: 142), who portrayed the *zaddik*'s role as a vessel or as a socially mediating tube, rightly stressed that only through the prerequisite process of contracting "humility" (*shiflut*) can the *zaddik* fulfill his social role in the inclusion community, because in Beshtian terms "that fullness of arrogance . . . leaves little room for God or man." In a similar vein, Rabbi Yaacov Yosef (1963: 50) uses Jacob's ladder as a symbol for the *zaddik*'s prescribed humility:

> Man is a ladder fixed in the earth, whose head reaches the heavens (Gen. 28:12). . . . When he thinks he is far from the Lord—fixed in the earth and one of those who descend—he is in reality close to the Lord and his head reaches the heavens. But when . . . his head reaches the heavens . . . he is in reality far from the Lord . . . and he is one of the descenders.

Here again, however, the emphasis is on contraction whereby no strength is lost, in contrast to the quietistic or Eastern self-extinction principle, for as Yaacov Yosef related in the name of the Besht, "too much humility can be a danger to any man . . . if he bows too often and too low toward the earth, he may forget to lift his head to the heavens" (Dresner 1960: 163).

Two interrelated contracting-communication principles seem to facili-tate the evacuating-inclusion process and are preconditions for opening the community's "heart-vessel" to reabsorb the potentially deviant person with-out imposing alter-centric actualization on him. Although these are essen-tial commonsense contraction prerequisites for establishing communication, they seem to entail egalitarian ground rules that are too often overlooked and deserve brief mention. These are: (1) material contraction by means of symbolic change in outer appearance and (2) spiritual contraction by means of symbolic change in speech.

Material Contraction

The first prerequisite principle is conveyed by Rabbi Yaacov Yosef through what became his classic parable of the lost prince who is returned to his father. In this simple tale, which was "told and retold, altered and transfigured, alluded to and hinted at," as Dresner (1960: 177) put it, Yaacov Yosef construes the *zaddik*'s active modeling role of contracting himself in relation to the potential deviant. Although this story includes many details to which great significance was attributed, the most relevant aspects from the present perspective are as follows:

A king sent his nobles to retrieve his lost son, whom he had once sent to a village, but all of them failed to bring him back. In the meantime the prince had mingled with the villagers, learned their ways, and forgotten his royal manners. At last one of the nobles removed his elegant attire, dressed in plain clothing like that of the townsfolk, and succeeded in reestablishing communication with the prince and returning him to his father (cited by Dresner 1960: 177). This story was used by Yaacov Yosef and his disciples time and again to inculcate the techniques of material contraction by the symbolic wearing of simple clothes and speaking the language of the people to win their confidence.

Rabbi Nachman of Bratzlav used a parable with a similar symbolic motif in which the change of clothing—or even undressing—was used as an active contraction technique for reestablishing communication with a prince who believed himself to be a turkey and therefore sat naked under a table and ate only sunflower seeds.

> While all the doctors hired by his father, the king, could not cure the prince, there was one wise man who got also undressed, sat with the prince under the table, introduced himself as a turkey, and ate sunflower seeds until the prince found it strange that a wise man should behave in such a fashion. Thus they both decided that turkeys could dress, eat other food, etc., and finally both came out from under the table and behaved like humans again. (See Steinman 1951: 157)

It should be obvious that the symbolic alter-centered contraction accomplished by wearing simple clothes does not necessarily refer to a literal changing of clothes, although in Hasidic communities, as in other inclusion communities such as the kibbutz, the wearing of uniform clothing plays quite an important role. The symbolic effect of wearing simple clothes, matching those whom one is to meet, may be understood in Goffman's (1959) interactive role-taking terms of "self-presentation" in order to establish communication with the other.

Moreover, in contrast to the alter-centered concept of asymmetric exchange, which theoretically pervades the relationship between material

Zebulunism and spiritual Issacharism, it is Veblen's "conspicuous consumption," the parading of flashy clothing and material-success signs, that precipitates the exclusion process by widening social gaps or sharpening social-class boundaries between the Zebulunian material creditors and the Issacharian spiritual debtors. It is therefore contraction in extravagant, external symbols of success that preserves a community's monistic harmony and facilitates the basic feeling of trust necessary for the reinclusion of potential "debtors." Consequently, although Goffman's (1959) "presentation of self" may be understood as a manipulative technique, an awareness of the meaning of egalitarian versus extravagant outer appearance and the flaunting of material-success signs, from the present alter-centered perspective, is important as the first step in the alter-centered actualizing salvation.

Spiritual Contraction

The second communication principle, which may be termed "verbal contraction," refers to the need of the spiritually inclined person to contract his broad, abstract, spiritual language—somewhat similar to the Maggidic father who talks to his child in small letters (see Chapter 7)—in order to converse on a more concrete level with the materially inclined man by using nonassertive analogies and simple parables. I have already discussed at some length how the deassertive communication style becomes imperative in Hasidic interpersonal relations. Here it should be further stressed that within an ego-centered dualistic social framework one of the major factors contributing to the exclusion process that widens social gaps and sharpens class boundaries may be traced to the overarticulate assertive snobbish language often used by the so-called upper classes or pseudointellectuals in their interaction with those considered subordinate in the social hierarchy. Verbal contraction, meaning climbing down from true or imagined "high-class" language to speak in everyday "material" terms, thus becomes a major inclusion technique that creates the necessary egalitarian atmosphere by minimizing social gaps and consequently enhances interpersonal communication. The *zaddik*'s well-known modeling descent from his spiritual-sophisticated or abstract-assertive language to converse with the people in the marketplace likewise constitutes the basis for the inclusion process. Moreover, according to the Hasidic multiple actualizing salvation paradigm of "in all thy ways known Him" (see Besht 1975b: 33), in which the power of letters and words plays an important role, the medium of talking or listening to simple stories and small talk also becomes a vital means of actualization. Rabbi Yaacov Yosef stated that "even in simple stories one should be able to feel the presence of the Creator. . . . There are men who can pray while speaking with a friend about plain things" (Dresner 1960: 188).

The *zaddik*'s modeling behavior in verbal contraction in order to make space for the inclusion of the needy other is best exemplified by the story of a group of Hasidim who attended one of the Besht's counseling talks. When it was over, each one expressed the belief that the Besht had spoken only to him. Dresner (pp. 189–190) relates in the name of the Besht:

> Every evening after prayer the Baal Shem went to his room. Two candles were set in front of him and the mysterious Book of Creation was put on the table among other books. Then all those who needed his counsel were admitted in a body, and he spoke with them until the eleventh hour.
>
> One evening when the people left, one of them said to the man beside him how much good the words which the Baal Shem had directed to him had done him. But the other told him not to talk such nonsense, that they had entered the room together and from that moment on the master had spoken to no one except himself. A third, who heard this, joined in the conversation with a smile, saying how curious that both were mistaken, for the rabbi had carried on an intimate conversation with him the entire evening. Then a fourth and a fifth made the same claim, and finally all began to talk at once and tell what they had experienced.

A good example of how material and verbal contraction facilitates inclusion is the kibbutz, which was inspired by Hasidic ethics and socialistic utopianism (see Spiro 1971; Buber 1958b: Fishman 1972). Alter-centered inclusion is applied there in terms of insistence on members wearing similar, simple clothing (and the consequent structural prevention of class-differentiating "conspicuous consumption") and on members speaking in the same egalitarian language, which makes communication easier. Indeed, in his anthropological study of the kibbutz, Spiro (1971: 165) points out that "any departure from the style of dress found in the kibbutz is viewed with critical disdain . . . [because] clothing, as is well known, is often important for the marking of status distinctions." He further indicates (p. 156) that, in regard to what can be termed "spiritual flaunting," "although the intellectual is admired *qua* intellectual, he does not enjoy great respect *qua chaver* (member of the kibbutz) unless he combines efficiency in physical labor with his intellectuality."

It is a plausible hypothesis that, because of a process of natural selection, people who might otherwise have suffered from material or spiritual "democratic disabilities" (i.e., deviance), as a result of forced independence of one kind or another, find their way to the kibbutz alter-centered-inclusion community.[2] There, permissive mutual interdependence in terms of subtle social control (preventing verbal or material flaunting) and the legitimation of the interdependence between the *tarbutnikim* (the spiritually inclined people) and the *mishkistim* (the materially inclined people) is the rule as Spiro so vividly described (1971: 156). Because there are no sociohistorical descriptions of the authentic Hasidic community, perhaps a good description of how contraction for inclusion filtered down from the Jewish *shtetl* (the small, Jewish, Eastern European town that according to Spiro essentially represents a Hasidic community) is Spiro's comparison between the *shtetl* and the kibbutz. Spiro (1971: 32) states:

> The following description of the *shtetl* applies, without qualification, to Kiryat Yedidim [the fictitious name of the kibbutz he studied]. . . . Locked doors, isolation, avoidance of community control, arouse suspicion. . . . "Home people," *heymisheh mentschen*, . . . are free to come in whenever they like at any time of the day. . . . Withdrawal is felt as attack, whether physical or psychological, and isolation is intolerable. "Life is with people." . . . Everywhere people cluster to talk, at home, in the market place, on the street. Everyone wants to pick up the latest news, the newest gossip. . . . The freedom to observe and to pass judgment on one's fellows, the need to communicate and share events and emotions is inseparable from a strong feeling that individuals are responsible to and for each other.

The kibbutz may then serve as a model alter-centered inclusion community where permissive interdependence between materially inclined people and the spiritually inclined people is structually facilitated but not imposed. This is not to suggest that in everyday life excessive collectivizing control is not imposed on people in many contemporary kibbutzim, as Spiro indicates. The kibbutz model is presented merely to elucidate the need for a "differential democratic" system for people who might otherwise encounter "democratic disabilities" on either the material level or the spiritual level.

While material and spiritual contraction are no more than commonsense prerequisites for egalitarian communication, they seem to entail an implicit inclusion philosophy that may be conceived as the foundation of the diagnostic-inclusion technique that I call "deciphering inclusion."

NOTES

1. Except for rare personalities, as in the case of the Besht himself, the notion of a single *axis mundi* (center of the world) Moses leader type (*zaddik hador*), in the Hasidic literature the term *zaddik* was mostly used in the plural to refer to the possibility of many "spiritual types" who are to function in various communities (see Green 1977; Y. Weiss 1977: 84, 85). This reality, which concurs with our sociological definition of contraction, is attested to by the simple sociohistorical fact that already during the second generation after the Besht the movement disseminated into many branches, which coexisted in relative harmony so that each Hasidic community "contracted" itself, so to speak, to make space facilitating the existence of other similar communities.

2. Essentially the biblical "refuge cities" (Num. 35:11) to which people could escape should also be construed as inclusion communities, because people were not exiled to these cities but went there willingly and because, according to commentary, a special control-support system was to function there as a rehabilitation system.

(12)

The Deciphering-
Inclusion Process

In discussing the Hasidic theme of organic interdependence, Piekarz (1978) cites various sources describing the deviant members of the community as the sick organs of the communal body that will affect the healthy organs if not properly treated. Moreover, I indicated earlier that according to the principle of mutual responsibility and mutual emulation, the bilateral, double-mirroring process of inclusion requires that "when a pious man sees a wicked act . . . he must blame himself . . . and when the people see an improper action on the part of the *zaddik*, they must blame themselves. . . . The leader should correct himself in order that the people might be corrected, and the people must correct themselves in order that the leader might be corrected." (Yaacov Yosef 1963: 335, trans. by Dresner 1960: 207)

Indeed, in construing the passage "Who is a wise man? A man who learns from everybody" (Fathers 4:1), Rabbi Yaacov Yosef (1963: 259) uses the reflective-mirror metaphor to state that it is the "wise man who learns from everybody like the one who looks in the mirror and knows his fault by seeing the other's fault." Our technique of mutual emulation stipulated accordingly how mutual correction is accomplished by means of self-correction. The most radical and controversial idea in Hasidic social theory—again, as role-modeled by the *zaddik*—is probably the notion that in order to preserve or restore the organic unity of the inclusion community and reach a higher level of alter-centered actualization, the conforming people (who might mistakenly believe that they are superior or higher while they are actually equal to the deviants) must first "descend" to the level of the deviants in order to restore the equilibrium of the inclusion community as an organic whole. That is essentially the means of mutual alter-centered actualization and the preservation or restoration of the organic unity: The perfect whole (*komah shelemah*), which can be achieved through unifying matter and form and the prevention of the disastrous process of separation (*perud*) caused by the breaking of vessels and hearts, paradoxically requires not the imposition of social control and conformity on the material or spiritual deviant but the contracting descent of others to his level—to the extent that in order to uplift the deviant, they must experience something of the devious sins, mental problems, or temptations with which the latter presumably lives.[1]

The radical point here is that it is the organic metaphor of the head or eyes depending on the proper functioning of the feet which stipulates that unity and social development can be achieved or restored, not through exclusion of the malfunctioning organs but, on the contrary, only through the contracting reinclusion of the social elements (organs) in danger of lingering decay. Such a contraction-reabsorption process can be accomplished only by evacuating space for both healthy and ailing "social organs" and bringing both to a common level that enables them to grow and thus prevents deviants from breaking away or becoming lost. Thus, in discussing how an egalitarian organic unity can be established between the spiritually and materially inclined people, Nigal (1962: 66) indicated that Rabbi Yaacov Yosef used the term "medium" (*memutza*) to stress that the connecting point between the *zaddik* and the people can be created only by bringing both to a meeting point, because "it is possible to bring two opposites closer only through a medium (*memutza*) point. . . . This medium includes the limits of both sides and in this way a closeness and contact is established between the polarities" (see Yaacov Yosef 1963: 341). But here again, contracting descent to reach the medium point for creating contact refers to the act of self-condensation, not self-annihilation, Hence, Yaacov Yosef (1963: 468) repeatedly cautions that when a person goes down into a pit to reestablish the necessary contact (*hitchabrut*) and save his friend (the deviant), he should first tie himself with a rope (i.e., not extinguish himself) so that he may subsequently rise out of the pit together with his friend. In other words, the holistic or monistic approach to organic healing and personal development can be accomplished only through the "deciphering" process of mutual emulation, which helps one to understand that the contaminating *defect* in one organ (the presumed deviance of some people who encountered salvation difficulties) has a definite *effect* on the healthy organs (the presumed conformity of other people). However, rather than lead to negative contamination, this relationship between the organs should be utilized for mutual growth. This monistic-organic conception of society is thus epitomized in the cabalistic paradoxical imperative stating, "Privileged is the one who holds the hand of the guilty" (see Yaacov Yosef 1963: 40).

To understand the meaning of the deciphering inclusion technique, it would be worth citing at some length Dresner's (1960: 193, 194) translation of Rabbi Yaacov Yosef's (1963: 686, 687) radical interpretation of the following biblical verse:

Thou shalt not see the *hamor* [donkey] of thy brother or his sheep driven away and hide thyself from them; thou shalt surely return them unto thy brother. And if thy brother be not nigh unto thee, and thou know him not, then thou shalt bring it home to thy house, and it shall be with thee until thy brother inquire for it, and thou shalt return it to him. . . . And so shalt thou do with every lost thing of thy brother's, which he hath lost and thou hast found; thou mayest not hide thyself. (Deut. 22:1–3)

Yaacov Yosef's reformulated or reinterpreted version of the above passage reads:

"Thou shalt not see the *hamor* [donkey] of thy brother driven away and hide thyself from them"—that is, you . . . should not see that the common people (*homer*²), who are indeed your brothers for there is in you an aspect of them, are driven from the path of righteousness to the path of evil, and then hide yourself from them. You should not hide yourself from them as if all this had no relation to you. For it does. Because of the underlying unity there is an aspect of their transgression in you as well, and, as it were, you (do not simply see their transgression but), are being shown it with a finger in order that you might feel your own failing. . . . "But if thy brother be not nigh unto thee and thou know him not"—that is, you search yourself to find an aspect of the transgression which you see in your brother, but "you know him not," because you do not find this fault in yourself since he is "not nigh unto you" as your brother, in this sin. "Then thou shalt bring it home to thy house"—that is, you should turn away from all other concerns, seclude yourself in meditation within your house, and "bring it"—the sin which you have seen in your brother—constantly before your eyes . . . until after this self-examination you "find" that he is your brother in that sin, and you turn in repentance from that taint of the sin which is in you. Then you will return him as well. "And so shalt thou do with every lost thing of thy brother's which he hath lost"—for sin is called a lack or loss—"and you have found"— that is, have found in yourself also. Therefore, "Thou mayest not hide thyself," in order to fulfill the commandment: "Thou shalt love thy neighbor as thyself," which is a great principle of the Torah.

The principle of contracting descent, which evacuates room to facilitate inclusion of the other in the community, requires a shrinking of one's inflated ego by recognizing how the other's faults are actually part of your own personality or behavior. Accordingly, superiority, which sharpens boundaries and widens social gaps, is only an illusion that must be corrected by self-contraction. This contracting process of cognitive descent or mutual emulation, discussed earlier, seems to surpass all the self-help principles practiced in Alcoholics Anonymous, Synanon, or even psychoanalysis. While these methods require a cognitive descent *before* one becomes a professional therapist or an ex-alcoholic or an addict helper, in contracting descent it is insufficient for the helper to empathize with the "deviant" by recognizing or admitting that he had experienced similar deviations in the *past;* he must recognize that an aspect of the other's fault is within him right now, and with that recognition (reached through the technique of holding his fault constantly before his eyes) he contracts himself and makes space for the deviant other in his world. It now becomes the common world for both of them, because the helper has stepped down from his pseudo-superior seat as *zaddik,* therapist, capitalist, imperialist, artist, spiritualist (and one might include a list of other "ists") to meet his brother on his level.

Dresner (1960: 192) cites various sources to emphasize the experiential principle of the helper's contracting-descent: "The prophet Hosea had to undergo the consummate pain of being wedded to a harlot before he could truly comprehend the harlotry of his people Israel, the wedded one of God. The sage Hillel said: 'Judge not thy neighbor until thou art come into his place.' " Similarly, it is told that the Besht once reproached a *zaddik* who had delivered reprimanding sermons to his congregants by asking, "What do you know of chastising? You yourself have remained unacquainted with sin all the days of your life, and you have nothing to do with the people around you. So how should you know what their sinning is?" (cited in Dresner 1960: 192).

The radical principle of deciphering and experiencing deviance for the sake of mutual development and organic inclusion can now be explained in social-psychological terms by distinguishing between two techniques for diagnosing and handling deviants.

Differentiating versus Integrating Diagnostic Labeling of Deviants

Laing (1965: 36) suggests that the process by which people are declared insane or psychotic involves a conjunction, or rather disjunction, between two persons. Thus he points out that "the critical test of whether or not a patient is psychotic is lack of congruity, an incongruity, a clash between him and me. . . . It is only because of this interpersonal disjunction that we start to examine his urine and look for anomalies." Accordingly, people have "no difficulty regarding another person as psychotic if, for instance, he says he is Napoleon, whereas I say he is not; or if he says I am Napoleon, whereas I say I am not." It is through this dualistic and differentiating diagnostic process of identifying the idiosyncratic behaviors and characteristics of the deviant which *differ* from the idiosyncrasies of the authorized diagnostician that people are labeled, handled, and most often excluded as deviants.

Laing therefore argues that to know how people suffering from what I term material or spiritual dissonance differ from others is obviously not what the deviant wants or needs to solve his ontological problems and be maintained or reincluded in the so-called normal society. While this is not to imply that people handling deviants do not try to understand the etiologies of deviance, we would agree with Laing that in the final analysis this "diagnostic understanding" is usually based on a differentiating-dualistic process anchored in a predetermined, prejudiced Greco-Latin medical conception of deviance that a priori limits an understanding of the existential meaning of a particular disordered behavior.[3]

In order better to understand the unique existential meaning of various disordered behaviors, which is admittedly sometimes very difficult because of the absence of reciprocity on the part of the deviant, Laing proposes the method used by the expositors of hieroglyphics. Drawing on many sources (among them Freud), Laing (1965: 31) suggests that the method of deciphering ancient texts, which depends to a large extent on the relationship between the ancient author and the contemporary expositor, "has been carried further forward and made more explicit . . . than the theory of the interpretation of psychotic 'hieroglyphic' speech and action." Indeed, expositors of ancient texts or experts on art and poetry would hardly assume that the ancient author or the ancient or contemporary artist or poet was or is insane, even though they may find the idosyncratic texts or works of art incomprehensible, bizarre, or most important, *different* from their perspective. Instead, they would undoubtedly blame themselves for lacking the talent, background, or understanding to decipher or explicate the meaning of the object or work in question. In attempting to overcome their narrow *Weltanschauung* and limited observational and interpretational capacity, our expositors would then seek in the observed object not those properties that are strange and consequently incomprehensible to them but rather elements that evoke for them the commonalities between their own experience and properties they are able to identify in the observed piece. By learning to identify in themselves the bizarre—or rather unknown—characteristics of the "other" (be it art or a person), they would then experience an inner growth and extension of their personality, which now includes a piece of the "other." This inclusion process, as Buber (1967: 97) saw it, is more than what is commonly known as empathy:

> Empathy means, if anything, to glide with one's own feeling into the dynamic structure of an object, a pillar or a crystal or the branch of a tree, or even of an animal or a man, and as it were to trace it from within, understanding the formation and motoriality of the object with the perceptions of one's own muscles; it means to "transpose" oneself over there and in there. Thus it means the exclusion of one's own concreteness, the extinguishing of the actual situation of life, the absorption in pure aestheticism of the reality in which one participates. Inclusion is the opposite of this. It is the extension of one's own concreteness, the fulfillment of the actual situation of life, the complete presence of the reality in which

one participates. Its elements are, first, a relation, of no matter what kind, between two persons; second, an event experienced by them in common.

Thus mutual deciphering inclusion, in Buber's terms of ego extension, may now be conceived as the epitome of alter-centered actualization not only in terms of the monistic diagnostic-integration approach to potential deviants, but also in terms of enhancing mutual actualization and personality enrichment. In this sense, personal growth by recognizing in yourself the commonalities shared with the apparent "deviant" is no mere rhetoric, since according to the Besht (1975a: 8), "evil is the chair of goodness," that is, what appears to be evil may actually serve goodness. In a similar context, the verse "Who is a wise man? A man who learns from everybody" (Fathers 4:1) was also interpreted by Yaacov Yosef (1963: 79) as referring to the "material deviant," from whose "vices" one may learn many "devices" that may be put to good use. Thus, the mutual-emulation double-mirroring technique derived from this verse receives here its concrete operational meaning. Our conclusion must then be, as Buber (cited in Friedman 1971: 82) stated, that "the inmost growth of the self is not accomplished, as people like to suppose today, in man's relation to himself . . . but in the making present of another self."

Accordingly, in the ego-centered differentiating and excluding diagnosis of deviance much is also lost for ego development in the production of the "one-dimensional man" (see Marcuse 1964). However, in the alter-centered integrating diagnostic process, the mutual deciphering technique, which requires interdependence of matter and spirit, enables the materially inclined person to expand his personality by deciphering the spiritual dissonance of the other and the spiritually inclined person to do so by understanding and incorporating material dissonance. Such mutual development may occur when, for example, a San Francisco businessman and a spiritual guru, while meeting in Esalan, learn to decipher and identify in themselves each other's dispositions and dissonances.

In this context the Besht's transformatory incorporating attitude toward deviants and deviance may be understood in terms of its contribution to personal growth:

> Who is the hero who conquers his impulse? . . . As in worldly matters . . . upon hearing an infiltrating thief, there is one who screams and thereupon the thief escapes, and there is one who prepares chains, and when the thief enters the room he ties him up with iron chains. So it is with the righteous. There is one who will not let any alien thought come near him . . . and there is one who utilizes the passion of love and evil fear to worship God. (Besht 1975a: 37)

The evil impulse or alien Oedipal thoughts are therefore to be not suppressed but incorporated and transformed for personal growth. Contraction in terms of deciphering inclusion is then the opposite of externalizing projection.

A case taken from my clinical records will further illuminate the difference between dualistic and monistic diagnosis. A young male bachelor in his late twenties with a long psychiatric record presented himself to me as the Messiah immediately after experiencing a severe social crisis. While traditional psychiatric diagnosis pointed out to him the disjunctive symptoms that differentiated him from the rest of society to prove his insanity, I kept stressing the commonalities between his and my own or anyone else's behavior, which differed quantitatively but not qualitatively. The common element was the technique of distracting or diverting attention from an unpleasant thought. I therefore indicated to him time and again that all people tend to divert attention from an anxiety-arousing source, such as an unpleasant thought or experience. In his case, being himself seemed to be unbearable at present, and it was certainly preferable to be a Messiah, especially since the Messiah has redeeming powers. While this integrating diagnostic technique of identifying the common element in our behaviors did not solve his social problem, it did relieve his anxieties and helped him come out of the psychotic crisis.

The organic conceptualization of deviance in terms of "I harbor part of your Messiah in me" may be culturally bound, however, so that organic unity would be limited to only those who have common archetypal "soul roots" (see Scholem 1972). Draguns (1974) has suggested, for instance, that patterns of disordered conduct may be understood as exaggerations of culturally accepted modes of adaptation stemming from specified socialization contexts. In a study of delusional contents among Israeli Jewish and Muslim psychotic patients (see Peretz 1977), it was found that despite their inevitable military indoctrination, none of the fifty-seven Jewish Israelis identified with figures representing warriors or conquerors, while five of the twenty Arabs identified with such "warriors" as Nasser and Arafat. This suggests that the archetypal Jewish Messiah is more deeply entrenched among Jews than recent ad hoc warrior role-models. The implication that I harbor a part of the other's spiritual deviation applies equally to material deviation. Alexander and Staub (1931: 35) suggested that "the only difference between the criminal and the normal individual is that the normal man partially controls his criminal drives."

Thus it is the electric contact between the plus wire and the minus wire that creates energy and light. It is the contact (*hitchabrut*) between the seemingly minus (deviance) in the other and the seemingly plus (conformity) within me that creates mutual development and constructs the organic whole out of the contracted "broken heart," which is more than the sum of its uncontracted parts. The process of inclusion on a physical-emotional level was described by Buber in discussing the function of touching contact which creates love between a man and a woman:

> A man caresses a woman, who lets herself be caressed. Then let us assume that he feels the contact from two sides—with the palm of his hand still, and also with the woman's skin. The twofold nature of the gesture, as one that takes place between two persons, thrills through the depth of enjoyment in his heart he will have—not to renounce the enjoyment but—to love. (Buber 1967: 96)

Thus there is indeed nothing more perfect and complete than the mended pieces of the broken vessels or the *contracted* and *contacted* pieces of the heart that was broken open to allow the *inclusion* of the other, whether in education, love, or communal relations.

Yaacov Yosef's (1963: 686, 687; Dresner 1960: 193) mutual deciphering inclusion dictum may now receive its full organic expression as a noncoercive, alter-centered means to prevent the "loss" of potential deviants:

> "But if thy brother be not nigh unto thee and thou know him not"—that is, you search yourself to find an aspect of the transgression which you see in your brother, but "you know him not," because you do not find this fault in yourself since he is "not nigh unto you" as your brother, in this sin. "Then thou shalt bring it home to thy house"—that is, you should . . . seclude yourself in meditation within your house, and "bring it"—the sin which you have seen in your brother—constantly before your eyes . . . until after the self-examination you "find" that he is your brother in that sin. . . . Then you will return him as well.

Monistic diagnostic integration, which seeks the common behavior properties present in both the conformist and the potential deviant, whether on the material level or the spiritual level, would seem to constitute the basis for the organic inclusion community (which Laing indeed attempted to build). In such a community, the potential deviant is prevented from falling into institutionalized secondary deviant behavior patterns, and the conformist and potential deviant may grow together through the organic deciphering understanding that develops between them.[4]

In conclusion, alter-centered actualization without coercion is possible in the inclusion community because people may have the freedom to be mutually and differentially interdependent on a horizontal level when exchange is asymmetric. The Zebulun may be dependent on the Issachar for his spiritual salvation, and the Issachar might depend on the Zebulun for his material salvation. Yet within the differentially democratic inclusion community, neither remains a guilty deviant debtor, because the multiple ideal-labeling system facilitates the multiple actualization of "in all thy ways know Him." According to Hasidic alter-centered individualism, so-cial mobility is unlimited; hence each person may actualize himself in his own rung (*madregah*) by studying, rejoicing, working, and mainly by help-ing the other in rational-technical or mystical-irrational terms. The inclu-sion community is thus not a "locality performance" but an interpersonal medium of socialization.

In differentially democratic alter-centered inclusion communities, mo-nistic harmony may be established because potential deviants—who would suffer from forced independence and its concomitant social indifference in the ego-centered exclusion society—are not sent back to the isolating community *after* they falter (despite or because of the intrusive treatment methods applied to them) but are prevented from dropping out of the community in the first place through its subtle control-support system. Such a centralized control-support system seems indeed to operate in some contemporary Hasidic communities (Poll 1969), in the kibbutz (Spiro 1971), and in the Japanese "total organization" firm (Rohlen 1974) or in the Synanon villages (Mowrer 1964). Although the above social systems differ from one another in many ways, their common denominator is that interdependence between matter and spirit, that is, work and leisure or other alter-centered asymmetric exchange mechanisms, are not *imposed* but are *offered* through the centralized inclusion communal structure. This communal socialization system emanating from mutual deciphering inclu-sion processes constitutes also the basis for material and spiritual alter-centered actualization.

NOTES

1. Traditional students of Hasidism who adhere to the textual-historical, analytical research methods (Scholem 1941; Pierkarz 1978; Weiss 1977) were divided as to whether the *zaddik*'s contracting descent, which is used here as a role-model for the uplifting of deviants, involves cognitive or active, involuntary or voluntary descent (i.e., premeditated or unconscious; see Weiss 1977; Pierkarz 1978). Such careful interpretation concerning the operational meaning of the *zaddik*'s descent comes to differentiate the Hasidic doctrine of descent for the sake of uplifting ascent from the heretical Sabbatean doctrine of the descent of the Messiah, which historically preceded eighteenth-century Hasidism and which, like Hasid-ism, became an active practice of cabalism. According to Scholem (1972), it had a great influence on the Hasidic doctrine of descent, while according to Pierkarz (1978) there are even earlier Jewish influences on the doctrine of descent. Thus the Sabbatean movement interpreted the cabalistic doctrine of correction (*tik-kun*)—through the liberation of the divine sparks from the prisons of earthly darkness (*kelipot*)—as a process by which the Messiah himself descends into the realm of evil, which not only legitimized sinful practices but culminated in the Sabbatean-Frankist doctrine of the holiness of sin. Hasidism, however, empha-sized a very cautious symbolic descent only to the extent that it can restore the organic whole. Moreover, contemporary writers such as Shoham (1979) have overlooked this very crucial predominant interpretation of Hasidic cabalism and

have consequently introduced cabalistic correction of or salvation from deviance in its distorted Sabbatean meaning of descending into sin. Later I shall address myself to the important psychological differences emanating from doctrines of destruction and contraction.

2. *Homer*, which is the Hebrew word for "matter," is composed of the same letters as *hamor* (donkey).

3. Interpretations of studies (see Rotenberg 1975) that have shown that, compared with physical scientists or laymen, professional psychologists were less accurate in their inferences about people suggest, for example, that training in psychopathological diagnosis accustoms people to making reckless stereotypic judgments of behavior.

4. Indeed, one of the characteristics in Von Weizacker's "inclusive therapy," which was inspired by Buber's "I and thou" philosophy, was that the doctor allowed himself to be changed by the patient (see Friedman 1971: 186).

(III)

The Psychological Perspective

James D. Page (1971):

"The prevailing mood of the manic person is one of elation. He is expansive, humorous, optimistic and carefree. . . . He vaguely realizes that his gaiety is a facade.

Melvin Zax and Emory L. Cowen (1972):

Manic behavior is a defense utilized to keep underlying depression from awareness.

The Besht (1700–1760):

"From this power of katnut (depression) he will come to gadlut (elation), as in coals: if there is one spark left he will be able to blow and reignite it till there is a big fire as before.

(13)

Ascent Through Descent: The Functional Dynamics of Monistic Deviance

In the foregoing sociological and social-psychological parts of this book, I have shown how a monistic culture reabsorbs deviant social elements into its mainstream through a process of sociological or interpersonal contraction. In the following psychological section, I shall discuss the monistic, functional dynamics of deviance (descent for the sake of ascent) on the *intra*personal level of intrapsychic contraction. In so doing, I shall stress that while it has been popular in various sociological traditions to analyze the positive functions of deviance, this perspective was never systematically applied to psychopathology and used to explain how deviance on the intrapersonal level may be functional per se for the deviant himself.

Sociologists adhering to the structural functional, symbolic interactionist, or phenomenological schools—beginning with Durkheim and Mead, who are usually cited as classics, and going on to Coser, Erikson, and Berger and Luckman—have made general claims that deviance may be structurally functional for the maintenance of society. As alluded to earlier, within these functional, phenomenological, or interactionist schemes, the question "functional for whom?" has never been seriously examined. Hence it is unclear whether deviance is functional for the social system at large or only for very specific segments of society.

The thesis to be developed below will argue (1) that traditional approaches to deviance are essentially socially dualistic, so that deviance is perceived as being selectively functional for the society of insiders but not for the deviant outsider and (2) that according to the monistic functional conception of deviance anchored in a mystic Hasidic "ascent through descent" perspective, deviance and psychopathology may be perceived as functional for the deviant himself, as well as for society at large.

Let us briefly consider first the dualistic functional approach to deviance. In one of his classic statements, Durkheim (1964: 102) asserted that crime or the most aberrant forms of behavior may often contribute to the development of social solidarity and the moral order, since "crime brings together upright consciences and concentrates them. We have only to notice what happens . . . when some moral scandal has just been committed. *They* stop each other on the street, *they* visit each other, *they* seek to come together to talk of the event and to wax indignant in common" (italics added). I have italicized the word "they," which appears three times in Durkheim's brief statement, because the question that should immediately come to mind is Who are "they"? It seems quite apparent that "they" are not the social deviants. Hence, while Durkheim's observations laid the foundations for a theory of social solidarity by explaining how deviance may contribute to the development of a collective conscience in which all members of the group (including deviants) are invited to take part, his theory was also used as a basis for the dualistic sociology that separates deviants from conformists. Indeed, George Herbert Mead (1928: 557), the father of the symbolic interaction theory, inadvertently(?) combines dualistic and monistic components in his statement about the function of deviance: "The attitude of hostility toward the law breaker has the unique advantage of uniting *all* members of the community" (italics added).

While Mead's statement shows no awareness of the inherent contradiction between the dualistic (alienating) function of "hostility toward the law breaker" and the monistic function of "uniting all members of the community," later functionalists such as Coser (1968: 286) are straightforward in expressing their dichotomizing view of deviance: "It is against the ground of their deviance that the righteous achieve comforting affirmation of their normality." Coser is quite clear about who "they" are and how deviance is functional not for the deviant "outsider" but for the "righteous" "insider."

The segmental dualistic function of deviance is most clearly formulated in Simmel's (1950: 402) concept of the "stranger" "who is fixed . . . within a particular spacial group . . . essentially by the fact that he has never belonged to it from the beginning" and in Erikson's (1966: 11–13) boundary-maintaining conceptualization, which tends to remind us of Berger and Luckman's (1966) universe-maintaning mechanism:

> The deviant is a person whose activities have moved ouside the margins of the group. . . . Boundaries remain a meaningful point of reference only so long as they are repeatedly tested by persons on the fringes[1] of the group and repeatedly defended by persons chosen to represent the group's inner morality. Each time the community moves to censure some act of deviation . . . it sharpens the authority of the violated norm and restates where the boundaries of the group are located.

Erikson, who actually portrays the relationship between deviants and conformists as an open class struggle, admits, however, that society needs the
deviant to sharpen the boundaries between these two class systems. Hence
special religious and secular confrontations are constantly activated to
maintain these class-dichotomizing boundaries:

> Religious ritual, dance ceremony, and other traditional pageantry can dra-
> matize the difference between "we" and "they" by portraying a "symbolic
> encounter between the two." . . . Whether these confrontations take the
> form of criminal trials, excommunication, hearings, court martial, or even
> psychiatric case conferences, they act as boundary maintaining devices.

It thus follows that in a dualistic functional view of deviance, the lack
of a conceptualization of deviance as functional for the deviant himself is
not accidental but rather quite consistent with the social-boundary, or
rather social-gap, maintaining philosophy. According to the monistic functional conception of man in society, however, deviance and evil are considered not as independent entities but as the flip sides of goodness and
conformity or as functional dynamic phases in the cosmic and human devel-
opmental rhythm of "ascent through descent." My emphasis on both conditions—that deviance-evil is not an independent entity and that "ostensible" deviance may be conceived as a necessary stage in the dialectic process
of "ascent through descent"—is meant to sharpen the contrast between the
contractional volitionary concepts "ascent through descent"[2] and the
quietistic-nihilistic approach to deviance that posits a somewhat deceivingly
similar "ascent through descent" notion of existential self-actualization.

Before I introduce the contractional intrapersonal "ascent through descent" model of functional deviance, a few words must be said about the
inherent difference between monistic and dualistic conceptions of good and
evil. The theologian Porter (1902:93), who compared the Jewish and Cris-
tian doctrines of sin, stated, "Man was to the Hebrew a unity. Body and
soul were but the outer and inner sides of one being, [whereas to Christians]
body and soul were regarded as two essentially contrasted and really unrelated things." Thus, Porter maintained, "the resulting [Christian] ehtics,
the idea that virtue is to be attained by the conquest and subjugation of the
body, in which evil has its seat and its power, were radically opposed to
Hebrew thought" (p. 94). Here, essentially, is the core of the contrasting
conceptions of good and evil (which may be considered the idealogical
ancestors of deviance and conformity) and the methods for changing from
evil to good that emanated from these two doctrines.

According to the Jewish monistic conception of man, what appears to
be evil can be utilized to serve good ends. The evil impulse (*yetzer hara*), for
example, is conceived as a dynamic force necessary for life (somewhat

similar to Freud's notion of the sublimated sex drive). To the perhaps paradoxical question of whether the evil impulse is good, there is a classic and much cited answer in Jewish commentary: "Certainly, for without it man would not build a house, nor marry, nor beget children, nor engage in trade" (*Breshit Rabba* 89:7). Therefore man need not torture himself over his past passions, for salvation is achieved by reinterpreting his evil desires in light of the positive energy they instilled in him.

It may be of interest to note that the Hebrew word for impulse, *yetzer*, is derived from the same root as *yetzira*, which means literally creativity, and from the Hebrew word *yetzur*, which means "creature," "being," or rather "being human" and actually suggests that impulsiveness equals being human, alive, and creative or that one cannot conceive of human creativity without natural impulses and passions. Thus good and evil or deviance and conformity are not two separate entities but are functionally interrelated to the point that seeming "evil" (deviance) serves goodness (conformity). "Evil is the chair of goodness" is the Besht's favorite metaphor to stress that evil actually serves goodness. "The real uniqueness is the divine, and how can it include two opposites in one subject, good and evil? . . . But in actuality it is non-contradicting, since evil is the chair of goodness" (Besht 1975a: 8). The verse "Turn from evil and do good" is repeatedly interpreted by the Besht as "Use evil to do good" (p. 15). Descending (deviating) is accordingly conceived as a temporary phase that is necessary if we are to be able to ascend and develop socially and personally.

The "Ascent Through Descent" Paradigm

The outlook that life and nature proceed in cyclic up-and-down or back-and-forth rhythms has been described and documented in many areas and disciplines. An overall consideration of how nature renews itself (see Eliade, 1974) and blossoms each spring after the resting period of the barren winter, or how the sun rises and the cosmos springs to life each morning after the night's darkness, allows for a general cosmic "ascent through descent" interpretation of nature's operation. Although somewhat overdeterministic in its attempt to present a "scientific," predictably cyclic approach to life, the recent "biorhythmic" method (e.g., Gittelson 1980), which indicates how to chart and cope with individual physical, emotional, and intellectual cycles, may be another example of an "ascent through descent" approach to life. According to the Hasidic *Weltanschauung*, the cosmic up-and-down cycle termed *ratzo vashov* (running and returning) refers to a continuous functional process of cosmic and human oscillations between states of *katnut* (smallness or narrowness) and *qadlut* (greatness or broadness). This constant ebb and flow between states of depressive smallness and energizing greatness is seen as a never-ending vital force necessary for cosmic and human life, renewal, progressional change. As the Besht (*Sefer Habesht* 1975: 63) stated, " 'all living[3] is running and returning' [Ezek. 1:14] and man's life is in the secret of smallness and greatness."

An interpretation of the role of mysticism in history, such as Scholem's (1972), views messianic movements of redemption, for example, the cabalistic outbreak in the sixteenth century (the ascending phase) as having followed an apocalyptic era of catastrophe (the descending phase), for example, the expulsion of Jews from Spain in the fifteenth century. Indeed, Scholem's statement that "this catastrophic character of redemption, which is essential to the apocalyptic conception . . . finds manifold expression: in world wars and revolutions, in epidemics, famine and economic catastrophe" (p. 12) seems to posit the world's progress through an ongoing process of ascending and descending phases of history. Returning to our present concern with descending processes of deviance per se, Merton's (1958) sociohistorical category of rebellious anomic waves that precede phases of social change and modernization may in fact be documented by case histories drawn from various cultural groups. Thus Scholem's (1972) description of the way the seventeenth-century heretical Frankist movement, which preached salvation through sin, was followed by the eighteenth-century Hasidic movement, which advocated salvation through radical but nonetheless conformist ecstatic prayers, may find its parallel in Christopher Hill's (1974) descriptions of the seventeenth-century English radical movements such as the Seekers, the Diggers, and especially the Ranters. The latter, for example, moved from antinomian deviation (just like the Frankists) by preaching that "adultery was not distinct from prayer" (Hill 1974: 315) to come back full circle to Puritan religiosity. As Hill summarized: "Ranterism easily passed over into its apparent opposite extreme, asceticism" (p. 318).

As will be argued later, however, these nihilistic "ascent through descent" movements do not necessarily represent monistic ideologies of functional deviance. Contemporary existential movements adhering to a social philosophy of the absurd (see Hinchliffe 1977), for example, essentially reject the cosmic-human purposefulness of "ascent through descent," since according to them life contains nothingness and hell equals otherness (other people, in Sartre's terms).

The basic difference between the dualistic "descent *and* ascent" approach to deviance and the monistic functional "ascent *through* descent" conception of deviance can best be illustrated by examining cross-culturally attitudinal interpretations of the psychopathological "ascent and descent" phenomenon known as manic-depressive psychosis. Indeed, our efforts to examine the possibility of developing a monistic functional perspective on psychopathology and deviance per se may well begin by reassessing common interpretations of manic-depressive behavior.

Ascent Through Descent:
The Manic-Depressive Case

According to the diagnostic manual of the American Psychiatric Association (DSM-I), manic-depressive reactions are generally described as "being marked by severe mood swings and a tendency to omission and recurrence" (see Ullmann and Krasner 1969: 414). Although the ancient Greeks and Romans observed that extreme states of excitement or elation and extreme depression or melancholy are cut from the same cloth, it was Kraepelin who is usually credited with first using the term "manic-depressive insanity" in the late nineteenth century, and Rado who asserted in the 1920s that "the manic condition succeeds the phase of self-punishment (depression) with the same regularity with which . . . the bliss of satiety succeeded to hunger" (see Ullmann and Krasner, 1969: 415).

I shall not unduly burden the reader with clinical or historical meticulosity about who first noticed that this struggle between Eros and Thanatos, life and death, or melancholic mourning (depression) and exciting "mornings" (mania) actually operates in an interrelated, cyclic regularity for specific "personalities" ("spiritual types") or for everyone, because what concerns us here is whether manic-depressive cyclic reactions are perceived in dualistic or monistic terms, that is, whether depression and mania are considered functionally or dysfunctionally related. In other words, the question from our perspective is: What is understood to be the predominant and desirable state in life, depression or mania? What is questioned here is not the interrelationship between these two mental states but whether the stress is on "manic-depression," in which depression could be conceived as a natural, temporary "rest" stage from the ideal striving toward joyful living, or on "depressive-mania," in which manic expressions that fail to receive institutionalized legitimation are interpreted as temporary "escapes" from the predominant life state, depression.

Here it is important to note that students interested in cross-cultural comparisons of altered states of consciousness have generally observed that while in comparing Eastern and Western psychotic behavior "significant differences between acute schizophrenics and shamans are not found. . . . In primitive cultures in which such a unique life crisis resolution is tolerated, the abnormal experience (shamanism) is typically beneficial to the individual" (cited in Pelletier and Garfield 1976: 23). That is to say, behavior considered as deviant, schizophrenic, or otherwise dysfunctional in the West may be viewed in the East as a culturally accepted life crisis that can be resolved beneficially. Indeed, Eliade (1964: 25), who defines the shaman as a "master of ecstasy," noticed that while most shamans come "from particular families in which nervous instability is hereditary," they enjoy a prestigious position in their societies because of their ability to control their "schizophrenic-manic" or even epileptic dispositions: "It is not to the fact that he is subject to epileptic attacks that the Eskimo or Indonesian shaman, for example, owes his power and prestige; it is to the fact that he can control his epilepsy" (p. 29). Similarly, Silverman noted in his comparative analysis of shamanism and schizophrenia (1967) that, while both schizophrenia and shamanism are "the result of a specific ordering of psychological events," such as feelings of fear, failure, guilt, and estrangement, "the essential difference between the two lies in the degree of cultural acceptance of the individual's psychological resolution of a life crisis. Thus, the same behaviors that are viewed in our society as psychiatric symptoms may, in certain other societies, be effectively channeled by the prevailing institutional structure or may perform a given function in relation to the total culture" (p. 23). Moreover, while according to Silverman's survey (p. 29) the shaman's prestige depends in part on his ability "to be continually able to 'enter' and 'return' from the far-flung reaches of the cosmos . . . similar kinds of ritualistic behavior when performed by a person in a schizophrenic state lead to absolutely nothing at all that has cultural significance, other than as verification of his insanity."

Most interesting here is Castaneda's (1974: 190) fictional-anthropological(?) account of how Don Juan taught him to control conditions propitious to fostering hallucinations. Castaneda's most dramatic example of learning to experience small doses of hallucinations is the following:

> I heard a formidable growl and Don Juan's voice shouting "run for your life!" And that was exactly what I did. . . . We advanced cautiously towards the animal. It was sprawled on its back. As I came closer to it I nearly yelled with fright. I realized that it was not dead yet. Its body was still trembling. Its legs, which were sticking up in the air, shook wildly. The animal was definitely in its last gasps. . . . I knew at once what the animal was. I walked over to it and picked it up. It was a large branch of a bush (p. 118).

Learning to cope with darkness may be a good example of what can be termed controlled entry and exit into functional psychosis (temporary detachments from reality).

Here are three consecutive citations: one about Castaneda's frightening hallucinatory experience, the second on his ability to control the experience by following Don Juan's instructions, and the third in Don Juan's explanation of how one stores personal power to control the entities of the night.

> [1]. I heard a clicking sound . . . and then a very large dark mass lurched out of the dark area. It was square, like a door perhaps eight or

ten feet high. The suddenness of its appearance made me scream. For a
moment my fright was all out of proportion.

[2]. . . . Suddenly I seemed to regain control of myself and was able
to turn around and for a moment I ran just as Don Juan had wanted me
to.

[3].What happened to me last night, Don Juan? You stumbled on
some entities which are in the world, and which act upon people. You
knew nothing about them because you have never encountered them. . . .
If you knew they were so dangerous, why did you leave me alone then?
There is only one way to learn. . . . If you want to know what power is, and
if you want to store it, you must tackle everything yourself.

The point in both cases (the shaman's and Castaneda's) is that in the
West it is only the "recognized" artist who is allowed to see hallucinatory
animals in branches, while ordinary people might be caught in a no-exit
psychosis when unexpectedly confronted with a hallucinatory condition,
because Western culture neither legitimizes such experiences nor provides
desensitizing-immunizing methods for controlling them. It has been shown,
however, that under experimental conditions with sensory deprivation (see
Nordland 1967) normal Western subjects are capable of having the same
hallucinatory experiences as shamans, which could be functionally desensitizing, if systematically induced.

Returning to our treatment of the manic-depressive cycle, it follows
that while in the Eastern shamanistic world ecstatic and even epileptic
attacks are not only tolerated but often employed functionally as desirable
and controllable mechanisms for handling natural (though problematic) life
cycles, in the West such schizophrenic or "manic" cyclical waves are usually
subdued—or rather denied by suppression—as deviant dysfunctional states.
As a result, such natural ascending-manic expressions may take the form of
periodic, uncontrollable, "overdose" explosions. It is remarkable that while
even Western writers interested in the psychological meaning of mystical
experiences (such as E. D. Starbuck, William James, and Evelyn Underhill)
have described descending-depressive moods as being functionally related to
the ascending-manic development of the mystic's personality, in contemporary psychiatric textbooks ascending-manic elation is unequivocally perceived as a facade and a defense against the predominant depressive state of
life prescribed by the Calvinist Protestant ethic. Thus Underhill (1949:
168), for one, acknowledged the natural growth cycle of oscillations between states of pleasure and states of pain, and upon describing the depressive phenomenon known as "the dark night of the soul" she states:

Psychologically . . . the "Dark Night of the Soul" is due to the double
fact of the exhaustion of an old state and the growth toward new states of

consciousness. . . . The great mystics, creative geniuses . . . have known instinctively how to turn these psychic disturbances to spiritual profit."
(p. 386)

In conventional psychiatric textbooks, however, we nonetheless find systematic and repetitive statements explaining manic elation as a defense and a facade for covering the underlying predominant state of depression. In one psychopathology textbook the manic person is described as "humorous, optimistic and carefree.[4] He describes himself as being on top of the world and full of pep. He radiates exuberance and vitality . . . [but] he vaguely realizes that his gaiety is a *facade,* a kind of desperate whistling in the dark" (Page 1971:235; italics added). In another typical textbook, which relies on one of the most widely cited studies on manic-depressive disorders done by a team referred to as the Washington Group, Zax and Cowen (1972: 200–201) conclude:

> The Washington Group regarded manic behavior as a defense utilized to keep underlying depression from awareness. When it followed depression it was seen as a straightforward escape mechanism. Where mania was followed by depression the mania was simply thought to have failed as a defense. The Washington Group believed that hypomania is a continual life style for many people, who use such behavior as a means of self-protection against potential depression.

It follows from the above and other "definitive" discussions of manic-depressive reactions (see Beck 1975: 97) that since even milder cases of mania (hypomania) cannot be considered a "desirable," normal state of being, but rather "self-protection" against the predominant state of depression, how much more deviant are the severe cases, where mania is portrayed as a facade, defense, or escape from the culturally prescribed norm of flat, controlled, and inhibited—that is, depressed—behavior.

Using simple logic, one may conclude that while any natural cyclic up-and-down rhythm can be perceived either as moving from the "up" condition to the "down" state or the opposite Western psychiatry seems to view the manic-depressive cycle as a "descent through ascent" cycle in which depression is the predominant state in life.[5] Consequently, while ancient or Eastern mystical philosophy legitimized dances or festivals[6] in the form of cyclical manic expressions, characterizing them as a "high" level of consciousness that facilitates control over natural, periodic crises, in the West such natural "manic" needs are considered deviant states that should be controlled and suppressed. As a result, natural manic expressions apparently take the form of uncontrollable explosions, as alluded to earlier.[7]

If one wishes to argue that the culturally relativistic position attributing significance to the social emphasis on either mania (ascent) or depression (descent) as the predominant states in life has no impact on the empirical prevalence and incidence of this unfortunate mental disorder, let us look at some cross-cultural observations concerning the manic-depressive phenomenon.[8] Kraepelin (1909) has already noted that in Java, for example, melancholia and mania were rare. Similarly Kiev (1972) reported in his psychiatric cross-cultural survey that in Kenya and in other African countries there is little depression. Researchers such as Carothers, Lambo, and others who were mentioned in Kiev's survey noted, however, that while among the African natives depression was relatively rare, mania was more frequent when compared to its incidence among whites. Lambo has suggested that depression is to be found more among "individualistic, competitive, and aggressive striving Protestant cultures" (Kiev 1972: 75), because these cultures produce unusual psychological stress and internal sin-oriented self-reproach. In a similar vein, Hoch and Zubin (1954: 46) cite a study which found that among "colored races" in the United States "the rarity of melancholia and the prevalence of mania . . . is twenty times more common than in whites," which may suggest that the institutionalized legitimation of manic behavior among "colored races" (epitomized in jazz, and spiritual dancing) may often be interpreted by white people as manic disorders while it may not necessarily be so conceived by the "colored races" themselves. This is not to say that depression is entirely absent in cultures where mania is more frequent; it only means that its recognition as an undesirable disorder varies across cultures. Thus Bebbington (1978) cites several studies which show that in numerous non-Western languages there is not even a word for depression, and in Japan, for example, the word *kanashi* (sad) can also mean "beautiful" and "affectionate."

It is hence important to stress that more than anything else it is the changes in socialization and value inculcation which in our own culture may affect the "prevalence" of manic or depressive phenomena. Arieti (1959), who has written what is considered by mainstream psychiatry to be the authoritative chapter on manic-depressive psychosis in the *American Handbook of Psychiatry*, suggested that the significant decrease in the incidence of manic-depressive "illness" in recent decades is due mainly to the decline of the Puritan ethic. In his opinion, the heavy burden of religious duty, guilt, and punishment previously placed on the "inner-directed" individual was associated with an increased incidence of depression. Although Arieti's conclusions are highly questionable—especially in view of studies indicating that the incidence of manic-depressive disorders was found to be relatively higher among other-directed (group-dependent) people living in cohesive communities (e.g., Eaton and Weil 1955)—the impact of cultural and socialization factors on the subject under consideration cannot be overlooked from either point of view.

It is precisely because socializing patterns may indeed affect the behavioral plights with which the rational Western man is faced, because of the prohibition on any institutionalized expression of irrational insecurities, or manic needs in any but controlled rational behavior, that it is worth examining the functional dynamics of the Hasidic, monistic, functional "ascent through descent" paradigm of deviance.

Ascent Through Descent: The Hasidic Model

A classic sociohistoric case demonstrating how a monistic socialization perspective may transform deviance and especially manic-depressive reactions into functional life cycles is, again, eighteenth-century Hasidism. Let us therefore consider the sociohistorical emergence of Hasidism from the present "ascent through descent" perspective. Intrinsic to Jewish survival throughout two thousand years of exile was the belief in a Messiah who would fulfill the biblical prophecies and gather together the scattered remnants of the House of Israel. However, as Rabinowicz (1970: 24) states, "like shooting stars, false Messiahs flashed across the skies of Jewish history, so that the flame of Messianism glowed through the darkness of the endless exile. But in the wake of each falling star came disillusionment, despair and disaster," which only cast the people back into even deeper misery and hopeless suffering. We may then assume that when the Besht appeared on the stage in Eastern Europe, early in the eighteenth century, he found a severely depressed people still licking the wounds inflicted by pogroms and massacres and bewildered by the smoldering trail left by the seventeenth-century pseudo-messianic Sabbatean and Frankist movements. Moreover, the Besht found masses of ignorant people surrounded by a world just emerging from the Dark Ages and still overcast by clouds of medieval superstition, witch-hunting, fear, and plagues. He found masses who were persecuted from the outside world by Polish tyrants and from within by ruthless rabbinical oligarchs. But most important, the Besht found desperate masses who, influenced by their Christian neighbors, were first given to exorcism of evil spirits and may also have been influenced by the essentially Christian predestinal conception of the damned man that swept over great parts of Europe and asserted that depression and hell's suffering are the predominant, unalterable state of the poor man. As suggested earlier, to redeem their despair and anguish the Besht did not offer economic salvation to these poor masses, but he created what may be viewed in Thomas Kuhn's (1962) terms as a "paradigmatic revolution" by teaching his people how "mania"—adhesion, ecstatic prayer, and joy—may be perceived as the predominant, desirable states in one's life, whereas depression or other forms of "deviance" are to be perceived as inevitable, temporary, and functional resting stages of "descent for the sake of ascent."[9]

According to the Besht's "ascent through descent" paradigm, "man is called an ascender and a descender as it is impossible always to remain on one rung." Moreover, because it is not only impossible but also undesirable to remain on one mental level, the Besht stressed that "he shall always be not in conceit (*hitnasut*) and not in abasement (*shiflut*) and sadness (*atzvut*), only once so and once so" (*Sefer Habesht* 1975: 91), "since a permanent pleasure . . . is no pleasure therefore man ascends and descends" (p. 120).

A classic and instructive monistic presentation of the Hasidic "ascent through descent" life cycle[10] is provided by what can be viewed as one of the Besht's (*Sefer Habesht* 1975: 47) most significant interpretations, of the fifth verse of the Bible: "And it was evening and it was morning, one day" (Gen. 1:5). The Hebrew word *erev* (evening), says the Besht, is derived from the word *taarovet*, which literally means mixture, a state wherein everything is confused and blurred, while the Hebrew word *boker* (morning) is derived from the word *bikoret*, which literally means control, suggesting when things are under control. Thus, for the Hasid who knows how to peel off the layers of darkness from the evening and elicit the sparking light of the morning, "evening becomes a throne for the morning, and so both together, evening and morning, are called one day" (*Sefer Habesht* 53).[11]

In order to explain how "evening" (depressive, blurred states) and "morning" (optimistic, controlled states) may indeed become "one day" if the manic-depressive life cycle is perceived monistically, so that morning follows the state of evening and not vice versa, I shall present the operational phases of the Hasidic "ascent through descent" model. But first it is appropriate to examine the significance of this model in the material-spiritual context proposed in earlier chapters.

"Ascent" and the Spiritual Meaning of Materialism

So far this discussion of the "ascent through descent" model has been related mainly to what I have termed "spiritual deviance" (e.g., the manic-depressive cycle), although deviance per se, as shown earlier, may take on either a material form or a spiritual form in a negative dialectic process. I accordingly argued that the negative or positive solution to the dialectic dissonance that one may encounter in the course of interacting with various ecologies may be either material (e.g., by adopting or acquiring a new material actualization role) or spiritual (by accepting a new spiritual salvation goal).

I shall now propose, however, that while the above scheme is basically plausible, on a deeper level of analysis only the descending phase of the dialectic dissonance process can be divided into material and spiritual forms of deviance; the ascending solution must, in the final analysis, include a spiritual component. Hence, while one may encounter a cognitive strain in regard to one's material ecology or spiritual ecology, because of factors of predisposition and/or socialization, and thus tend to deviate either materially (e.g., steal, cheat) or spiritually (e.g., hallucinate, be withdrawn), the solution to this dissonance must be "spiritual" in a cognitive sense in order for it to carry an actualizing meaning, for otherwise the solution remains *anomic*, at least on a perceptual level. That is to say, while a solution to "material deviance" (e.g., stealing) might be essentially material (e.g., acquiring goods by working in a trade), the working experience by which the material dissonance is reduced inevitably requires a concomitant cognitive process of attributing existential actualizing meaning to that material solution, since otherwise its anomic tension will probably persist. Indeed, Durkheim (1963: 248–250) in his classic analysis of suicide especially in the face of prosperity indicated that anomic suicide following from the law of "the more one has the more one wants" can be prevented only by creating a feeling of "average contentment," which "causes the feeling of calm, active happiness, the pleasure of existing and living." And what is that "feeling of calm, active happiness, and the pleasure of existing and living" if not finding the spiritual actualizing solution to one's existential problem, be it in relation to spiritual dissonance or material dissonance.

From this spiritual existential perspective, the material overtone of the Mertonian anomic model of deviance is limited and somewhat misleading, because it is not the bridging between material means and material success goals (Merton 1958) or the provision of material opportunities (Cloward and Ohlin 1960) that minimizes anomie and deviance. Rather, it is the spiritual meaning one may learn to attribute to any existential experience, including anarchic antimaterial or, paradoxically, even anomic experiences, as Viktor Frankl (1965) has so eloquently demonstrated, that may mitigate or even prevent the expressive outlet of anomic deviant conduct. In this sense one may now understand Yaacov Yosef's (1963: 341) statement (which might otherwise appear somewhat contradictory to his general egalitarian social conception of matter and form): "As it is the main purpose of creating man who was born in matter and spirit so that he will strive all his life to make spirit out of matter." Thus, to "make spirit out of matter" would refer to the cognitive transformation process which attributes spiritual meaning to material achievement. Consequently, in the Hasidic ethical system, the operational phase of descending refers to both material and spiritual descent; the ascending phase, however, stands mainly for a spiritual process of attributing meaning. Moreover, as we will show later, it is the "spirit-matter" conceptualization of the "ascent through descent" model that provides the most compelling evidence to support the self-contractional (as opposed to self-annihilative) interpretation of Hasidic "active quietism." Because descending and ascending, as conceived here, is congruent with the Hasidic insistence on man's free will (see Besht 1975a: 42), it likewise refers to a conscious process of self-contraction in which will and self-control can never be relinquished, as would happen in total self-annihilative quietism. Hence, descending must be understood as an intrapersonal process of alter-centered contraction, whereby the self evacuated room within himself for the inner, "alter," seemingly deviant part of himself, accepting it not as a static Jungian "shadow" but as a dynamic transformable *yetzer* (impulse), which literally means "being," a "creative" (*yetzirati*) "human creature" (*yetzur*).[12] It is thus the biblical categorical imperative of "Thou shalt rule over him" (Gen. 4:7) (the impulse) which draws the sharp distinction between the self-contracting and the quietistic self-annihilating or subconsciously driven conception of personality.

Let us now examine the functional operational phases that the Hasidic "ascent through descent" model encompasses. I should stress at the outset that although this model entails the essential components of a therapeutic process, my aim here is merely theoretical, and the discussion will therefore be general and eschew procedural action strategies.

NOTES

1. In articulating the function of social conflict, Simmel (1955: 13) stated similarly that "conflict is thus designed to resolve divergent dualisms: it is a way of achieving some kind of unity even if it be through the annihilation of one of the conflicting parties."

2. Although contraction on a sociological level has been presented as a horizontal scheme, on a psychological level contraction should be visualized as a vertical springlike condensation process (descent) which is supplemented by an expansion act aimed to regain an ever higher egalitarian vertical (though possibly slanted) level (ascent). Thus, descent in its various manifest forms is perceived not as a process of casting group members into lower irreversible deviant statuses in society, but as a temporary stepping down for a subsequent growth or comeback which indirectly contributes to the raising of the level of the whole community.

3. The original Hebrew word *Chayot* refers to animals and the verb "living."

4. It is of interest to note that in one textbook the major pathological symptom justifying hospitalization of "manic people" is expressed as follows: "Manic patients often get themselves into difficult situations and require hospitalization to prevent them from giving away all their money" (see Beck 1975: 97). Besides the fact that such a move raises serious questions about respect for the individual's civil rights, this tendency seems to reflect Western man's need to condemn and even banish one who violates the Protestant norm of egoistic and ascetic savings.

5. It is implicit in Freud's "Mourning and Melancholia" (1950: 153) that since in both conditions depression is caused by loss of a loved object, it would likewise be plausible in both conditions that if the lost libidinal object can be identified, "after a lapse of time it [depression] will be overcome." It is unclear, however, why Freud was so sure that in the case of a *real* loss (grief) "the ego becomes free and uninhibited again" (p. 154) whereas in the case of *symbolic* loss (melancholia) recovery is inevitably complex and difficult.

6. It is interesting that in his group psychology Freud (1965: 81) acknowledges

that the manner in which "the ego ideal . . . has to be periodically undone . . . is shown by the institution of festivals, . . . which owe their cheerful character to the release which they bring."

7. A good example of how, in a Western country such as the United States, the "manic" movements of the 1960s were generally not institutionalized but were subdued as uncontrollable, dangerous phenomena is found in the testimonies compiled in the book *Snapping*, which is typical of that decade. Conway and Siegelman (1978: 90, 91) state: "As new attitudes burst forth to fuel the sixties' environment of revolution and alternative lifestyles, a growing number of individuals began to find themselves adrift or run aground—and they began to react accordingly. Around the country, people began to "flip out" and go visibly crazy, engaging in violent and self-destructive behavior. Others, in contrast, "flipped in" and snapped, dropping into states of fantasy, terror and disorientation that were, in those early days, wholly unforeseen and inexplicable." It is not in order to take a stand in favor of or against these "humanistic" movements that I quote Conway and Siegelman but merely to show that no legitimate institutional means are available in the West to handle "manic" needs in a controllable manner, so that one might feel lost when imbued with ecstatic-manic feelings. A case in point illustrating how feeling simply good and elated is apparently so anormative in the United States to the point that one may feel guilty about it is the following confession: "I felt so good that my first reaction was a sharp pang of guilt, a feeling that I have stumbled into some forbidden region" (ibid., p. 61).

8. I am thankful to my students Debbie Ginsburg and Dror Zandberg for collecting part of the data reported here.

9. It is in commentaries such as those of the Maggid (1927: 79), who was one of the Besht's most prominent disciples and who repeatedly used the descent and ascent metaphor, that we can find the source of the popular Hasidic phrase "descent is for the sake of ascent."

10. An "ascent through descent" self-renewal interpretation of the Jewish ritual bath (*mikveh*) can be found in the following source: "The person enters the *mikveh* in order to be included and return the defective soul and limbs to the place from where they came . . . like an embryo which disappears in his mother's womb . . . and when the person comes out of the *mikveh* . . . he is new . . . and will feel a new spirit" (De Vidash 1746: 101b).

11. A classic example illuminating how in Hasidic ethics evening may be turned perceptually into morning is Rabbi Nachman of Bratzlav's famous allegoric parable about the seven beggars, each of whom suffered from a different kind of invalidism but perceived his "lack" as an advantage. For example, the blind beggar insisted that his blindness is in fact an acuity of vision so great that he does not perceive the details of mundane existence and sees everything in perspective of eternity (cited and translated by Steinsaltz 1979: 176).

12. While in Buberian language I would prefer to term the evil *yetzer* a dynamic intrapsychic "it" and not a "non-I," as Frankenstein (1978: 130) indicated. I tend to agree with him that the transformation of the "it" into an inner "thou" should be conceived of as a reconstruction process so that "in therapy everything depends on structural changes, namely, on the reversal of all the experiences, responses and attitudes which have been crystallized throughout one's life, into a structure, by reerecting them on the basis of the original personality."

(14)

Functional Phases in the "Ascent Through Descent" Process

The Functions of "Descent"

MATERIAL DESCENT: DESENSITIZING IMMUNIZATION

While the Puritan socialization ethic is ascetic but material, the Hasidic socialization ethic is nonascetic and amaterial. Set in broader terms, while in Protestant "inner-worldly asceticism," to use Weber's (1967) terminology, any indulging (descent) in physical materialism (e.g., hedonism) is theoretically prohibited and frustrated while actualizing ascent (e.g., accumulation of wealth) is strictly rational-material, in Hasidism limited indulgence in physical-material descent is seen as a constructive immunization device against deviant rational materialism. Thus, although the Sabbatean notion that in order to fulfill the commandment and prescriptive norm of repentance one ought first actually to sin was essentially condemned by Hasidism as heretical (see Piekarz 1978), the idea that some controlled physical-material descent is instrumental for spiritual ascent was for several reasons quite popular in Hasidism, as among other Jewish movements.

First, it was conceived as natural and human to have physical-material passions. Second, passions were viewed essentially as energizing mechanisms; Rabbi Yaacov Yosef stated, "It is good for man to desire all earthly [material] things, and from it he will come to desire studying Torah and worshiping God" (cited in Piekarz 1978: 207). Accordingly, Piekarz suggests that many circles held to the view that "one who does not desire a woman resembles a donkey" (p. 209), and stories similar to the one telling of how the passion of a "street-corner idler" for a princess turned into passion for God (ibid.) were to teach material "ascent through descent" (mitzva habaa beavera). It is remarkable, however, that while Hasidism dealt with problems of material descent in earthly terms, such as indulgence in eating or in sexual passions, the problem of material deviance, as expressed in stealing or cheating, is entirely lacking in Hasidic literature. The immu-

(156)

nizing function of behavioral descent due to temptations of the evil desire (*yetzer hara*) is nonetheless repeatedly accounted for in general terms. For example, the Besht states:

> The evil impulse was given to try us in the way one tests a child, by making it difficult and confusing the simple to divert us . . . and if we are wise and we don't let Him defeat us, then God derives great pleasure, as in the case of the good, diligent son whose father has great pleasure when the guests test him . . . but the son is not defeated. (1975a: 37)

Thus "material descent" manifested in the temptations of the evil impulse is conceived as a desensitizing, immunizing, and strengthening or challenging device to teach man how to anticipate and overcome the obstacles that life entails. Moreover, the Besht interprets even the actual commitment of transgressions as serving good. The verse "There is no righteous man on earth who will do good without sinning [means] that when a person does only good the evil impulse seduces him, whereas when the evil impulse realizes that he has in him a part of the evil inclination, he will leave him alone" (Besht 1975a: 30).

SPIRITUAL DESCENT: RE-ENERGIZING MENTAL REST

I have already mentioned that inherent to the Hasidic conception of life is the notion that man's participation in the cosmic ebb and flow of *ratzo vashov* (running and returning) is expressed in his natural vacillations between mental states of *katnut* (smallness) and *gadlut* (greatness). In doing so I have also stressed that it is not depression per se that Hasidism denied, but its predominance as man's disposition. Thus "depressive evenings" are perceived as functional "rest periods" that precede the ideal and desirable state of "sunny mornings." Accordingly, the Besht states,

> The matter of running and returning is that everything always enthusiastically desires to cleave to its root upward . . . and if it is constantly in ecstasy it would cease to exist. . . . Therefore the Almighty arranged that he [man] will sometimes be engaged in physical needs. . . . During these times the soul rests and his mind will be strengthened to return to the work of God later, and that is: Life is running and returning (*hachayot ratzo vashov*). (1975a: 38)

Smallness and greatness are then interconnected mental states (see *Sefer Habesht* 1975: 64), as the Besht (1975a: 44) states: "To understand what is smallness and what is greatness, when a man studies with no understanding, then he is in smallness, as his mind is incomplete; but when he studies with understanding and enthusiasm, then he is on the level of greatness." Thus during a phase of smallness, a person sees matters from a narrow, pessimistic, and depressed perspective, which causes him to do things "only out of necessity and with great effort, without pleasure" (*Sefer Habesht* 1975: 63), while during the greatness phase he may view the very same matter with optimism, enthusiasm, and broader understanding.

Hence, according to the Besht, the ideal natural state is always to strive and move upward to life ecstasy and "morning," since "everything desires . . . to cleave to its root upward." But since this is impossible because nothing can be in a constant ecstatic state, temporary states of depressive smallness (*katnut*), during which one attends to simple, basic physical needs, are functional phases to be used as reenergizing mental rest periods. To utilize these rest periods of "spiritual descent" functionally, one should never lose control over one's free will and volition, since descent only means self-contraction, not quietistic self-destruction. Thus it is man's responsibility to be alert during such oscillatory phases and heed the human volitionary spark, so that "from this power of smallness he will come to greatness, as in coals: if there is one spark left he will be able to blow and reignite it till there is a big fire as before" (Besht 1975a: 48).

A case in point of how one may ascend from the depressive state of smallness (*katnut*) to the joyful state of greatness (*gadlut*) is Rabbi Nachman of Bratzlav, the Besht's great-grandson, who was known as an archetypal "manic-depressive" (see Piekarz 1972). His disciple-biographer, Rabbi Natan (see *Chaye Moharan* 1952: 85), tells how during one of his infamous depressive states,[1] Rabbi Nachman began

> to teach Torah from the situation of simpleness [depressive "smallness"] . . . which is called *prostik,* and he revived himself [ascended] during this state of simpleness from reliving [the experience] of his trip to the Land of Israel . . . and he explained that he knows nothing now and is now in fear. . . . And then he said that he is happy that he has had the privilege of being in the Land of Israel. . . . And then he was in great joy and reprimanded Rabbi Naftali for being a bit ashamed to play music. . . . And he was then very happy.

From the state of depression (simpleness, smallness) Rabbi Nachman ascended first by acknowledging the state and then by utilizing his spark of volition, by talking about a past joyful experience (his trip to Israel). Finally he succeeded in ascending to a state of *being* joyful, so much so that he began to try and revive others, for example, by urging Rabbi Naftali (who was apparently also feeling low) to play music. Indeed, Rabbi Nachman's teachings are permeated with doctrinal techniques instructing that "from melancholy one should rejoice," and "transform all the bitterness, sighing, and, sorrow and suffering into joy . . . words of nonsense, do funny things and joke around to make oneself happy . . . since melancholy and sadness overpower man more than anything else" (ibid., p.72).

In general, then, depression is viewed as an integral part of a cosmic oscillating rhythm. Hence, rather than resist it, man must utilize it as a resting stage. But when melancholy is dangerously overwhelming, it is within man's power and his responsibility to counteract it, as the Besht (*Sefer Habesht* 1975: 52) states: "When the disease of melancholy due to sadness and asceticism predominates, then one must . . . eat and drink and rejoice and eliminate the above disease . . . and all this must be weighed with the weight of his mind." That is, melancholy does not deterministically control man's mental state or his behavior but, on the contrary, is controllable by his spark of volition, the self, which can be contracted but must never be annihilated or extinguished and thus destroyed.

The Functions of Transformation Procedures

MATERIAL TRANSFORMATION: THE UPLIFTING OF SPARKS

I suggested earlier that even in the case of material anomie, when a person encounters a dialectic crisis or dissonance between his material aspirations (goals) and his material ecology (means and/or opportunities), this anomic dissonance is in a way spiritual (since the meaning one ascribes to material goals is essentially spiritual and cognitive). Put differently, material acquisitions that lack spiritual meaning would probably increase rather than decrease the anomic dissonance. Prior to the emergence of Hasidism in the eighteenth century, the Jewish masses were undoubtedly in a general spiritual and material state of anomie, as they could not actualize themselves either as spiritual Issachars or as material Zebuluns. The Hasidic doctrine of "spark-lifting" (which will be explained below) works counter to material anomie, not by providing increased or improved means or opportunities to reach material success goals, as would follow from the Western counteranomic paradigm (see Merton 1958; Cloward and Ohlin 1960), but by decreasing the valence or value of material success goals and providing a multiple ideal-labeling system. The multiple actualization system of "in all thy ways know Him," which permits the attribution of meaning to any material-earthly activity (means) regardless of its goal-oriented, material-success value, is the essence of the material "spark-lifting" doctrine in Hasidism. Thus let us again briefly trace the sociohistorical meaning of the spark-lifting concept in order to elucidate its corrective significance from the present standpoint.

As stressed earlier (see Chapters 1 and 6), the potential for evil or "seeming" evil is traced by the Hasidic-cabalic doctrine to the primordial "breaking of the vessels" (*shevirah*), in which the good elements, the divine sparks, came to be mixed with the so-called vicious elements, the shells (*kelipot*). The actualizing-salvation process (*tikkun*), which refers to the restoration of the divine order through man's "spark-lifting" behavior, can now be seen in its operational meaning in terms of material transformation.

It is thus man's responsibility to transform and consequently eliminate "seeming" evil through the world-correcting (*tikkun*) process of attributing existential meaning to earthly affairs (*gashmiyut*) that might appear to be mundane (e.g., eating, working, copulating, or rejoicing). Accordingly the Besht stated, "This is a great principle: in everything in the world there are the holy sparks. Nothing is empty of sparks—even trees and stones, even all that a man does, even a sin that a man commits entails sparks . . ." (1975b: 54). Assuming that every event, entity, or experience involves holy sparks that can be redeemed by peeling off the shells (and by raising the sparks up to their divine source), that is, doing whatever one does with the proper sanctifying intention (*kavana*), this cognitive transformation process of correcting can be said to operate as a relabeling process. Indeed, the Maggid (1927: 38) elucidates this transformatory spark-lifting process of *tikkun* (correction), according to which even sins may contain transformable holy sparks, by referring to the Talmudic saying "Through repentance, transgressions become merits" (Talmud, *Yoma* 86:2)—which suggests that repentance entails a relabeling power and helps to desensitize the evil impulse that leads to sinning. Moreover, the Beshtian multiple actualization principle of attributing meaning (*kavana*) to any earthly experience is illustrated in parables such as the one telling, "Once, when the Besht was observed eating excessively, he said, 'My intention in eating is to achieve what Moses achieved in the . . . two tablets of the Ten Commandments' " (Horodetsky 1951, vol. 1, p. 18), which suggests that by using the proper intention any experience may reach the existential actualizing peak that one might assume Moses felt when he brought the Ten Commandments to Israel.

Thus, for the materially inclined person, actualization through the attribution of spiritual meaning (spark-lifting) to earthly activities (*avoda begashmiyut*),[2] which is conceived as a part of the world-correcting process (*tikkun*), mitigates material anomic dissonance by providing a dialectic antithesis to the strain one may encounter in relating to one's material ecology. Accordingly, the Besht stated: "Man is comprised of matter and form . . . and is likewise attracted to materialism, copulation, eating, and drinking, which seems [to respond to] a higher need to select sparks so that spirit may subdue matter." (1975a: 25)

SPIRITUAL TRANSFORMATION: THE UPLIFTING OF ALIEN THOUGHTS

While Weber (1967: 149) predicated his cross-cultural universal theory of the genesis of systematized conduct and social change on the assumption that man's inevitable "physical, psychological and social sufferings of terrestrial life" produce and motivate various forms and processes of secularized salvation patterns, he never discussed possible behavior patterns resulting from *unsuccessful* attempts at salvation. In his role-theory analysis of schizophrenia, Sarbin (1969) posited that normality can actually be conceived as a function of one's relatively successful placement in relation to the different ecologies with which one must interact. Thus, successful placement in the social ecology can be accomplished by providing satisfactory answers to such questions of social identity as "Who am I in relation to other people?" Similarly, successful "placement in the transcendental ecology is achieved through forming acceptable answers to cosmological questions of the form: *What am I in relation to God?*"

Sarbin has further suggested that because only a small part of the cognitive and sensory inputs from the ecological world of occurrence can be matched (given meaning) with our cognitive structure (beliefs, values, knowledge), ambiguous inputs often force people to engage in unconventional cognitive activities in order to reduce the cognitive strain (anxiety) that is caused by the lack of satisfactory cognitive cues (whether one is healthy or sick, loved or hated, etc.). To instantiate stressful occurrences, such as social alienation, somatic illness, death, loss of job, fatal accidents, or other unanswerable inputs that make it difficult for a person to locate himself in any of these ecologies, he will scrutinize his distal and proximal ecologies to find alternative answers and/or he will employ various adaptive techniques to reduce the cognitive strain.

Examples of adaptive techniques usually employed to reduce cognitive strain by changing one's distal ecology are: efforts to change one's belief, knowledge, or value systems, or the use of the "redeployment of attention" technique, in which one distracts attention from the stressful input by concentrating on an alternative act or event. Examples of strain reduction through attempts to change the proximal ecology are: the use of tranquilizers, alcohol, narcotics, sleep, dancing, sex, or other releasing techniques.

Whether a particular adaptive technique may be generally or only privately successful in reducing cognitive strain would depend upon whether or not it has received legitimation from a relevant audience that usually provides negative or positive reinforcements. Thus, Sarbin contends (1969) that in a typical Western social ecology, which provides neither proper answers to stress-producing inputs (especially in relation to one's dissonance with the transcendental ecology) nor the positive social reinforcement for using various adaptive techniques, a large proportion of people who are ultimately labeled and incarcerated as schizophrenics use the attention redeployment technique after "withdrawing" from their disturbing social ecology. In other words, Sarbin claims that there is ample evidence indicating that most people engage, at one time or another, in casual attention redeployment as a means of reducing cognitive strain. In the rational West, however, the only available classification for people who, due to their lack of viable answers to fears arising from nonrational occurrences in their lives functionally redeploy attention to their private fantasy lives, is the ready-made label "mentally ill." If we accept Sarbin's theory, it follows that "schizophrenic attention redeployment" is actually a logical cognitive process that, in face of a lack of proper alternative answers, the absence of a satisfactory belief structure for handling strain-producing metaphysical inputs, and the negative social reinforcement for private or mystical adaptive techniques, is apprehended and rejected as mental illness.

I have indulged in a somewhat lengthy discourse on Sarbin's theory of schizophrenia in order to prepare the ground for suggesting that while Hasidic "uplifting of alien thoughts" may appear to be a naive, spiritual-transformation technique, it in fact entails the components for a "rechanneling of attention" theory that may be instrumental in redirecting thought disorders. In essence, the operational roots of neurosis and repressed guilt feelings, with which modern psychodynamic therapies deal, are thoughts. According to the presumably universal Oedipus complex, for instance, the child represses his forbidden desires or wishful *thoughts* (not real attempts) to copulate with his mother and kill his father. The assumption that people in all societies repress forbidden thoughts and develop neurotic guilt symptoms is challenged, however, by the Beshtian-Hasidic methods for handling "alien thoughts." Indeed, from Boisen's (1952) conclusion in his study of mental patients with problems of mystical identification, for example, it comes through loud and clear that it is only in the West, where social ecologies reinforce the notion that depression and damnation are man's natural states, that disturbed behavior may result from repressed, forbidden, "alien" thoughts. Thus Boisen states: "In most of our cases, the basic evil is . . . personal unworthiness due to the presence of unruly desires . . . which can neither be controlled nor acknowledged for fear of condemnation by the significant persons in one's life. These forbidden desires . . . behave like ill-digested food" (1952:288). In the Hasidic culture, however, alien thoughts are "garments and covers behind which the Holy One . . . conceals Himself" (see Buber 1958a: 204). Moreover, "sometimes an alien thought is sent to him" (see Besht in Buber 1958a: 205). It is thus repeatedly stressed by the Besht that alien thoughts and impulses are not to be repressed or chased away but should be transformed and utilized as positive energizers, mainly by rechanneling these thoughts.

A classic parable often used by the Besht to explain how cognitively to transform (redirect) an alien thought is the following:

> He should watch the thought . . . like adultery, he should bring it to its
> root. . . . He should think: it is part of the world of love. . . . If he

suddenly sees a beautiful woman . . . he shall think from whence does she have this beauty? If she were dead, she wouldn't have this face any more . . . therefore it comes from God's power that spreads within her (1975b: 28–31).

While the Beshtian cognitive method for transforming "alien thoughts" may appear to be a somewhat naive technique that resembles conventional techniques of neutralization and ventilating methods,[3] the notion that disordered thoughts should be redirected to their roots entails more than mere psychological rhetoric. Let us consider the following statement of the Besht:

> It is desirable to think in regard to the matter that I fear or love . . . whence the fear or love come from. It is after all from Him the Blessed One who implanted fear and love even in bad things, such as savage beasts, or from all the fallen traits which fell during the breaking of the vessels, and therefore . . . why should I fear one spark . . . as it is good to reconnect it with the great fear. And so it is with love and with regard to all traits. To elicit from them the spark and uplift it to its root . . . since this is the goal of our soul to uplift the broken [vessels] to its root. (1975b: 45)

The Hasidic-cabalistic doctrine of transforming, correcting (*tikkun*), and rechanneling "alien thoughts" to their divine root obviously represents a religious belief system which, if properly reinforced by a relevant audience (Hasidic community), undoubtedly makes it easier for the individual to place himself in relation to the social and transcendental ecologies. The psychological universal implication for rechanneling disordered thoughts may nonetheless be understood in the following way.

Let me illustrate briefly by again using the clinical case of the young man who redeployed his attention from thoughts about his failing self to his being a Messiah, or the case of an elderly spinster (cited by Sarbin 1967) who, after being deserted by her employers, began to hear voices (deploying attention from her loneliness) that were later identified as belonging to a man she loved thirty years earlier. While we may safely say that these people engaged in attention deployment to reduce their cognitive strain or stress, they were obviously forced to depend on input from their private fantasy world, since the West lacks norms for the functional handling of ambiguous anomic inputs (see Sarbin 1969), using adaptive outputs termed "hallucinations," for example, hearing voices or having "delusions" (being a Messiah). It became apparent from clinical experience, however, that while the rechanneling of the disordered thought to its root (reconnecting that thought to its original input) did not solve anyone's problem, it was more effective in reducing the hopeless feeling generated by conventional diagnosticians who usually label such people as "hallucinating schizophrenics."

Thus, if people are forced to withdraw from their social ecology to engage in what Sarbin (1969) called "silent syllogizing" (to reduce cognitive strain), reinforced by an "autistic audience," they eventually lose sight of the logical root and vital premises of the disordered thought and syllogism. While this is not to suggest that conventional therapists do not attempt to reconnect disordered thoughts to their roots (identify inputs), the dualistic process of diagnosing such people as schizophrenics enhances the "I *or* thou" exclusion process of excommunication called hospitalization. Consequently, the dualistic medical diagnosis of people as "different" from the rest of society may undo and counteract the reconnection of disordered thoughts to their "normal" input.

Spiritual transformation or rechanneling alien thoughts is therefore a reversal of the attention-redeployment process, which by reconnecting the distorted thought to its root may help to attribute new-old logical meaning to silent cognitive processes and may rehumanize behavior that would otherwise usually be diagnosed as hopeless schizophrenia. The notion of rechanneling disordered alien thoughts to provide the proper norms, inputs, belief systems, and positive social reinforcements may therefore comprise the essential components of an affective spiritual transformation phase in the process of "ascent through descent."

The Functions of Ascending Procedures

SPIRITUAL ASCENT: THE INDIVIDUAL DIMENSION OF ADHESION (DEVEKUT)

In contrast to the rational-material West, where there are no institutionalized norms to deal with stress-producing inputs coming from the transcendental ecology, as alluded to earlier, Eastern ecstatic, "ascent" practices such as shamanism is one institutionalized method for controlling and reducing cognitive strain. Shamanism provides the norms, belief system, and social, legitimation (positive reinforcements) for periodic, volitional, "ecstatic-manic" detachment from reality, which enables the shaman to reconcile stressful social and transcendental inputs (see Eliade 1964).

The function of ecstatic-ascension procedures is thus to reach the desirable state of manic joy and elation, while the transformation procedures described above refer to techniques of attributing meaning to mundane activities and states that would not lead to a sense of elation without recourse to cognitive rechanneling procedures. The cabalistic-Hasidic "ascent" practice of ecstatic *devekut* (usually termed *unio mystica*), meaning adhesion, attachment, and devoutness (see Scholem 1972: 203), has been known to Jewish mystics since the thirteenth century and is essentially "neither an exclusively Hasidic concept nor a novel invention of the Baal Shem [the Besht]." Like other ecstatic practices of meditation, Hasidic adhesion (*devekut*) is basically an individualistic salvation method to build around contemplating (possibly constantly), or rather visualizing, the name of God (which may be conceived as a religious mantra). A vivid description of this practice preserved from the thirteenth century may provide the best illustration. Scholem (1972: 207) states that this technique required about nine hours daily:

> For the spiritual activities of retreat and *devekut* [they] used to imagine the light of the *Shekhinah* [God] above their heads, as though it were flowing all around them and they were sitting in the midst of the light. . . . And while in that [state of meditation], they are all trembling as a natural effect, but [spiritually] rejoicing in trembling.

In one of the famous legends about the Besht (compiled in the collection *In Praise of the Baal Shem Tov*, see Ben-Amos and Mintz 1972: 50), there are about five versions of how the Besht trembled during prayers. In one a Hasid described the Besht's face during prayers as follows: "He saw that it was burning like a torch. The Besht's eyes were bulging and fixed straight ahead like those of someone dying, God forbid." According to another version, the Maggid attested that "when the Besht was inspired . . . he was not in this world. When the Besht put on his *kittel* (coat) it was wrinkled around his shoulders. The Great Maggid grasped the *kittel* in order to straighten it, and when he touched the Besht he himself began to tremble. He held the table that was there and the table began to tremble with him as well."

From these descriptions we may learn that Hasidic *devekut* involved what may be termed "temporary detachment from reality" (functional psychosis) derived from the notion of *iyun* (abnegation of self), as the Besht's classic statement (1975b: 17) asserts: "He should put himself as one who is not, as stated in the Talmud, and wisdom will be found from nothing (*ayin*), which means that he should think as if he is not in this world." It appears on the surface that the Besht taught his disciples the quietistic practice for reducing cognitive strain through temporary and controlled "psychotic detachment" from reality, which did not essentially differ from other ecstatic methods of quietistic self-annihilation. Scholem (1972), Weiss (1977), and others suggest, however, that while Eastern, Christian, and other ecstatic practices are usually "other-world-oriented" methods geared to isolate, separate, and drain the self of this world's content and society, Hasidic monistic doctrines of *devekut* became an active, "this-world-oriented" method that everyone can perform by contemplating faith (*emunah*) and the attribution of meaning or sanctifying intention (*kavana*) during normal social intercourse and everyday activities.

I shall not burden the reader with the many details and forms that comprise this spiritual method of ascent and epitomized Hasidic physiognomy. But I argue that although Hasidic adhesion is essentially an individualistic technique of spiritual ascent, its unique monistic meaning can be understood only by considering *devekut* in conjunction with its complementary social-material imperative of ecstatic *joy*. While Eastern ecstatic meditation seems functional in reducing the cognitive dissonance created by unexplainable, incomprehensible social or transcendental inputs, the conception that depression and suffering predominate in life still seems to underline these perspectives. Herman Hesse (1957: 13), for example, in his classic novel *Siddhartha*, provides a vivid description of how depressive suffering underlies the Eastern conception of life and salvation: "What is meditation? What is abandonment of the body? What is fasting? What is holding of breath? It is a flight from the Self, it is a temporary escape from the torment of Self. It is a temporary palliative against the pain and folly of life."

According to the "ascent through descent" conception, however, the descending phase of depressive *katnut* (smallness) is seen as a functional and preparatory stage in the process of steady ebb and flow that leads one toward an ascending phase of manic joyful greatness (*gadlut*). Illuminative of this "ascent through descent" *Weltanschauung* is Scholem's statement "There is a steady flow of life, up and down, and no state is void of its manifestation. There can be a modest form of *devekut* even in the minor state (*katnut*). It is limited, and without that exuberance and exhilaration that comes to man only when joy sweeps him off *katnut*" (1972:220).

Again juxtaposing the Hasidic meditation method of *devekut* with Hesse's (1957: 12) account of the Eastern "suffering-oriented" salvation practice, the difference between these philosophies becomes even more blatant. "Siddhartha learned many ways of losing the Self. He travelled along the path of self-denial through pain, through voluntary suffering . . . through hunger, thirst and fatigue. . . ." But individual spiritual adhesion combined with social-material joy (to be described later) constitutes the predominating ascending phase in the steady up-and-down flow of life that everyone must strive to achieve by using his will and "world correcting" (*tikkun*) obligation to "uplift sparks" and ignite first and foremost his own spark of joy and life.

While at this point the reader may notice that the uniqueness of the *devekut* method may be attributed to what is termed elsewhere (Rotenberg 1978) the reciprocal individualistic dimension, which differentiates it from other isolating "alienating individualistic" meditation practices, reciprocal individualization should be distinguished from what Jung (see Jacobi 1976) would term individuation. Reciprocal individualization or rather "individu-realization," which accentuates how volitional self-contraction and expansion is suited to each individual, can best be understood by examining the concept of "rung."

INDIVIDUATION AND THE CONCEPT OF "RUNG"

The notion that Hasidic "ascension" concurs with the principle of self-contraction, which forbids abandonment of the self and free will, follows directly from our reciprocal-individualistic conviction that each person dwells on his own "rung" of existence from where he may ascend to the highest level of his unique, self-realization potential. Concomitant with the multiple actualization principle of "in all thy ways know Him," descent should not culminate in reascending to the same level from where one began to descend but rather, according to the contracting "spring" metaphor mentioned earlier,[4] each person should strive to ascend to a higher or the highest possible rung on the ladder.

Thus the Besht (1975a: 10) asserts, "And running and returning (*ratzo vashov*) is because everything is eager to return to its root. . . . Then the soul rests from its enthusiasm and is strengthened to return to even higher adhesion." Similarly, the Maggid, who differentiated between individual reasons for descent and collective-cosmic descent, which causes the individual to fall or step down from his rung, insists that "in both cases the descent is for the sake of an even higher ascent" (see Scholem 1972: 222). The actualizing-therapeutic "spring" conception of descending for the sake of higher ascension also concurs with Scholem's (1972) Jewish "utopian" category of messianism (mentioned earlier) in which redemption consists of the reconstruction of a past plus a completely new and better future, in contrast to "restorative messianism" (e.g., the Christian), which refers only to the reconstruction of the past.

Adhesion (*devekut*) in terms of ascending on one's own ladder of rungs toward manic joy as the predominant state in life is clearly expressed by Rabbi Yaacov Yosef, who asserts that "the reason why man doe not stay on one rung is because permanent pleasure is no pleasure. Therefore he sometimes descends, so that if later he will ascend there will be more pleasure" (cited in Steineman 1957: 83). Thus real ecstatic ascent requires periodic temporary descent. The "rung" conception of joyful, spiritual ascent suggests, however, that ascent receives its full operational meaning not when spiritual adhesion is practiced individually as an act of solitary retreat, but when it is conceived together with ecstatic communal *social* joy.[5] Indeed, Yaacov Yosef (cited in Dresner 1960: 169) states that "there are different rungs for each man according to his nature and his faith, and no man must feel that he cannot serve on his rung, for from the very rung upon which he is located, he should join himself to the world of many rungs, all of which are the limbs of the community of Israel. From there he should pray and God will be with him and raise him." Accordingly, spiritual-ecstatic ascent combined with communal social-material joyful ascent—to join "the world of many rungs, all of which are the limbs of the community"—constitutes the epitome of the "ascent through descent" model to which our final discussion of that model will be addressed.

MATERIAL ASCENT: THE SOCIAL DIMENSION OF JOY

If indeed the Hasidic practice of individualistic, ecstatic adhesion (*devekut*), used to facilitate the reduction and control of cognitive dissonance between man and his transcendental ecology, essentially resembles other ecstatic-mystic methods (notably Eastern), the underlying and guiding Hasidic conception of life as an alter-centered (social-oriented) existence of joy, not suffering, seems to differ radically from other essentially ego-centered ecstatic methods emanating from relatively more pessimistic conceptions of man. True, Scholem (1941: 330) contends that two actualizing-salvation patterns can be distinguished in Hasidism: "The individualistic . . . salvation of the soul, and the second the truly messianic redemption which is, of course, a phenomenon concerning the whole body of the community." But while this reading might misleadingly suggest that Hasidic mystical practices are not a social phenomenon, Scholem admits elsewhere (1972: 1) that "Judaism in all its forms and manifestations has always maintained a concept of redemption as an event which takes place publicly . . . and within the community." Hence, the uniqueness of the Hasidic doctrine of "ascent through descent" must be understood from its messianic-utopian and social orientation. Actualizing salvation therefore refers to the intertwined practice of individual and social adhesion that pervades life, not by emptying (i.e., annihilating) and separating the self from life's suffering and society, but by constantly contracting the self and descending to the material-earthly existence in order to reemerge from it and ascend to ever higher levels of spiritual existence.

The conception of manic joy as the predominant and desirable state in life, to be reached through combining both social-material joy and individual-spiritual meditation is clearly reflected in the simple fact that both these methods were presented as prescriptive techniques to be used for reaching the state of ascending adhesion. Indeed, Shochat (1951: 13), who suggested that the *social* form of the Hasidic joy imperative essentially constitutes the main innovative contribution of Beshtian Hasidism (as compared to early Hasidism), cited Rabbi Yaacov Yosef, who stressed that ecstatic adhesion is in fact impossible without the interpenetrating impact of social-material joy on individual-spiritual contemplation, because "through the body's joy it causes the soul to rejoice in its cleavage to God." Thus Yaacov Yosef's (1963: 451) parable about the prince who overcame his sadness by providing drinks for the masses, who essentially infected him with their joy, became a motif in Hasidic literature illuminating the dynamics of mutual contagion. Here Yaacov Yosef alludes to the vital relationship between matter and spirit, which seems necessary for ascending adhesion and the consequent difficulty that either materially or spiritually inclined people have in reaching adhesion without the mutually contagious impact of these two on each other. As he states (Shochat 1951:13), "it is impossible for the soul to rejoice in the spiritual until matter rejoices in the material [earthly]." Hence, cleaving and ecstatic adhesion takes on the concrete dimension of social cleavage (*devekut*). Accordingly, Yaacov Yosef (1963: 451) goes on to state: "The generality resembles the individuality in this respect, since those material people cleave in unification to the *zaddikim* who are the spiritual people, only that spiritual people are ashamed to rejoice. . . . Therefore it is necessary to make the material people happy, whether with food or with music, so that there will be place for the spiritual people to rejoice in adhesion."

The level of ecstasy in terms of the behavior engendered by such joyful social activities as singing, drinking, and dancing is described in the following legend about the Besht (see *Shivchey Habesht*, Ben Amos and Mintz 1972: 80):

> Once on Simhat Torah [the festival of Rejoicing with the Torah], the followers of the Besht were happy, dancing and drinking a lot of wine from the Besht's cellar. The Besht's pious wife . . . entered his room and said to him: "Tell them to stop drinking and dancing, since you will not have any wine left over for the *kiddush* and *havdalah*" [Sabbath rituals which require drinking some wine]. The Besht said to her jokingly: "Well said. Go and tell them to stop." When she opened the door, however, and saw that they were dancing in a circle and that flames of fire were burning around them like a canopy, she herself took the jugs . . . and brought them as much wine as they wanted.

Another parable illustrating the dynamic features of social adhesion, cited in the name of the Besht (see Geshury 1956: 32), tells about a king who, after no longer feeling elation during the daily concert given by his favorite violinist, decided to invite a new audience every day to revive the music and even more to revive the musician. Finally, after he found it too difficult to produce a new audience daily, he blindfolded the violinist and told him that there were new listeners present, so that his music would be addressed to the fictitious audience that had presumably never heard his wonderful music before. Implicit here is the Hasidic principle that ascent and social-personal growth are bilateral, in the sense that not only does the father or God influence the son but man influences heaven, the son influences the father, and it is the audience that must constantly reawaken the soul's music in order that the soul (violinist) may reciprocate and revive the people. Elsewhere (Rotenberg 1978: 198) I have termed this dynamic principle of reaching ecstatic ascent through socially oriented contractional descent the "feather blanket" principle for producing reenergizing joy. Let me reformulate briefly this interactive principle of social-ecstatic joy, in the present "spiritual-material" terms.

THE "FEATHER BLANKET" DYNAMICS OF SOCIAL JOY

The reflective interdependence between spiritual singing and dancing and the material body can be compared to the effect of a feather blanket on the human body. When a person feels very cold and covers himself with a feather blanket, his body must first warm up the blanket slightly; only afterward does the blanket in return produce increasing warmth. To feel real spiritual joy, capable of counteracting melancholic sadness, the singing and dancing of people striving to ascend together must often begin on a mechanical-material level in order to "warm up" the melody and the dance, and only thereafter can the ascending song and dance reproduce the spiritual joy. Yet, concurrent with the contraction principle, the Besht (1975a: 48) states that the bellows can inflame the fire only "if there is one spark left with which to reinflame the big fire," so the coals of the melody (the free will) should never be entirely cold. In other words, it is neither extreme self-insulating individualism nor extreme collectivism, in both of which, according to Buber (1967), people run away from themselves and their personal responsibility—once *from* the crowd and once *into* the crowd—but rather the "I and thou" reciprocal individualism (see Rotenberg 1978) where people never lose their individualistic spark of volition but contract themselves to make space for others that facilitates mutual reciprocal reenergization. Indeed, the periodic social gatherings among contemporary Hasidic groups, during which the Hasidim sing and dance together, or the *"hora"* dances in *kibbutzim* seem to function as a reciprocal-individualistic medium during which the interaction between the material and the spiritual, operates as an antimelancholic bellows. Hence, drinking and dancing are perceived not as hedonistic ends but as material acts of the "bellows" necessary to nourish the spirit. Man's earthly material activity is accordingly conceived as an integral part of the cosmological rhythm (*ratzo vashov*) necessary for the world's renewal and reproduction of positive (spiritual) energy in order that people may ascend higher and higher, not as a mob and not as hermits but in reciprocity, each one on his own ladder of rungs. Compelling descriptions of how the "feather blanket," joy-producing principle was activated as a social-material and anti melancholic device to ascend spiritually are ample. Thus during the High Holidays, which are days of repentance for past sins, when people might fall into gloomy retrospective thoughts, it was precisely the social-material dancing, singing, and drinking that was used to ascend spiritually, as Horodetsky (1951: vol. 4, p. 83) reports:

Even during the High Holidays they [the Hasidim] would periodically dance in a circle, which included everybody, and they would sing and play special melodies and the *zaddik* would also take part in the dance. . . . This moment they would rise above reality, forget everything, dancing and singing for long hours and not feeling fatigue. During intermissions they would drink a little alcohol and tell holy stories and then return to dance.

Material Deviance and "Prospective Therapy"

So far I have shown how the need to control transcendental inputs is met by the Hasidic practice of social-material joy and/or by the individual technique of ecstatic meditation. Although I have alluded to the interdependence between matter and spirit, I have not discussed the social-material joy-oriented ascending pattern in relation to material deviance per se or the individual-spiritual ascending technique in relation to spiritual deviance, because ascent, as suggested earlier, is essentially a spiritual process of attributing meaning to both material and spiritual experiences. It is true that preserving the analytical consistency of the spirit-matter conceptualization in regard to the "ascent through descent" model required some theoretical "arm-twisting," despite the general distinction, because the Hasidic ethical system is not built to allow for a neat sequential differentiation between various material and spiritual behavior patterns.

In concluding my discussion of ascending procedures in terms of social-material joy, however, I should mention that there is ample evidence that according to Hasidic ethics, material ascent (drinking, dancing, working, social joy) is indeed prescribed mainly to combat material deviance, as it is anchored in what I termed the "prospective therapy" perspective (Rotenberg 1978). I have shown that in contrast to the personal-history-based, past-oriented despair and self-torture that accompanied Christian restorative-introspective conversion methods and is featured in contemporary psychodynamic "retrospective therapy," self-torture over past material deviance (actual sinning) is strictly prohibited in Hasidic culture. I have thus cited Schatz-Uffenheimer (1968), who points out that the three major imperatives prerequisite for the Hasidic life-style are the prohibitions against despair, dejection, and regret. As Schatz-Uffenheimer indicated, retrospective self-examination involves the ego-centric weighing of sins against merits, which prevents one from the prospective-active worship of God so that paradoxically in Hasidism past-oriented sadness, doubt, and despair are considered to be the worst transgressions, that is, retrospective self-torture stands in diametric opposition to two Hasidic principles. Such behavior concentrates on man's egoistic attempts to save his own soul instead of redeeming the holy sparks of the total community, and it casts doubt on man's ability to affect his future and change himself. Buber (1958a: 164–165) cites the Rabbi of Ger, who warned against past-oriented self-torture:

He who has done ill and talks about it and thinks about it all the time does not cast the base thing out of his thoughts . . . and so he dwells in baseness. He will certainly not be able to turn . . . and in addition to this he may be overcome by gloom. . . . Rake the muck this way, rake the muck that way—it will always be muck. Have I sinned, or have I not sinned? . . . In the time I am brooding over it, I could be stringing pearls for the delight of Heaven.

As far as future-oriented change is concerned, "turning" or repentance (*teshuva*) requires nothing more than an instantaneous *future*-oriented cognitive decision to change (see Schatz-Uffenheimer 1968), and concurrent with Scholem's "utopian therapeutic" perspective, the Talmud (*Berachot* 34:2) states that "in the place where *baaley teshuva* (repenters) stand the fully righteous do not stand," because the former may ascend higher than the latter.

The point here is that joy, in terms of the future-oriented, antisadness prospective therapy, may logically refer mainly to material deviance, in terms of past sins per se more than to depression and melancholy, because it is in the nature of man to *be depressed* over past material sins, not over *past depression*. Although this is not to suggest that past material and spiritual deviance may not eventually interact or that the social-material joy-oriented "ascent" perspective is more effective than other correctional or therapeutic methods for the combating of material deviance, it does imply that the future-oriented "prospective" approach appears to be more instrumental in preventing the irreversible retrospective-labeling effect that prevents rehabilitation of material deviants in the West (see Lofland 1969). Indeed, to prevent the process of the negative self-fulfilling prophecy (Merton 1958), which might culminate in derogatory self-labeling (see Rotenberg 1978) if one overindulges in retrospective self-torture, the Besht's (1975a: 14) prescriptive norm instructs:

Even if he stumbled into sin, he should not be overly sad because such feelings of sadness or regret for past sins are temptations of the evil impulse. Sometimes the evil inclination will mislead a man by telling him that he committed a great sin. . . . In this case the evil impulse simply wishes to sadden him. . . . One must be careful to detect this deceit and say . . . if in truth it was a sin, then God will have more joy on my account if I pay it no heed and refuse to be saddened by my transgression.

Social joy may therefore be conceived in terms of material activities geared to counteract the detrimental consequences resulting from past material deviance. Ascent, as pointed out earlier, is nonetheless meaningless unless it is accompanied by the cognitive process of attributing meaning; hence any ascending procedure, while being relatively material, must in the final analysis be understood in a spiritual relabeling sense.

The "Ascent Through Descent" Model: Concluding Remarks

The "ascent through descent" model has presented as a general theoretical perspective for a functional, dynamic, socio-personality theory and not as an action strategy outlining therapeutic techniques. It thus contrasted the elitist and dualistic functional approach to deviance with the monistic perspective, in which deviance per se may be perceived functionally. Moreover, the "ascent through descent" model constitutes the psychological perspective of our monistic, sociopsychological paradigm in which self-contraction is conceived as an intrapersonal process.

This dynamic perspective conceives of the world in terms of the cosmic-human ebb and flow described above, in contrast to actualization doctrines and psychotherapeutic theories positing life as a deterministic existence of suffering and depression. Volitionary self-contraction and expansion conceives of manic optimism as the predominant and desirable state in life. This monistic approach to life also assumes that, in a Kantian sense, the very socialization process that legitimizes "manic needs" and inseminates "manic joy" as the predominant ideal state in life may change the individual or collective reality, as Beshtian Hasidism has demonstrated since the eighteenth century. The cyclic "ascent through descent" model should therefore be understood not as a denial of depression but as a perspective that is careful to differentiate between "manic depression" and "depressive mania." Hence "weeping may endure for an evening but singing cometh in the morning" (Ps. 30:6), and it is thus the sunny "morning" succeeding the gloomy "evening," and not the reverse, that facilitates living through the dark night of dialectic questioning. Consequently it is intuition and faith that imbue us with the strength to climb on the giant shoulders of logical rationalism in order to see the steps of the redeeming Messiah through the clouds of catastrophe. Likewise, it is the paradoxical, monistic conception of deviant descent that supports the ladder on which we may ascend and grow, and it is to this notion of paradox that the Epilogue will be devoted.

NOTES

1. During the last phase of his life, Rabbi Nachman went to live with an "enlightened" (and nonreligious) Jew in the town of Uman, presumably in order to fulfill the Hasidic dictum requiring the *zaddik* to descend in order to uplift others. In this period he was often depressed, perhaps because by this point he was already declining (see Piekarz 1972).

2. It is worth mentioning here that the labor ideology (mainly in regard to agriculture) preached by A.D. Gordon (1951) in early twentieth-century Palestine contained many of the Hasidic "spark-lifting" connotations of attributing actualizing meaning to earthly work through enthusiasm and sanctification. Indeed, Gordon's frequent use of Hasidic-cabalistic terms such as ascent and descent have led Schweid (1979) to identify Hasidic-cabalistic influence on his thought. It should be stressed, however, that Gordon's negative use of the term "contraction" as an egoistic act of withdrawal and isolation from the world, distorts the original positive meaning of a voluntary process of evacuating space for others.

3. Not all Hasidic groups adhere to this Beshtian principle. According to rational philosophy, advanced by the Hasidic branch known under the name *Chabad*, alien thoughts should be expelled, i.e., repressed (see Shneurson 1956). It thus remains a good empirical question whether neurotic guilt feelings are comparatively lower among Hasidic groups that follow the Beshtian doctrine for uplifting alien thoughts.

4. Rabbi Menachem Mendel of Premishlen (cited by Elstein 1980: 57) uses the image of a crane to explain the dynamics of "ascent through descent": "Since from the power of descent . . . he will ascend to a very high place . . . like a person who wants to throw a stone lowers his hand with the stone in it, in order to throw it up to a high place."

5. Here the ecstatic communal activities of Rabbi Carlibach (known as "the dancing rabbi") among social dropouts may be a case in point.

Epilogue:

The Philosophical Perspective

Albert Camus (1955):

The absurd man thus catches sight of a burning and frigid, transparent and limited universe in which nothing is possible but everything is given, and beyond which all is collapse and nothingness.

Rabbi Nachman of Bratzlav (1772–1810):

That is the way it ought to be . . . that there should be questions kushyot concerning the Almighty. The essence of work and free choice is that one remains always in doubt (question).

(15)

Toward a Philosophical Sociology of Paradox

A popular Hasidic story tells about a young man whose occupation was to stand on the hill near his town in order to be able to see the Messiah approaching from afar and announce his coming, so that the people of the town would have sufficient time to prepare for his reception. When asked what kind of a job that is for a nice Jewish boy, he was said to have replied that indeed it was not such a remarkable job, but at least it was a steady one. The very fact that this story is so popular in Jewish circles seems to reflect the deeply entrenched monistic belief that it is in fact the constant, steady waiting and hoping for the Messiah that constitutes life. Life means yearning and living with unceasing hope and faith through the dark questioning night between blurred depressive states of evening (*erev-ta'arovet*) and joyful clear phases of morning (*boker-bikoret*) when things get under control again. Thus, life is neither "evening" nor "morning" but the question state in between; the ability and will to strive, hope, and see the light of the sun but not be blinded by it; the ability to force the sun to shine by uplifting the "world correcting" spark and create light in the dark; the ability of the son to force the father to contract and interact. Life as a dialectic "hypothesis" or "question" between the antithetic "evening" and the synthetic "morning," between seeming evil and good, between realism and idealism, means living in a paradox and with contradictions in which both evening and morning coexist by the power of mutual contraction and man learns to see the reliable, oscillating cosmic rhythmic wisdom that forces the evening moon to contract itself more in relation to the bright morning sun. "And God made the two great lights: the greater light to rule the day, the lesser light to rule the night" (*Gen.* 1:16, see esp. Rashi's commentary). "Thinking is learning all over again how to see," argued Camus (1955: 32). Creative thinking would therefore refer to the ability to see new compositions in old given elements, to envision how the sunny morning emerges from the dark evening without having to eliminate either one of the conditions. In this epilogue I shall attempt to argue that it is neither from the dualistic either/or perspective characterizing the existentialist sociology of the absurd nor within the functional-conflict approach to deviance but only within the monistic paradox emanating from the social-contraction principle that deviance, in terms of the "ascent through descent" model, may be functional for the deviant himself.

Dualism and the Either/Or Dilemma

Either/or was the anti-Hegelian phrase coined by Kierkegaard (see Bretall 1946: 19) to express the impossibility of preserving contradictory ideas of "thesis" and "antithesis" to be included in a new "synthesis." Exclaimed Kierkegaard, "Either/or is the pass which admits to the absolute . . . either/ or is the key to heaven . . . and is the way to hell. . . . Will you, said Mercury, have youth, or beauty, or power, or a long life, or the most beautiful maiden, or any of the other glories we have in the chest? Choose, but only one thing." Kierkegaard then concluded, "The only absolute either/or is the choice between good and evil, but that is also absolutely ethical." Indeed, even a "humanistic" Western thinker such as Erich Fromm (1980: 119) seemed to have disregarded the function of human regression for the sake of progress, because he saw only two absolute either/ or ethical-social possibilities:

> Man can choose only between two possibilities: to regress or to move forward. He can either return to an archaic pathogenic solution or he can progress toward, and develop, his humanity. We find this formulation of this alternative . . . as the alternative between light and darkness . . . between blessing and curse, life and death.

Hence, according to Fromm, for Western man "ascent through descent" and living in contradiction[1] between "evening" and "morning" is impossible, because "this conflict in itself requires a solution, and basically there are only the regressive or the progressive solutions" (ibid.). This either/or dilemma in fact comprises the essential difference between dualistic functionalism and the monistic functional conception of deviance, which I discussed earlier. Let us now consider how the possibility of deviance ("evening"), which I claim may be functional for the deviant himself, is treated by the existential sociology of the absurd.

The Absurd and the Either/Or Dualism

In his "to be or not to be" treatise of the absurd, Camus deals with the either/or question of desperate suicide versus nihilistic living in a meaningless world: "Living under that stifling sky forces one to get away or to stay. . . . This is how I define the problem of suicide and the possible interest in the conclusions of existential philosophy" (1955: 22). His verdict against suicide (p. 44) calls for a vote in praise of hedonistic existence, not because it envisions the possibility of creative-intuitive hope emanating from living in paradox within the hypothetical question state between the "evening" and the "morning" but precisely because there is absolutely no hope, no future, no cosmic-rhythmic wisdom:

> The absurd man thus catches sight of a burning and frigid transparent and limited universe in which nothing is possible but everything is given, and beyond which all is collapse and nothingness. He can then decide to accept such a universe and draw from it his strength, his refusal to hope, and the unyielding evidence of a life without consolation. But what does life mean in such a universe? . . . Indifference to the future and a desire to use up everything that is given.

In his critical account of the absurd, Hinchliffe (1977: 29) argues that similar to Camus' perception of the world as being meaningless, Sartre's pessimistic novel *Nausea*, for example, expresses a similar recognition of our being as living creatures in a senseless world of nothingness. Thus Sartre's hero in *Nausea*, Roquentin, who cut himself off from society, insists that "we must if we are sincere, feel, when we look at the world, nausea, a sense of the absurd" (ibid.). For the absurd man there is *either* death, meaninglessness, and a world of nothingness *or* a nihilistic, ego-centered here-and-now existence in face of a hopeless future. But while Camus and Sartre sometimes struggle with the monistic possibility of living within the questioning paradoxical state between "evening" and "morning," in the sense that "living is keeping the absurd alive" (see Camus 1955: 40), the so-called new sociology of the absurd seems to present an absolutely dualistic *either* life *or* death position.

Thus Lyman and Scott (1970: 1) state unequivocally that "the Sociology of the Absurd . . . captures the fundamental assumption of this new wave: The world is essentially without meaning"; hence not manic mornings but depressive evenings, "alienation and insecurity are fundamental conditions of life." Moreover, while on the face of it sociologists of the absurd construct a volitionary monistic "ascent through descent social-contraction" model (striving for meaning in a meaningless world), they in fact present a dualistic, quietistic, and social-gap oriented either/or paradigm. Let me explain. It is probably not too surprising, but nonetheless self-defeating from the humanistic-existential point of view, which these "absurdists" claim to represent, that ego-centered social-class dualists such as Machiavelli and John Calvin are chosen and presented by them as the ideological ancestors of "the sociology of the absurd." Lyman and Scott (1970: 17) state: "Machiavelli, we believe, is the father of the Sociology of the Absurd because of his insistence on the essential meaninglessness of the world and his perception of how most men impute a meaning to their illusions." Similarly, they claim that according to Max Weber "the Calvinist conception of life and afterlife revealed a God who ruled the universe arbitrarily. . . . Calvinists responded to this not by resignation . . . but rather by an intensive search for signs of their election or damnation. . . . Weber thus suggested that when the world reveals its meaninglessness, the men who discover this plunge into a course of action."

True, both Machiavelli and Calvin saw man as an actor, yet not as a monistic I *and* thou performer but as an I *or* thou dualist who finds meaning in his egoistic achievements by oppressing others, whether through the Calvinist competitive process of defining his election by damnifying and stepping on others or through the Machiavellian, egoistic, violent, and subtle techniques of deceiving, manipulating, and striking fortune, as Lyman and Scott (1970: 13) proudly cite Machiavelli, their modeling master: "Fortune is a woman, and if you wish to master her, you must strike and beat her, and you will see that she allows herself to be more easily vanquished by the rash and the violent than by those who proceed more slowly and coldly." In short, the absurd man is a hedonistic, aggressive Hobbesian wolf who strives for meaning through the dualistic process of survival of the fittest by cunning, deception, and oppressing others. The absurd man believes that he can attribute meaning to his life in a senseless world, but one may wonder how meaningful his life would be without his ability to rely on the regularity of the cosmic wisdom that provides him with daily sunlight, seasonal rain, and natural food.[2]

Absurd on a psychological level may be examined in terms of its either/ or life-or-death or rather death-and-rebirth orientation. The dilemma here is whether striving for meaning is seen as a voluntary oscillating "ascent through descent" process in which both "evening descent" and "morning ascent" may coexist to facilitate a dynamic volitionary striving upward through the question state of "night" or whether striving upward is conceived as a deterministic rebirth process through the total annihilation of the will and the self by plunging into sin, profanity, or self-destructive nonbeing. While Jung takes general cognizance concerning the functional dynamics of regression for the sake of progression, and it would hence require more than a comment to determine whether his "shadow" conception refers to a predestinal given that man must learn to accept as part of his preordained damnation or whether he may learn to transform the "shadow" creatively, in relation to the death-rebirth process Jung nevertheless states that "the reality of evil and its incompatibility with good . . . leads to the crucification and suspension of everything that lives . . . . We all have to be crucified with Christ" (cited in Edinger, 1974: 152). Jung's crucification ordeal is thus conceived as a dualistic either good or evil dilemma according to which salvation is not a volitionary "ascent through descent" process but a deterministic death (crucification) and rebirth experience in which we accept our predestined damned "shadow" as a static given.

Shoham's (1979: 11) existential psychology of the absurd likewise discusses the dynamics of ascent through descent. It is nevertheless probably not accidental that his case studies are taken from Jacob Frank's antinomian nihilistic movement and "Saint" Jean Genet's "rebirth" from the gutters-womb of crime and blasphemy. Shoham's conception of cabalistic ascent (and descent?) is described as a self-annihilating pantheistic process whereby man reaches the state of nonbeing: "Our participation, per contra, is a tumultuous struggle up stream to reach the promised land of non-being." Accordingly, ascent is accomplished through a process of descent into the absolute state of nothingness and baseness, because "if purity and holiness were scattered in all directions by the breaking of the vessels, some of these fragments of sacred goodness would be stranded in dirt, impurities, and squalor. One must descend and dive in the mud to collect these shining gems. One must wallow in profanity and sin to retrieve the holy particles that have been lost therein" (ibid., p. 13). While Shoham may indeed present or represent a conventional interpretation of a quietistic or existential "psychology of the absurd," one may well wonder how the existential, voluntary, actualizing attribution of meaning can be exercised by a "nonbeing"[3] who through the quietistic regressus ad uterum is left only with the choice between death and nihilation (i.e., self-destruction) or a hedonistic life and nihilism (i.e., world destruction).

Thus absurd, on a sociological level, stands for a Machiavellian, dualistic, either/or, survival-of-the-fittest manipulation, and on a psychological level it implies either death and total self-annihilation (of the will) in a meaningless world or a deterministic rebirth of uncontrolled hedonism.

The Paradox and Functional Monism

The Random House Unabridged Dictionary defines "absurd" as "ridiculously senseless, illogical or untrue; contrary to all reason or common sense and laughably foolish or false." Conflict is defined as "collision," "disagreement," "opposition," or "a battle or struggle," and "paradox" is defined as "a statement or proposition seemingly self-contradictory or absurd but in reality expressing a possible truth." Heretofore we have been dealing with schools of thought. I shall now attempt to outline the socio-sophical components of the concept of paradox. While by definition, absurd stands for ridiculous senselessness and untruth, and conflict implies a dialectic collision between two opposites that may be resolved by a battle or struggle, culminating in a new synthesis that swallows the previous thesis and antithesis, the paradox facilitates the coexistence of seemingly opposite positions interconnected by an inner truth. The paradox accordingly stands for the hypothetical state between thesis and antithesis, which may thus functionally combine good and evil, sternness (midat hadin) and compassion (midat harachamim), deviance and conformity, rationality and irrationality, physics and metaphysics, the natural and the supernatural, or depressive evenings and manic mornings and other contrasting elements without eradicating either position or element.

Living in paradox thus positively defined should be distinguished from Paul Tillich's (1965: 176) existential "negative paradox," in which "the hidden pleasure produced by despair witnesses to the paradoxical character of self-negation. The negative lives from the positive it negates." According to this negative formulation of the paradox, "accepting meaninglessness is in itself a meaningful act." And the "meaning of life is reduced to despair about the meaning of life" (ibid., p. 175), which must inevitably lead either to suicide or to the absurd hedonistic "psychopathization" of damnation by "accepting oneself as accepted in spite of being unacceptable" (p. 164).

Living in contradiction and paradox also differentiates between the Hegelian-Marxist either/or dialectic conflict, according to which the synthesis swallows the thesis and the antithesis, and the Buberian monistic dialogue, in which life emanates from the creative sphere in between the coexisting, mutually contracting I and thou, which embrace but do not eliminate each other (see Bergman 1974a). Let us now examine the functional meaning of life as a hypothesis or of living in contradiction and paradox between coexisting polar elements that are not remolded through an either/or battle into a new synthetical state.

As suggested earlier, the difference between idolatry and monotheism may be portrayed as the difference between worshiping the concrete rational material "known" (be it wooden or iron idols, science, or people) and the worshiping of the transcendental, supernatural "unknown" God (whom man worships due to the reality of the irrational, "unreal," and unanswerable). According to Weiss (1974: 138), Rabbi Nachman of Bratzlav's theology is based precisely on this "paradoxical faith: [because] there is no faith but where there is doubt, namely the question (kushya)." Indeed, Rabbi Nachman states that "in what the mind understands there is no need for faith, and the essence of faith is where the mind ceases and he does not understand it with his mind—there faith is needed" (Likutey Moharan, cited in ibid., p. 141).

It is often said that for the Jew, who lived a very precarious life for thousands of years but nevertheless survived and outlived most of the ancient nations, not to believe in miracles is to be unrealistic. From this theosophical assumption of recognizing the reality of the unreal—which means that faith and hope are needed precisely because life entails discrepancies, irrational uncertainties, and questions for which no rational answers may be found—Rabbi Nachman constructed his systematic dialectic-dialogue theory of the paradox, which puts the hypothesis, or the question, in the center of the world.[4]

In the Bratzlavian theosophy, the paradox of living in contradiction and in the "questioning hypothesis" or *kushya* state (which in Hebrew dialectics means literally "difficulty" or "challenging complaint") characterizes the relationship between both man and God (son and father) and rational empiricism and irrational intuition. Thus Rabbi Nachman states, "That is the way it ought to be . . . that there should be *kushyot* (questions) concerning the Almighty, and that is what is proper and suitable for Him. Blessed be He according to his greatness and highness since . . . He is very much above our knowledge . . . and therefore it is imperative that there will be *kushyot* concerning Him" (*Likutey Moharan Tenina* 52, cited in Weiss 1974: 112).[5]

Following the mutual-contraction process and the world-correcting (*tik-kun*) dictum, whereby men may use *chutzpa* (see Chapter 1) to challenge heaven into a questioning dialogue, where son questions father and so on down to all interpersonal relations derivable from the contractional mutual-emulation principle, it is then the questioning hypothesis which gives birth to and breeds the continuous dialectic dialogue that functionally combines the seemingly opposing elements in life. How does the questioning hypothesis emanate from the contraction principle? Weiss (1974: 123) contends that Rabbi Nachman attributed the creation of the paradoxical questioning hypothesis to the archaic, primordial act of divine contraction:

> The first momentum movement of creation was also the hour of appearance of the question and its beginning predominance in every reality . . . the vacuum that was created due to the act of contraction whereby the Godly contracted itself to provide space for the creation of the world . . . . This evacuated divine space is the very essence of the . . . contradictory dialectics since the world must be based on two mutually contradictory assumptions: God's immanence and his transcendence in relation to the world.

Thus mutual contraction especially on the educational-interpersonal level, in the sense of dimming one's overassertive existence to evacuate space for the other, but staying in the background, conceals the rational-absolute answers to facilitate creative-intuitive questioning. The creative authenticity of Jewish humor, from Shalom Aleichem down to Woody Allen, lies not in its mocking others or slapstick self-assertiveness but in its deassertive self-contraction, which evacuates space to make the other feel at ease with his own faults.

In this sense, questions mean not "to be *or* not to be" but "to be *and* not to be" at the same time, that is, not to be there with all the synthetic, rational answers but to be there in the background to urge the creative, intuitive, questioning hypothesis. Rational answers connote finality and stalemate; questions imply continuous dialogue and creativity. Thus, life proceeds from question to question, each one already entailing the seeds of the next. This is the essence of Talmudic dialectic which may have echoed down to the popular notion that a "Jew always answers a question with a question," namely, that for him the "question" constitutes life.[6] Moreover, life oscillates between the descending "evening" and the ascending "morning," between rational empiricism and intuitive questioning that do not cancel each other out but rather facilitate their creative coexistence because the "rational receives its vitality from the irrational." To designate the interrelationship between the rational and the irrational, Rabbi Nachman used the two concepts "inner mind" and "engulfing" or "encircling mind" (see Weiss 1974: 116). The rational mind refers to the inner mind (which indeed, due to its rational basis, penetrated one's mind) and the encircling mind refers to the intuitive irrational (which indeed, one cannot conceive and interpret logically in one's inner mind but is nonetheless there). The difference between the two intertwined forms of thinking is that the rational inner one refers to the "mind which one acquires through many introductions" and the intuitive one refers to the spontaneous mind, the "mind which comes to a person without any introduction."

The relationship between the "inner mind," which resembles the Bergsonian rational matter or rather the Maggidic *bina* (building knowledge), and the encircling mind, paralleling Bergson's spiritual or the Maggidic *chochma* (potential knowledge), is not in that the intuitive is a nebulous preconscious knowledge but rather a clear creative spontaneous flash of the mind that has not yet been processed and substantiated by the inner rational mind. Here the popular expression of "open-mindedness" colors the vital relationship between the "inner rational mind" and the external "intuitive encircling mind." Thus, the "inner rational mind" is not closed or locked up but remains open and is constantly nourished by one's intuitive, creative "encircling" mind. Hence it is man's active hoping and waiting for the Messiah with creative "wondering" (see Heschel 1966) but with nonetheless unceasing faith, and it is man's creative swimming in the ocean of intuitive questions, not his landing on the safe shore of rational synthesis (see Weiss 1974: 120), that breeds life into the continuous dialogue between contrasting elements that are paradoxically and functionally interrelated. Moreover, according to Rabbi Nachman, rational final answers eliminate the creative free will: "The essence of work and free choice is that the mind of knowledge does not know (see *Likutey Moharan* 141; Weiss 1974: 146). Thus in the rational synthetic "redeemed world" of the millenarian Messiah who has already come there is no choice, because restorative past-oriented salvation (see Chapter 3 and Scholem 1972) refers to the rational "known, while in the utopian future-oriented hypothetic world that has not yet been redeemed, free will is constructed on the paradoxical relationship between the mystic unknown world of the future and the rational known world of the past, which complement each other.

The creative relationship between seemingly contrasting elements inherent in the questioning hypothesis that connects them calls for a brief reformulation of the *tikkun* concept, in light of the proposed philosophical "sociology of the paradox."

Monistic "Tikkun" and the Paradox

A famous Hasidic story tells of a simple farmer who came into the synagogue in the midst of the High Holiday prayers and sat down to chant the alphabet, which was all he was able to read in Hebrew. When asked by the respectable, frowning members of the community exactly what he was trying to do besides cause a turmoil, he is said to have answered, "Unfortunately, I only know how to read the alphabet. I trust that God, who knows what I want to say, will rearrange the letters into the proper words."

I stressed earlier that the cabala attributes great significance to the symbolic meaning of reconstructing words by rearranging their letters so that they take on a new, usually contrasting meaning. Thus, by rearranging the word *ani* (I or me) into *ain* (nothingness) the imperative verb of *iyun* (self-designification) is derived. Rearranging seemingly contrasting elements thus constitutes the paradoxical essence of the monistic notion of *tikkun*. In the monistic world, all elements may in principle be functionally interrelated. Their seeming dysfunctional, contrasting, and often clashing appearance results mainly from the improper connection between them. Thus, *tikkun* (correction), in the monistic world of paradoxes, is actually a matter of rearranging seemingly contrasting elements. The Hebrew word *nitukk* (separation, disconnection) becomes *tikkun* by rearranging its letters. God's holy sparks, which fell down into the depth of the earthly abyss, are merely misplaced; hence the creative "spark-lifting," correcting (*tikkun*) process is a matter of restoring order and reintegrating the original monistic whole by replacing and rearranging the divine sparks where they belong, up in heaven. Indeed, the symbol of fertility and creation upon which the perpetuation of life and existence depends is explained in the cabala (see Tishby 1975) as a process emanating from a proper arrangement between the two contrasting symbolic creatures: male and female. Life, creation, and continuity are possible only when male and female are arranged together in certain physical positions. Thus paradoxical *tikkun*, which would facilitate creative continuous relationship between seemingly polar contrasting elements, requires the prevention of *perud* or *nitukk*, (separation or disconnection) and the creative connecting rearrangement of male and female or any other paradoxical, contrasting elements. In this way *tikkun*, be it socio-historic, therapeutic, or political, can make evil the throne for goodness in a Beshtian sense by using the rearranging "spark-lifting" transformation process of attributing new existential meaning to previously distressing phenomena or by creating new gestalts out of old dysfunctional structures that were perceived as unchangeable givens. Thus, creativity means indeed nothing else but the creation of new compositions out of old elements.

The Contraction Paradox and Tolerance

We may now conclude our differential analysis of the dualistic either/or or synthetic dialecticism and the monistic hypothetical dialogue by contrasting absurd and conflict with the paradox in the rephrased terms of the problem of *tolerance*. In essence, the definition of the paradox as standing between two opposite positions of thesis and antithesis that coexist as separate, contrasting, but functionally related entities may be treated on a philosophical level as well as on the social, practical level as a problem dealing with the possibility of tolerance. The concept of tolerance refers to the possible coexistence of diametrically opposed positions, ideologies, or convictions which by definition must remain polar entities, for if they were to be swallowed and molded into a single new synthesis, by a dialectic process, there would be no opposing positions that could be mutually tolerant. In other words, while the strong convictions of true believers essentially preclude tolerance of dissidence from those convictions (e.g., religious or political orthodoxies), only those with strong convictions can in fact be considered tolerant in relation to equally strong but opposing beliefs.

I stress that only equally strong opposing positions facilitate true tolerance, because one may assume, as Halberstam (1980) has recently suggested, that the more I am convinced that the other's belief is erroneous, weak, and nonthreatening to my conviction, the more "tolerant" I may be toward his position; but then it is highly questionable whether we are still speaking about tolerance or what I would rather term "social indifference." Let me illustrate. If a young boy neglects his studies or drops his pocket money into the river and his father does not interfere or reproach him for his behavior (but rather reimburses him for the "lost" money), we would probably describe the father's behavior not as tolerance but as indifference or even negligence. If, however, the father is a Protestant nationalistic capitalist and his son grows up to become a devout cosmopolitan communist but they live together peacefully, we may speak about mutual tolerance—

although by definition they cannot really tolerate each other's position because real communism in the dialectic-synthetic sense of conflict described above requires the destruction of exploitative free enterprise.

How, then, is tolerance possible? Halberstam (1980: 10) has eloquently suggested that contemporary "openness to divergent views stems less from a mien of tolerance than from the endemic lack of convictions; having transcended the 'age of belief' we are left without heresies as well." I would suggest, further, that the popular notion of social tolerance so prevalent among so-called liberal, democratic circles may reflect social indifference or patronizing tendencies rather than egalitarian tolerance. If the rich are "tolerant" toward the poor, or rational intellectuals are "tolerant" toward the uneducated or the poor, they not only demonstrate indifference to poverty and ignorance, but actually by their tolerant behavior widen the guilt-debt social gap between the patronizing strong creditors and the weak debtor clientele as long as equally strong opposing positions are not structurally institutionalized in the social system. If, however, a multiple ideal-labeling system provides the institutionalizing tools for the development of equally effective but divergent educational, mystical, and other actualizing mechanisms, we may speak about mutual tolerance.

Consequently, it is not the ego-centered absurd with its mono-antithetic ideal-labeling system of hedonistic, manipulative, actualization dictums that would make tolerance possible. Neither is it the dialectic either/or conflict in which the rational class struggle is to culminate in a mono (new?) ideal-labeling system, for true tolerance can be effected only by a multiple ideal-labeling paradox in which equally strong and opposing positions may coexist by virtue of the mutual-contraction principle.

In the multiple contracting paradox, in contrast to the rational *dialectic* conflict where the mono-synthesis is to predominate, the hypothesis, the questioning *dialogue* between thesis and antithesis, predominates. Hence the Marxist dialectic's conception of deviance as conflict concurs with a dualistic either/or class struggle between the ruling class and the exploited class, because the conflict may be resolved only through a violent revolutionary "synthetic" uneven "duel" process[7] whereby one class must be eliminated or swallowed by the other.[8] Indeed, the analysis of a Marxist conflict-oriented criminologist such as Quinney (1977: 32) begins with "the material conditions of life" because there is only one actualization ideal—that of "the materialist method and conception of reality"—and so crime is conceived essentially as a material problem that is an either/or "integral part of the class struggle and the development of capitalism" (p. 91) I say either/or class struggle because conflict may by definition be resolved even within a Sartrean existential dialectical system only, as Laing and Cooper (1971: 174) have argued, in "negative violence and antagonistic reciprocity between classes" and individuals who must destroy each other.

It follows that not only according to the "spirit of capitalism," but also according to the Marxist conflict-oriented dialecticians, there is only one Calvinist ideal salvation label, that of rational materialism. Hence, unless eliminated by the revolutionary dialectic process, the wealthy capitalist will perpetuate and widen the social gap between the exploiting creditors and the exploited debtors.

Thus, within the conflict-oriented dialectic conception of personal history, self-assertion and individualistic growth are possible only through hating[9] and killing the old Oedipal father, since according to the either/or conflict philosophy, the "I or thou" existence means "to be or not to be" rather than a dialogical I *and* thou "to be too" existence. In a sense, according to this formulation of the dialectic conflict, Freud was a Marxist who taught man how to ascertain his existence by eliminating the ruling Oedipal fathers, and Marxists are Freudians who suffer from economic castration fears of the Oedipal ruling class.

From the theoretical position of the paradox, however, it was precisely because Zebulunian materialism and Issacharian Talmudic rationalism enjoyed structurally equal and independent ideal-labeling status due to the imperative of mutual contraction that it was possible for eighteenth-century Hasidic mysticism to be institutionally *tolerated* as a new, equally ideal actualization label. Accordingly, in the structurally contracting multiple actualization system, not only intolerance of tolerance but also tolerance toward intolerance is institutionally and constitutionally impossible.

It is not because the rational Issachar, the material Zebulun, or the mystical intuitive Hasid lacks strong conviction that tolerance is possible, for by definition strength is not lost in the process of mutual contraction but condensed to facilitate the enrichment caused by allowing the diversity of multiple ideals and convictions to intersect and dispute freely. It is thus the structural predominance of the wondering, questioning hypothesis emanating from the practical meaning of the paradox that forces contraction and tolerance (which becomes thus practically obsolete[10]) on polar positions and legitimizes the multiple actualization of "in all thy ways know Him."

In conclusion, the philosophical sociology or the social philosophy of the paradox summerizes and epitomizes the social-contraction perspective developed in this book. It is thus not material rationalism or intuitive mysticism, not alienating individualism or massifying collectivism, not I or thou, not evil or good, not punitiveness (*din*) or compassion (*rachamim*), not deviance or conformity, not normality or abnormality, not damnation or election, not the depressive evening or the manic morning, not the physical or the metaphysical, not the antithesis or the synthesis but the questioning hypothesis, the intermediate phase of faith in between and the creative volitionary hope and light that man created during the night, the spark he kindles in the dark, that bestows meaning on life.

NOTES

1. Although Simmel's sociological conceptualization of the conflict (see Chapter 13) appears highly dualistic, in regard to the psycho-philosophical meaning of life he wrote: "According to the common view, life always shows two parties in opposition. One of them represents the positive aspect of life . . . while the very meaning of the other is non-being, which must be subtracted from the positive elements before they can constitute life. This is the common view of the relation between success and failure . . . . The highest conception indicated in respect to these contrasting pairs appears to me different: we must conceive of all these polar differentiations as of *one* life . . . . We must allow the total meaning of our existence to grow out of *both* parties. In the most comprehensive context of life, even that which as a single element is disturbing and destructive is wholly positive" (Simmel 1955: 16).

2. In his analysis of the Jewish concept of trust (*bittahon*), Werblowsky (1964: 107) states that according to rabbinic literature "there is . . . a natural way in which things work, and it is precisely by adapting himself to it and relying on its regularity that man can do his job and discharge his duties without fear.

3. While Laing's (1967: 138) theory of attributing existential meaning to "insane" behavior is similar to Viktor Frankl's (1965) monistic existentialism, he nonetheless uses the either/or, death-rebirth terminology, which might explain the contradiction between his therapeutic system and his recognition of the outside world as nothingness.

4. The conception of life as a questioning hypothesis should be understood in Heschel's (1966: 58) terms of radical amazement and unceasing wonder in facing cosmic wisdom, rather than in terms of the despairing doubt that characterizes existentialism, which conceives the world as being meaningless. Thus Heschel states: "To a mind unwarped by intellectual habit, unbiased by what it already knows; to unmitigated innate surprise, there are no axioms no dogmas; there is only wonder, the realization that the world is too incredible, too meaningful for us. The existence of the world is the most unlikely, the most unbelievable fact."

5. Paradoxically, this would mean that according to the Bratzlavian doctrine, dogmatic ritualism would border with heresy.

6. Rabbi Nachman (*Likutey Moharan* 141) says that the Talmudic concept *tiku* (meaning no answer, no legal decision) is spelled in Hebrew with the same letters as *tikkun* (meaning correction). Because it turns out that the difference between *tikkun* (correction) and *tiku* (no answer) is only the n at the end of the word "correction" (*tikkun*) (which in Hebrew means only shortening the last letter of *tikkun*), one should always cut the end, the finality, in matters and leave things in an open dialogical state of *tiku* (no final answer).

7. In this romantic conflict-oriented tradition whereby disputes were settled through the dualistic elimination of the opponent, at least theoretically both sides had an equal opportunity to win the battle, unlike the Oedipal-Marxian conflict in which one side is by definition weaker than the other.

8. It is a fact that in contemporary Israel communist economies such as kibbutzim exist in harmony alongside capitalist enterprises.

9. Indeed, one should question the legitimate basis for putting parents on a life-long psychoanalytic trial stand as culprits who are to be blamed for their children's incapacity to fulfill their self-actualization needs.

10. I am indebted to I. Tashma for his insight on this point.

Bibliography

Angon, S. Y. 1959. *Sipurim Veagadot* (Hebrew). Jerusalem: Schocken.

Alberti, R. E., and Emmons, M. L. 1977. *Stand Up, Speak Out, Talk Back!* New York: Kangaroo Books.

Alexander, F., and Staub, H. 1931. *The Criminal, the Judge and the Public.* New York: Macmillan.

Allen, F. A. 1964. *The Borderland of Criminal Justice.* Chicago: University of Chicago Press.

American Psychiatric Association. 1968. *Diagnostic and Statistical Manual.* Washington, D.C.: American Psychiatric Association.

Arieti, S. 1959. Manic-Depressive Psychoses. In *American Handbook of Psychiatry*, vol. 1, ed. S. Arieti. New York: Basic Books.

Bandura, A. 1969. *Principles of Behavior Modification.* New York: Holt.

Baron, S. W., et al. 1976. *Economic History of the Jews.* New York: Schocken.

Bebbington, P. E. 1978. The Epidemiology of Depressive Disorders. *Culture, Medicine and Psychiatry* 2:297–341.

Beck, A. T. 1975. *Depression.* Philadelphia: University of Pennsylvania Press.

Becker, E. 1968. *The Structure of Evil.* New York: Free Press.

Becker, H. S. 1963. *Outsiders.* New York: Free Press.

Beer, M. 1968. Issachar and Zebulun. In *Bar-Ilan Year Book.* Ramat-Gan: Bar-Ilan University Press.

Bellah, R. N. 1970a. *Beyond Belief.* New York: Harper & Row.

———. 1970b. *Tokugava Religion.* Boston: Beacon.

———. 1973. *Emile Durkheim on Morality and Society.* Chicago: University of Chicago Press.

Ben-Amos, D., and Mintz, J. R., eds. 1972. *In Praise of the Baal Shem Tov.* Bloomington: Indiana University Press.

Ben Shlomo, J. 1965. *The Mystical Theology of Moses Cordovero* (Hebrew). Jerusalem: Bialik Institute.

Benz, E. 1958. *Die christliche Kabbala.* Zurich: Rhein-Verlag.

Berger, B. M. 1963. The Sociology of Leisure. In *Work and Leisure*, ed. E. O. Smigel. New Haven: College and University Press.

Berger, P. L., and Luckman, T. 1966. *The Social Construction of Reality*. Middlesex: Penguin.

Bergman, S. H. 1974a. *Dialogical Philosophy from Kierkegaard to Buber* (Hebrew). Jerusalem: Bialik Institute.

———. 1974b. *History of Philosophy: From Nicolaus Cusanus to Age of Enlightenment* (Hebrew). Jerusalem: Bialik Institute.

———. 1977. *A History of Philosophy: Jacobi—Fichte—Schelling* (Hebrew). Jerusalem: Bialik Institute.

Bergman, Y. 1940. *Hatzedakah B'Yisrael* (Hebrew). Jerusalem: Tarshish Books.

Bergson, H. 1978. *Creative Development* (Hebrew trans.). Jerusalem: Magnes Press.

Besht, I. 1975a. *Keter Shem Tov* (Hebrew). Jerusalem: Rosen.

———. 1975b. *Zavaat Harivash* (Hebrew). New York: Kehat Pub. Society.

Blau, P. M. 1964. *Exchange and Power in Social Life*. New York: Wiley.

———. ed. 1975. *Approaches to the Study of Social Structure*. New York: Free Press.

Boisen, A. T. 1952. The Genesis and Significance of Mystical Identification in Cases of Mental Disorder. *Psychiatry* 15:287–296.

Boorstin, D. J. 1974. *Democracy and Its Discontents*. New York: Random House.

Bretall, R., ed. 1946. *A Kierkegaard Anthology*. Princeton: Princeton University Press.

Brightbill, C. K. 1960. *The Challenge of Leisure*. Englewood Cliffs: Prentice-Hall.

Browne, H. 1974. *How I Found Freedom in an Unfree World*. New York: Avon.

Buber, M. 1958a. *Hasidism and the Modern Man*. New York: Harper Torchbooks.

———. 1958b. *Paths in Utopia*. Boston: Beacon.

———. 1960. *Bepardes Hachasidut* (Hebrew). Tel-Aviv: Devir.

———. 1963. *Israel and the World*. New York: Schocken.

———. 1967. *Between Man and Man*. New York: Macmillan.

———. 1974. *Pointing the Way*. New York: Schocken.

———. 1978. *Tales of the Hasidim: Early Masters*. New York: Schocken.

Burns, T. R. 1977. Unequal Exchange and Uneven Development in Social Life: Continuities in a Structural Theory of Social Exchange. *Acta Sociologica* 20: 217–245.

Cameron, N. 1963. *Personality Development and Psychopathology*. Boston: Houghton Mifflin.

Campbell, J. 1977. *The Portable Jung*. Middlesex: Penguin.

Camus, A. 1955. *The Myth of Sisyphus*. New York: Vintage.

Castaneda, C. 1974. *Journey to Ixtlan*. Middlesex: Penguin.

Chaim of Volozin. 1871. *Nefesh Hachayim* (Hebrew). Vilna.

Charles, R. H., ed. 1917. *The Testaments of the Twelve Patriarchs*. London: SPCK.

Chaye Moharan (Hebrew). 1952. Jerusalem.

Clinard, M. B. 1978. *Cities with Little Crime: The Case of Switzerland*. Cambridge: Cambridge University Press.

Cloward R., and Ohlin, L. 1960. *Delinquency and Opportunity*. Glencoe, Ill.: Free Press.

Cloward, R. A., and Piven, F. F. 1974. *The Politics of Turmoil*. New York: Vintage.

Cohen, A. A. 1971. *The Myth of the Judeo-Christian Tradition*. New York: Schocken.
Cohen, A. K. 1955. *Delinquent Boys*. New York: Free Press.
Conway, F., and Siegelman, J. 1978. *Snapping*. Philadelphia: Lippincott.
Cooley, C. H. 1902. *Human Nature and the Social Order*. New York: Scribner's.
Coser, L. A. 1956. *The Functions of Social Conflict*. New York: Free Press.
———. 1968. Some Functions of Deviant Behavior and Normative Flexibility. In *Approaches to Deviance*, ed. M. Lefton, et. al. New York: Appleton-Century-Crofts.
De Vidash, E. 1746. *Reshit Chochma* (Hebrew). Kushtandina.
Dinnerstein, D. 1977. *The Mermaid and the Minotaur*. New York: Harper & Row.
Doi, T. 1973. *The Anatomy of Dependence*. Tokyo: Kodansha International.
Draguns, J. G. 1974. Values Reflected in Psychopathology: The Case of the Protestant Ethic. *Ethos* 2.
Dresner, S. H. 1960. *The Zaddik*. New York: Schocken.
Dubnov, S. 1975. *Toldot Hachasidut* (Hebrew). Tel-Aviv: Devir.
Durkheim, E. 1963. *Suicide*. Glencoe, Ill.: Free Press.
———. 1964. *The Division of Labor in Society*. New York: Free Press.
Dushkin, A. M. 1939. Character Education and Teaching Processes. In *Problems of Hebrew Secondary Education in Palestine*, ed. L. Roth. Jerusalem: Rubin Mass.
Eaton, J. W., and Weil, R. J. 1955. *Culture and Mental Disorder*. Glencoe, Ill.: Free Press.
Edinger, E. F. 1974. *Ego and Archetype*. Baltimore: Penguin.
Eisenstadt, S. N. 1968. Introduction to *Max Weber on Charisma and Institution-building*. Chicago: University of Chicago Press.
———. 1971. *Social Differentiation and Stratification*. Glenview, Ill.: Scott, Foresman.
———. 1977a. *Revolution and the Transformation of Societies*. New York: Free Press.
———. 1977b. Sociological Theory and an Analysis of the Dynamics of Civilization and of Revolutions. *Daedalus* 2:59–70.
Eisenstadt, S. N., and Roniger, L. 1980. Patron-Client Relations as a Model of Structuring Social Exchange. *Comparative Study of Society and History* 1:42–77.
Eliade, M. 1964. *Shamanism: Archaic Techniques of Ecstasy*. London: Routledge & Kegan Paul.
———. 1974. *The Myth of the Eternal Return*. Princeton: Princeton University Press.
Elstein, Y. 1980. Teshuva Bederech Yerida Al Pi Tefisat Hachasidut Bedoroteha Harishonim. *Hagut* 3:53–67.
Ergas, Y. 1926. *Shomer Emunim* (Hebrew). Berlin: B. Cohen.
Erikson, K. T. 1966. *Wayward Puritans*. New York: Wiley.
Faunce, W. A. 1968. *Problems of an Industrial Society*. New York: McGraw-Hill.
Feinberg, J. 1973. *Social Philosophy*. Englewood Cliffs, N.J.: Prentice-Hall.
Fensterheim, H., and Baer, J. 1975. *Don't Say Yes When You Want to Say No*. New York: Dell.
Festinger, L. 1968. *A Theory of Cognitive Dissonance*. Stanford: Stanford University Press.

Fishman, A. 1971. Hayahadut Beyachasa el Hametziut Haempirit. *Molad* (Hebrew) 18:684–690.

———. 1972. Lehashpaat Hachasidut Al Hamishna Hasozialit Harishonit Shel Hapoel Hamizrachi (Hebrew). *World Jewish Congress*, vol. 2. Jerusalem.

Flor-Henry, P. 1974. Psychosis, Neurosis and Epilepsy. *British Journal of Psychiatry* 124:144–150.

Flusser, D. 1964. Pharisees and Stoa According to Josephus. *Iyun* 14:318–329.

———. 1970. Salvation Present and Future. In *Types of Redemption*, ed. Werblowsky and Bleeker. Leiden: E. J. Brill.

François, W. 1967. *Automation: Industrialization Comes of Age*. New York: Collier Books.

Frankena, W. K. 1963. *Ethics*. Englewood Cliffs: Prentice-Hall.

Frankenstein, C. 1978. *Sincerity and Equality* (Hebrew). Tel-Aviv: Hapoalim.

Frankl, V. E. 1965. *The Doctor and the Soul*. Middlesex: Penguin.

Freedman, J. L. 1970. Transgression, Compliances and Guilt. In *Altruism and Helping Behavior*, ed. J. Macaulay and L. Berkowitz. New York: Academic Press.

Freud, S. 1938. *The Basic Writings of Sigmund Freud*. New York: Random House.

———. 1950. Mourning and Melancholia. *Collected Papers*, vol. 4. London: Hogarth.

———. 1956. *Group Psychology and the Analysis of the Ego*. New York: Bantam.

Friedman, M. S. 1971. *Martin Buber: The Life of Dialogue*. New York: Harper Torchbooks.

Friedman, M. 1977. *Society and Religion* (Hebrew). Jerusalem: Yad Ben-Zvi.

Fromm, E. 1960. *The Fear of Freedom*. London: Routledge & Kegan Paul.

———. 1980. *The Heart of Man*. New York: Harper & Row.

Funkenstein, A. 1974. Imitatio Dei Umusag Hatzimtzum Bemishnat Chabad (Hebrew). In *Rafael Mahler Book*, ed. S. Yevin. Tel-Aviv: Hapoalim.

Galin, D. 1974. Implications for Psychiatry of Left and Right Cerebral Specialization. *Archives of General Psychiatry* 31:572–583.

Gendron, B. 1977. *Technology and the Human Condition*. New York: St. Martin's.

Geshuri, M. S. 1956. *Music and Dance in Hasidism* (Hebrew), vol. 1. Tel-Aviv: Nezach.

Gittelson, B. 1980. *Bio-Rhythm*. New York: Warner.

Goffman, E. 1956. *Asylums*. Chicago: Aldine.

———. 1959. *The Presentation of Self in Everyday Life*. New York: Doubleday.

Gordon, A. D. 1951. *Haadam Vehateva* (Hebrew). Jerusalem: Hasifriya Hazionit.

Gouldner, A. W. 1966. The Norm of Reciprocity. In *Role Theory, Concepts and Research*, ed. B. J. Biddle and E. J. Thomas. New York: Wiley.

Green, A. 1977. The Zaddik as Axis Mundi in Later Judaism. *Journal of the American Academy of Religion* 45:327–347.

Guttman, J. 1899. Aus der Zeit der Renaissance. *Monatschrift für Geschichte und Wissenschaft des Judentum* 43.

Halberstam, J. 1980. The Paradox of Tolerance. Unpublished paper read at the Long Island Philosophical Society.

Haring, D. ed. 1956. *Personal Character and Cultural Milieu*. Syracuse, N.Y.: Syracuse University Press.

Heifetz, H., ed. 1978. *Zen and Hasidism*. London: Theosophical Publishing House.

Heschel, A. J. 1966. *Man Is Not Alone*. New York: Harper & Row.

Hesse, H. 1957. *Siddhartha*. New York: New Directions.

Hill, C. 1974. *The World Turned Upside Down*. Middlesex: Penguin.

Hinchliffe, A. P. 1977. *The Absurd*. London: Methuen.

Hobbes, T. 1969. *Leviathan*. Cleveland: Meridian.

Hoch, P. H., and Zubin, J. 1954. *Depression*. New York: Grune & Stratton.

Homans, G. 1961. *Social Behavior: Its Elementary Forms*. New York: Harcourt Brace.

Hommes, O. R. 1971. Depression and Cerebral Dominance. *Psychiatry, Neurology, and Neurochemistry* 74:259–270.

Hook, S. 1962. *The Paradoxes of Freedom*. Berkeley: University of California Press.

Horodetsky, S. A. 1951. *Hasidism and the Hasidim* (Hebrew). Tel-Aviv: Devir.

Huizinga, J. 1949. *Homo Ludens: A Study of the Play Element in Culture*. London: Routledge & Kegan Paul.

Idel, M. 1980. Franz Rosenzweig and the Kabbalah. Unpublished paper.

Ishizu, T. 1970. The Basis of the Idea of Redemption in Japanese Religion. In *Types of Redemption*, ed. R. J. Z. Werblowsky and C. J. Bleeker. Leiden: E.J. Brill.

Jacobi, J. 1976. *The Psychology of C. G. Jung*. New Haven: Yale University Press.

Jacobs, L. 1978. *Hasidic Prayer*. New York: Schocken.

Johnson, C. L., and Johnson, F. A. 1973. Interaction Rules and Ethnicity. *Social Forces* 54:452–466.

Kant, I. 1960. *Religion Within the Limits of Reason Alone*. New York: Harper.

Kaufmann, H. 1970. *Aggression and Altruism*. New York: Holt.

Kaufmann, W. 1977. Retribution and the Ethics of Punishment. In *Assessing the Criminal Restitution, Retribution and the Legal Process*, eds. R. E. Barnett and J. Hagel. Cambridge, Mass.: Ballinger.

Kiev, A. 1972. *Transcultural Psychiatry*. New York: Free Press.

Klostermaier. 1973. *Liberation, Salvation, Self-Realization*. Madras: University of Madras.

Kraepelin, E. 1909. *Psychiatrie*, vol. 1. Barth.

Kuhn, T. S. 1962. *The Structure of Scientific Revolutions*. Chicago: University of Chicago Press.

Laing, R. D. 1965. *The Divided Self*. Middlesex: Penguin.

———. 1967. *The Politics of Experience*. New York: Ballantine.

Laing, R. D., and Cooper, D. G. 1971. *Reason and Violence*. New York: Vintage.

Lederman, E. K. 1972. *Existential Neurosis*. London: Butterworth.

Leibowitz, Y. 1979. *Sichot Al Pirkey Avot Veal Harambam* (Hebrew). Tel-Aviv: Schocken.

Levin, N. 1977. *While Messiah Tarried: Jewish Socialist Movements*. New York: Schocken.

Lewin, K. 1964. *Field Theory in Social Science*. New York: Harper.

Lofland, J. 1969. *Deviance and Identity*. Englewood Cliffs: Prentice-Hall.

London, P. 1969. *Behavior Control*. New York: Meridian.

Lyman, S. M., and Scott, M. B. 1970. *A Sociology of the Absurd*. New York: Meredita.

Macarov, D. 1980. *Work and Welfare*. Beverly Hills: Sage.

Macaulay, J., and Berkowitz, L., eds. 1970. *Altruism and Helping Behavior.* New York: Academic Press.

Maggid, Dov Baer of Mezeritz. 1927. *Maggid Devarav LeYaacov* (Hebrew). Lublin.

Maimon, S. 1954. *Autobiography of Solomon Maimon.* London.

Malinowski, B. 1961. *Argonauts of the Western Pacific.* New York: Dutton.

Marcuse, H. 1964. *One Dimensional Man.* Boston: Beacon.

Marriott, M. 1976. Hindu Transactions: Diversity Without Dualism. In *Transaction and Meaning,* ed. B. Kapferer. Philadelphia: Institute for the Study of Human Issues.

Marx, W. 1980. Schelling's "Of Human Freedom": The Essence of Evil and Its Role in History. Jerusalem: paper given at the Department of Philosophy.

Matza, D. 1964. *Delinquency and Drift.* New York: Wiley.

Mauss, M. 1954. *The Gift.* Glencoe, Ill.: Free Press.

May, R. 1950. *The Meaning of Anxiety.* New York: Ronald Press.

Mead, G. H. 1928. The Psychology of Punitive Justice. *American Journal of Sociology* 23:557–602.

———. 1934. *Mind, Self and Society.* Chicago: University of Chicago Press.

Mendels, J. 1970. *Concepts of Depression.* New York: Wiley.

Merton, R. K. 1958. *Social Theory and Social Structure.* New York: Free Press.

Merton, R. K., and Gieryn. 1978. Institutionalized Altruism: The Case of the Professions. In *Sociocultural Change Since 1950,* ed. L. Smith and M. Singh Das. New Delhi: Vikas.

Mill, J. S. 1910. *Liberty in Utilitarianism.* London: Oxford University Press.

Mowrer, O. H. 1964. *The New Group Therapy.* New York: Van Nostrand.

Murti, T. R. V. 1970. The Concept of Freedom as Redemption. In *Types of Redemption,* ed. R. J. Z. Werblowsky and C. J. Bleeker. Leiden: E.J. Brill.

Mussen, P. 1967. Early Socialization: Learning and Identification. In *New Directions in Psychology III,* ed. G. Mandler et. al. New York: Holt.

Nagel, T. 1975. *The Possibility of Altruism.* Oxford: Clarendon.

Nakane, C. 1970. *Japanese Society.* Berkeley: University of California Press.

Nelson, B. 1969. *The Idea of Usury.* Chicago: University of Chicago Press.

Nietzsche, F. 1969. *On the Genealogy of Morals.* New York: Random House.

Nigal, G. 1962. *Manhig Ve-Eda* (Hebrew). Jerusalem: Yehuda Press.

———. ed. 1974. *Rabbi Jacob Joseph of Polenoye* (Hebrew). Jerusalem: Mossad Harav Kook.

Nisbet, R. A. 1977. *The Quest for Community.* London: Oxford University Press.

Nordland, O. 1967. Shamanism and "the Unreal." In *Studies in Shamanism,* ed. C. M. Edsman. Stockholm: Almqvist & Wiksell.

Otto, R. 1976. *Mysticism East and West.* New York: Macmillan.

Padover, S. K. 1965. *The Meaning of Democracy.* New York: Lancer.

Page, J. D. 1971. *Psychopathology.* New York: Aldine Atherton.

Parsons, T. 1964. *The Social System.* New York: Free Press.

Pelletier, K. R., and Garfield, C. 1976. *Consciousness East and West.* New York: Harper & Row.

Peretz, L. 1977. The Messianic Psychotic Patient. *The Israel Annals of Psychiatry* 15:364–374.

Piekarz, M. 1972. *Chasidut Bratzlav* (Hebrew). Jerusalem: Bialik Institute.
——. 1978. *The Beginning of Hasidism* (Hebrew). Jerusalem: Bialik Institute.
Piven, F. F., and Cloward, R. A. 1972. *Regulating the Poor*. New York: Vintage.
Plaut, W. G., ed. 1963. *The Rise of Reform Judaism*. New York: World Union for Progressive Judaism.
Polak, F. 1973. *The Image of the Future*. San Francisco: Jossey-Bass.
Poll, S. 1969. *The Hasidic Community in Williamsburg*. New York: Schocken.
Pope, W., et. al. 1975. On the Divergence of Weber and Durkheim: A Critique of Parsons' Convergence Thesis. *American Sociological Review* 40:417–427.
Popper, K. 1950. *The Open Society and its Enemies*. Princeton: Princeton University Press.
Porter, F. C. 1902. The Yezer Hara. *Yale Bicentennial Publications, Biblical Semitic Studies*. New York: Scribner's.
Potok, C. 1967. *The Chosen*. New York: Fawcett.
Quinney, R. 1977. *Class, State and Crime*. New York: David McKay.
Rabinowicz, H. M. 1970. *The World of Hasidism*. London: Hartmore House.
Rand, A. 1975. *The New Left: The Anti-Industrial Revolution*. New York: New American Library.
Rappoport, A. S. 1918. *Pioneers of the Russian Revolution*. London: Stanley Paul.
Rawls, J. 1971. *A Theory of Justice*. Cambridge, Mass.: Harvard University Press.
Rempel, H. D. 1976. On Forcing People to Be Free. *Ethics* 87:18–34.
Rieff, P. 1961. *Freud: The Mind of the Moralist*. New York: Anchor.
——. 1966. *The Triumph of the Therapeutic*. Middlesex: Penguin.
Robinson, S. M. 1958. A Study of Delinquency Among Jewish Children in New York City. In *The Jews: Social Patterns of an American Group*, ed. M. Sklare. Glencoe: Free Press.
Rogers, C. R. 1965. *Client Centered Therapy*. Boston: Houghton Mifflin.
Rohlen, T. P. 1974. *For Harmony and Strength*. Berkeley: University of California Press.
Ross, T. 1980. Rabbi Kook's Conception of the Divine. Jerusalem: Unpublished paper.
Rotenberg, M. 1974. Conceptual and Methodological Notes on Affective and Cognitive Role-Taking (Sympathy and Empathy): An Illustrative Experiment with Delinquent and Non-delinquent Boys. *Journal of Genetic Psychology* 125:177–185.
——. 1975. Cognitive Role-Taking Among First and Third Year Social Work and Pharmacy Students. *International Social Work* 28:53–58.
——. 1978. *Damnation and Deviance: The Protestant Ethic and the Spirit of Failure*. New York: Free Press.
Roth, C. 1940. *The Jewish Contribution to Civilization*. Cincinnati: Union of American Hebrew Congregations.
Rothschild, M. M. 1969. The "Hallukkah" (Hebrew). Jerusalem: Rubin Mass.
Russell, B. 1945. *A History of Western Philosophy*. New York: Simon & Schuster.
Sarbin, T. R. 1964. Anxiety: Reification of a Metaphor. *Archives of General Psychiatry* 10:630–638.
——. 1967. The Concept of Hallucination. *Journal of Personality* 35:359–380.

―――. 1969. Schizophrenic Thinking: A Role-Theoretical Analysis. *Journal of Personality* 37:190–209.

Sartre, J. P. 1951. *Iron in the Soul.* London: Hamish Hamilton.

―――. 1959. *Nausea.* New York: New Directions.

Schatz-Uffenheimer, R. 1968. *Quietistic Elements in Eighteenth Century Hasidic Thought* (Hebrew). Jerusalem: Magnes.

―――. 1976. *Maggid Devarav Le-Yaacov* (Hebrew). Jerusalem: Magnes.

Schelling, F. W. J. 1936. *Of Human Freedom.* Chicago: Open Court.

Scholem, G. 1941. *Major Trands in Jewish Mysticism.* New York: Schocken.

―――. 1970. Opening Address in *Types of Redemption,* ed. R. J. Z. Werblowsky and C. J. Bleeker.

―――. 1972. *The Messianic Idea in Judaism.* New York: Schocken.

―――. 1976. *Devarim Bego* (Hebrew). Tel Aviv: Am-Oved.

―――. 1977. *Elements of the Kabbalah and Its Symbolism* (Hebrew). Jerusalem: Bialik Institute.

Schulze, W. A. 1957. Schelling und die Kabbala. *Judaica* 13:65–98.

Schutz, A. 1967. *The Phenomenology of the Social World.* Evanston, Ill.: Northwestern University Press.

Schweid, E. 1979. *Hayachid Olamo Shel A. D. Gordon.* Tel-Aviv: Am Oved.

Seeman, M. 1959. On the Meaning of Alienation. *American Sociological Review* 24:783–791.

Sefer Habesht Al Hatora (Hebrew), vol. 1. 1975. Jerusalem.

Segal, S. P., and Aviram U. 1978. *The Mentally Ill in Community-Based Sheltered Care.* New York: Wiley.

Sennett, E. R., and Sachson, A. D., eds. 1970. *Transitional Facilities in the Rehabilitation of the Emotionally Disturbed.* Manhattan: University Press of Kansas.

Sennett, R. 1977. *The Fall of Public Man.* New York: Knopf.

Shelleff, L. 1976. Beyond the Oedipus Complex: A Perspective on the Myth and Reality of Generational Conflict. *Theory and Society* 3:1–44.

Shmueli, E. 1980. *Seven Jewish Cultures* (Hebrew). Tel-Aviv: Yachdav.

Shneurson, S. Z. 1956. *Tanya* (Hebrew). New York: Kehat.

Shochat, A. 1951. On Joy in Hasidism. *Zion* (Hebrew) 16:1–2.

Shoham, S. G. 1977. *The Tantalus Ratio* (Hebrew). Tel Aviv: Cherikover.

―――. 1979. *Salvation Through the Gutters.* Washington: Hemisphere.

Silverman, J. 1967. Shamans and Acute Schizophrenia. *American Anthropologist* 69:21–31.

Simmel, G. 1950. *The Sociology of Georg Simmel.* Glencoe, Ill.: Free Press.

―――. 1955. *Conflict and the Web of Group-Affiliation.* New York: Free Press.

Singer, P. 1981. *The Expanding Circle: Ethics and Sociobiology.* New York: Farrar, Straus, & Giroux.

Skinner, B. F. 1972. *Beyond Freedom and Dignity.* New York: Bantam.

Sombart, W. 1963. *The Jews and Modern Capitalism.* New York: Collier.

Soule, G. 1955. *Time for Living.* New York: Viking.

Spiro, M. E. 1971. *Kibbutz Venture in Utopia.* New York: Schocken.

Steinman, E. 1951. *Kitvey Rabi Nachman Mibratzlav* (Hebrew). Tel Aviv: Keneset.

―――. 1957. *Shaar Hachasidut* (Hebrew). Tel Aviv: Newman.

Steinsaltz, A. 1979. Beggars and Prayers. New York: Basic Books.

Stephen, L. 1950. The English Utilitarians, vol. 1. London: Duckworth.

Strong, S. M. 1943. Social Types in a Minority Group: Formulation of a Method. American Journal of Sociology 48.

Strouse, J. 1975. Women and Analysis. New York: Dell.

Suzuki, D. T. 1971. Mysticism, Christian and Buddhist. New York: Harper & Row.

Talmon, Y. 1972. Family and Community in the Kibbutz. Cambridge, Mass.: Harvard University Press.

Talmud. 1938. Translated by M. S. Soncino Press.

Teshima, J. Y. 1978. Self-Extinction in Zen and Hasidism. In Zen and Hasidism, ed. H. Heifetz. London: Theosophical Publishing House.

Thomas, W. I. 1928. The Child in America. New York: Knopf.

Tillich, P. 1965. The Courage to Be. New Haven: Yale University Press.

Tilliette, X. 1970. Shelling, Une Philosophie en Devenir. Paris.

Tishby, I. 1975. The Doctrine of Evil and the Kelippah in Lurianic Kabbalism (Hebrew). Jerusalem: Akademon.

Tishby, I. 1971. The Wisdom of the Zohar (Hebrew). Jerusalem: Bialik Institute.

Titmuss, R. M. 1970. The Gift Relationship. London: Allen & Unwin.

Trotsky, L. 1970. My Life: An Attempt at an Autobiography. New York: Pathfinder.

Tucker, R. 1967. Philosophy and Myth in Karl Marx. Cambridge: Cambridge University Press.

Turner, V. 1972. Myth and Symbol. In International Encyclopedia of the Social Sciences, vols. 9–10, ed. D. C. Sills. New York: Macmillan.

Ullman, L. D., and Krasner, L. 1969. A Psychological Approach to Abnormal Behavior. New York: Prentice-Hall.

Van den Haag, E. 1978. Liberty: Negative or Positive. Harvard Journal of Law and Public Policy 1:63–86.

Veblen, T. 1934. The Theory of the Leisure Class. New York: Modern Library.

Vital, H. 1882. Mavo Sheaarim (Hebrew). Krakaw.

———. 1890. Etz Chayim (Hebrew). Jerusalem: Levy.

Von Hirsch, A. 1976. Doing Justice. New York: Hill & Wang.

Warren, R. 1963. The Community in America. Chicago: Rand McNally.

Weber, M. 1967. The Sociology of Religion. Boston: Beacon.

———. 1968. Economy and Society. New York: Bedminster.

Weiss, J. G. 1974. Studies in Bratzlav Hasidism (Hebrew). Jerusalem: Bialik Institute.

Weiss, R. S., and Riesman, D. 1963. Some Issues in the Future of Leisure. In Work and Leisure, ed. E. O. Smiegel. New Haven: College and University Press.

Weiss, Y. 1977. Reshit Zemichata Shel Haderech Hachasidit (Hebrew). In Studies in Hasidism, ed. A. Rubinstein. Jerusalem: Zalman Shazar Center.

Wells, H. G. 1971. A Modern Utopia. In Utopias, ed. P. E. Richter. Boston: Holbrook.

Werblowsky, R. J. Z. 1964. Faith, Hope and Trust: A Study in the Concept of Bittahon. In Papers of the Institute of Jewish Studies, ed. J. G. Weiss. Jerusalem: Magnes.

Wilensky, M. 1970. Hasidim and Mitnagdim (Hebrew). Jerusalem: Bialik Institute.

Wills, G. 1979. Inventing America. New York: Vintage.

Wittgenstein, L. 1965. *The Blue and Brown Books.* New York: Harper.

Witten, M., et. al. 1977. State Abandons Mentally Ill to City Streets. *The Village Voice,* October 31, 1977, p. 44.

Yaacov Yosef Hakohen. 1963. *Toldot Yaacov Yosef.* Jerusalem: Agudat Beit Vayeli-faly.

Zax, M., and Cowen, E. L. 1972. *Abnormal Psychology.* New York: Holt.

Zborowski, M., and Herzog, E. 1952. *Life Is with People.* New York: International Universities Press.

Zilboorg, A. G. 1941. *A History of Medical Psychology.* New York: Norton.

Index

Abraham, 13
  as the Zaddik, 121
Absurd, either/or dualism and, 178–181
  sociology of, 179
Absurd freedom and independence, 98–100
Absurd man, 178–179
Achdut and hitkalelut (unification and generalization), 72
Active quietism, Hasidic, 71
  Christian individualistic/passive quietism and differentiation of, 73
  interpersonal contraction and, 71–75
Adams, George, 106
Adhesion (devekut), individual dimension of, 164–167; See also Devekut.
Agnon, Shumel Yosef, 19
Alberti, R.E., and Emmons, M.L., 91
Alien thoughts, Beshtian cognitive method for transforming, 163
  in the Hasidic culture, 162
  uplifting of, 160–164
Alienation, Protestant individualism and, 69
Allen, F.A., 106
Alter-centered contraction
  balanced (symbiotic) and imbalanced (parasitic), 33

main cognitive and affective components of, 82–83
  model of, neo-Issacharian-Zebulunian, 23
  mutual-aid tradition and, 34–35
  shnor tradition and, 35–38
  sociological sources of, 40
Alter-centered inclusion in a kibbutz, 126–127
Alter-centered individualism and interpersonal contraction, 69–80
Alter-centered salvation, 7
  messianic universalism and, 38–40
  principle of, breakdown of, 58
  system of, process of intrusion or exclusion and, 105–106
"Alter-centric" or other-centric salvation system, 6
Alterism
  bilateral experiential actualizing salvation and, 32
  contractional versus contractual altruism and, 28–41
  definition of, 29
  individual freedom, "exclusion" systems and, 97–109
  Zebulun and Issachar and, 32
Alteristic contraction. See Alter-centered contraction.
Alteristic relationships and altruistic relationships, philosophical difference between, 29